"A treat to read." – Milt Dunnell, *The Toronto Star*

"Filled with anecdotes and offers insights into the makeup of dozens of famous athletes . . . Frayne became a sports writer at a time when Ring Lardner, Damon Runyon and Grantland Rice were better known than many of the athletes they wrote about. At 72, [Frayne] has joined that exclusive company." – *Winnipeg Free Press*

"It's hard to do justice to Trent Frayne . . . How to paint the proper picture of a writer of great facility who always liked the characters better than the games, who retained perspective and conscience in a world of facades?" – Stephen Brunt, *The Globe and Mail*

"A true pleasure to read." – *Toronto Sun*

"Frayne has a gift for putting words into the mouths of his subjects – wry, sometimes folksy wisdom that turns professional golfers into philosophers and lends his aging athletes a poignant dignity." – *The London Free Press*

TRENT FRAYNE was born in Brandon, Manitoba, in 1918. A sports writer for more than forty years, he has contributed countless columns to newspapers from the *Winnipeg Tribune* to four Toronto dailies, as well as to a score of magazines. He is also the author of more than a dozen books, including *The Queen's Plate*, *Goaltender* (with Gerry Cheevers), and *The Mad Men of Hockey*. Trent Frayne is married to author June Callwood. They live in Toronto.

TRENT FRAYNE

The Tales of an Athletic Supporter

M&S

An M&S Paperback from
McClelland & Stewart Inc.
The Canadian Publishers

An M&S Paperback from McClelland & Stewart Inc.

First printing October 1991
Cloth edition printed 1990

Canadian Cataloguing in Publication Data

Frayne, Trent, 1918-
The tales of an athletic supporter

"An M&S paperback."
ISBN 0-7710-3213-7

1. Frayne, Trent, 1918-   .   2. Sportswriters -
Canada - Biography.   I. Title.

GV742.42.F7A3 1991   070.4'49796'092   C91-094372-9

Cover design by Martin Gould
Cover illustration by Terry Mosher

Printed and bound in Canada

McClelland & Stewart Inc.
The Canadian Publishers
481 University Avenue
Toronto, Ontario
M5G 2E9

Contents

Preface

It was not my intention to write a memoir – ever. Memoirs, I always felt, were for non-athletes such as Winston Churchill, Pierre Trudeau, and Connie Smythe, who even as a youth couldn't put the puck in the ocean.

But I often have lunch with two close, non-athletic friends and occasionally I would recount to them what Reggie Jackson did in the clubhouse or Red Smith said at the Queen's Plate. These two friends – Joey Slinger, who writes a brilliant humour column in the *Toronto Star*, and Mike Enright, the host of the CBC network show *As It Happens* (he's cerebral but he's tall) – one or the other of them would say, "For God's sake, get that stuff down before you atrophy."

My dear wife, to whom I owe all that I have become (like old), also heaped encouragement on me ("That's the 11th time I've heard that anecdote. Why don't you put it in a book?"). No, in truth she kept saying it would be a good idea to sit down and assemble some reflections on my half-century or so in the toy department.

Still, all such entreaties proved unavailing until one night my agent, Jack McClelland, said to me, "Why don't you get off your butt and send me some athletic supporter stuff? You're a jock, aren't you?"

So with an inspired title unwittingly supplied by Jack, what follows is what happened.

Before going, I want to thank the book's copy editor, Richard Tallman, who did a wonderful job on the spelling and grammar and punctuation, and who knew such things as that "speciman" is not the singular of "specimen" and that when I applauded John Lardner's self-deprecativeness I really meant his self-deprecation.

Chapter 1

It's true, you meet all kinds

The trouble with going out to the West Coast, Sam Taub was saying, is that there are no good-looking women out there any more. Sam Taub was 91 at the time, seated with a group of sports scribes at a large, round, paper-covered table in the catacombs of Yankee Stadium.

"I used to like going out there when there were them beautiful movie stars like Pola Negri and Clara Bow and Pearl White," Sam Taub continued, removing a chewed heater from his mouth and waving it in the air. "Now all the good lookers are dead."

Sam was conducting this lament an hour or so before the start of the second game of the 1977 World Series between the New York Yankees and the Los Angeles Dodgers, guys sitting around over a beer or a cup of coffee talking idly until it was time to go up to the press box. Even at 91, Sam rarely missed a ball game at the Stadium, never an important ball game. He used to go up there with a guy he'd known for years, James T. Farrell, the novelist who wrote the Studs Lonigan books years ago.

Parked between Sam and James T. Farrell was Red Smith, who at the time was probably the best and certainly the best-loved sports scribe in the known galaxy. And next to him sat a guy with the unlikely name of Shirley Povich, who had been writing a column called Good Morning in the *Washington Post* for several decades. All of them had something to say, none of it earth-shaking but most of it entertaining or amusing or, for all anybody knew, even true. However, as Red Smith once remarked of a guy named Dumb Dan Morgan, a fight manager of his acquaintance, "Dan doesn't always resort to the truth when the truth isn't important."

I often think of that night in the stadium catacombs because it epitomizes what I've liked best about nearly half a century on the sports beat writing about the children's games that seem to enchant millions of grownups. The joy of being a scribe hasn't come as much from watching the games, which tend to be repetitious, as from occasional encounters with people whose view of the world is at the very least unusual and at the very most bizarre and quite often surprising.

Sam had other things on his mind apart from the women of Hollywood as he sat chewing on this cigar of his, which he never seemed to be without. "I quit smoking 83 years ago," Sam volunteered, removing the cigar for a moment to enunciate. "I was eight at the time and I lived in the South Bronx. By then I had tried everything and made my priorities." He returned the dead heater to his impassive kisser.

Dapper little Sam, hardly larger than a small jockey, used to broadcast fights with Graham McNamee, a guy who in his time was as familiar with a microphone as Howard Cosell became, and was charged with being obnoxious by no one. Even before that, Sam worked on the *Morning Telegraph* with a former lawman, Bat Masterson. "Yeah, the same Bat," Sam said this night. "Bat came to New York in the early 1890s. He and his wife Pearl practically raised me. He got me my first job as a copy boy on the *Telegraph*."

Sam peered thoughtfully at the ceiling and his audience silently digested his reminiscence. Then the novelist James T.

Farrell, casting a brief glance in my direction, said that he had once visited Vancouver but that he didn't know much about Canada.

"I know two Canadians, Ron Taylor and Morley Callaghan," he said. "I know Taylor from when he pitched for the Mets. And I always said Morley Callaghan is a better writer than Hemingway." I mentioned this to Morley when I met him in an elevator in the Sutton Place Hotel in Toronto a year or so ago, and he didn't seem moved one way or another by Farrell's observation. "I liked the Lonigan books," Morley said.

Actually, Farrell, a scrawny little guy with wiry grey hair and a baggy suit, knew three Canadians. He knew me. A few years earlier Ray Gardner, who was an admirer of the Studs Lonigan novels and an editor at the *Toronto Star* when I worked there in the early 1970s, sent me off to New York to talk to Farrell and write a piece about him. I'd spent a day and a half listening to him in his dishevelled flat at 71st Street and 1st Avenue.

A couple of years later I left the *Star* for a sports column at the *Toronto Sun* and one of my first assignments was the World Series of 1975. There, I encountered Red Smith in the press lounge on the roof at Fenway Park where the Boston Red Sox were hosts to the Cincinnati Reds. Smith had often come to Toronto for the Queen's Plate and the occasional George Chuvalo fight, and he was such a charming and friendly man that there on the roof he immediately extended his hand and asked me how the new job was going.

"To tell you the truth," I said, "I'm having a tough time with the deadlines. I'm finding it hard to come up with a lead in a hurry."

His eyes twinkled.

"Well, you know," he said, smiling. "If you're stuck, you can always try, 'In the fifth inning . . . '"

And now, in the Yankee Stadium catacombs, he'd invited me to join him and his friends, a most thoughtful man, as warm toward obscure visitors as to any of the towering intellects of the press box. I don't know if he ever met anybody he disliked for long, although in print he often scorched the hides of George

Steinbrenner, the Yankee owner, whom he always referred to as George III, and Bowie Kuhn when Kuhn was the baseball commissioner. He was a gentle, warm-hearted, enormously friendly man who in his visits to Toronto would stand up half the night smoking Camel cigarettes and drinking scotch high-balls, enchanting racing officials, boxing fauna, and fellow scribes with embellished tales of the events he had written about in the old *New York Herald-Tribune*, and after it folded, the *New York Times*. Before that, away back in the days of the Great Depression, Red Smith worked on the *Philadelphia Record*, writing seven columns a week and covering the games of the old Philadelphia A's as well, as many as 2,000 words a day, day after day.

He saw his share of Philadelphia's other team, too, the woebegone Phillies, and this night in the catacombs, glass in hand, blue eyes merry behind a pair of black hornrims, he talked of one of his favourite ballplayers, Hack Wilson, a squat barrel of a Cubs outfielder, the goat of the 1929 World Series who became the toast of Wrigley Field a year later when he walloped 56 homers, the National League record. (Actually, Red's all-time favourite ballplayer was likely Willie Mays. This night he said that Abner Doubleday didn't invent baseball for the American masses, he did it to accommodate Willie Mays. "Willie was born to play baseball," Red said.) However, on the topic of Hack Wilson, Red noted that in 1932 the Cubs shipped him to Brooklyn where he was inherited by Casey Stengel two seasons later when Stengel made his bow as a big-league manager.

The point of Red's story was the loathing this fading old outfielder had for a pitcher named Walter (Boom Boom) Beck and how that antipathy came about (it was said of Beck that the first boom in his name was for the ball hitting the bat, the second for the ball hitting the outfield wall).

One hot afternoon in Philadelphia's ramshackle old Baker Bowl where the Phillies played until 1938, Beck was pitching and Hack was out in right field nursing the residue of a hard, hard night. It wasn't one of Beck's better performances, even by his standards. Rival hitters kept ricocheting the ball off a tin facing on the right-field wall, a trick that wasn't all that difficult since the right-field foul line stretched only 280 feet to the wall. Wilson was near exhaustion from chasing the bouncing balls and silently cursing the inept Beck. After one foray across the grass in pursuit of the ball Hack stood gasping, head down, hands on knees, getting a respite while Stengel came wearily out of the Dodger dugout and trudged to the mound to replace Beck.

Boom Boom was enraged by this affront from his manager. He thought he ought to stay in the ball game. He turned angrily and hurled the ball on a line into right field. When it struck the tin facing out there, poor Hack heard the crack and thought it was yet another base hit. His head came up and he whirled and lumbered after the skipping baseball, caught up to it, clutched it, and turned and flung it with all of his fast-ebbing strength toward the infield. Other players stood transfixed, staring.

That night in the Stadium's bowels, laughing over Hack Wilson's plight, I remembered Jake Milford telling me of the time Eddie Shore traded him from the Springfield Indians to the old Buffalo Bisons of the American Hockey League. For the benefit of James T. Farrell in this hockey wasteland I mentioned that Jake had become the general manager of Jack Kent Cooke's Los Angeles Kings a few years earlier, in 1973.

Jake was a lovely, soft-spoken, stocky fellow from Winnipeg who had been advised of the trade by Shore, the Springfield owner, and told to report immediately to Buffalo. When Jake got there he bought the morning paper, the *Courier-Express*, at the train station and turned to the sports pages while he had a cup of coffee. His own name caught his eye.

Milford Acquired
for 2 Hockey Nets

"Eddie hadn't told me the details," Jake recounted years later, chuckling. "I wasn't all that surprised about the nets because Shore was a strange sort of guy, but I was a trifle disconcerted a little later on when he complained that the Buffalo team had led him to believe they'd be *new* nets. Apparently the ones they sent him were used."

I could have told a great many tales this night about Shore's mistreatment of his players – almost everybody who ever played for him has a horror story. One I hadn't heard was told to me quite recently, in fact, by that celebrated television commentator, Don Cherry, who had played in his younger days for three and a half seasons on teams owned by Shore, a man Don called "the meanest guy I ever played for." He remembered once being compelled to skate for four hours and 20 minutes, around and around the rink, because Shore had caught him glancing at a clock as the end of a practice neared.

I didn't dwell on Shore, though, or on Grapes either. Back then hardly anybody had heard of Grapes except inveterate hockey fans. In 1977 he had not yet been invented as a television star. That happened in 1982 when a TV producer named Ralph Mellanby remembered having enjoyed watching interviews with Don when he coached the bruising Boston Bruins and, later, the terrible Colorado Rockies. Ralph recommended that *Hockey Night in Canada* hire Grapes as a commentator and the airlanes haven't been safe since.

I've written three or four times about Grapes over the years, as I have about some of the other people and places in this book – in *Maclean's* magazine, where I've contributed stuff off and on for 40 years, and in the three newspapers in Toronto. Actually I sold a piece to *Sports Illustrated* magazine before there was a *Sports Illustrated* magazine. To explain that one, I have to go back to 1952 when Stanley Woodward, a once-famous sports editor of the old *New York Herald-Tribune*, left the newspaper business to become editor of a new independent magazine called *Sports Illustrated*. I must stress that this one had nothing to do with Time Inc., the current magazine's owner; this one was strictly independent – and, unhappily, short-lived.

But before it folded I went to see Woodward, a hulking giant with a crewcut who wore eyeglasses with enormously thick lenses. He took me to lunch and agreed as we stood at the bar and drank a couple of martinis to give full consideration to a piece I proposed on Turk Broda, the Maple Leaf goaltender. I'd already written about Turk in *Maclean's* and was later to write about him there again as well as in in the old *Star Weekly*. After I got back home I spent a week putting together a 3,000-word article on Turk, mailed it off to Woodward, and was delighted to receive a cheque for $200 for it a week or two later.

Woodward's magazine fought a losing battle and went belly up after a year. In 1954 Henry Luce's Time Inc. decided to bring out a weekly sports magazine. It made its first appearance on August 16 that year and was called *Sports Illustrated*. Luce's empire had a great deal more money than Woodward's backers and after five persistent years and $10 million in losses it began to break even and today it's one of the top money-makers.

Obviously, then, retelling a story – or as my friend and former *Maclean's* articles editor Pierre Berton used to say, "recycling" one as I've done occasionally in this book – is no recent development.

Anyway, getting back to Don Cherry, after Mellanby's recommendation was acted upon by the *Hockey Night* people, Grapes turned out to be the most refreshing, ungrammatical, opinionated, entertaining, funny, outrageous, exhilarating, and occasionally boring commentator in the genteel world of sports broadcasting. His impulsive outbursts delighted and infuriated tens of thousands of people every winter and, of course, his personality was (and is) the antithesis of the accepted bland Canadian image.

"I react. I can't rehearse," Grapes said one morning when I went to visit him in one of a growing chain of restaurant bars called Don Cherry's Grapevine that began spreading across Ontario in the late 1980s. "If I have to say something twice it's no good. One time, at Rochester, I'm playin' for Joe Crozier and I go, 'Joe, I think that . . . ' And Joe interrupts and goes, 'Grapes, don't think. You'll hurt the hockey club.'"

For a long time Grapes had this dopey pooch, a female English bull terrier named Blue, that he'd talk to. Once, Blue bit Don's long-suffering wife, Rose, and it caused a lot of consternation. "You're gonna have to get rid of her," a friend told Don.

"I know," Grapes concurred readily enough. "Me and Blue will really miss her."

Grapes was outraged on the air when nine Soviet players arrived on National Hockey League rosters for the 1989-90 season. "I worked in construction for 25 years while I was playin' and after," he complained. "I know what it's like to have somebody take your job. And listen, when a Russian gets $700,000 to play hockey here, $350,000 goes to the Russian federation to make their hockey players better. It's like Wayne Gretzky says, nobody ever gave *his* folks anything."

Speaking of whom, one June afternoon in 1989 I went to the southwestern Ontario town of Brantford where the highway sign on the outskirts still proclaims in the orange and blue colours of the Edmonton Oilers that this is the birthplace of Wayne Gretzky. All through the decade of the 1980s, Wayne the Wizard took the offensive side of hockey to a new dimension, and after he was forced out of town by the greedy owner, Peter Pocklington, he was still on the minds and in the hearts of the Oilers when they went into the decade of the 1990s with yet another Stanley Cup title, beating the Boston Bruins by four games to one last May.

Kevin Lowe, the thoughtful veteran who anchored the Oiler defence for a decade, said that on the afternoon of the team's wrapup victory in Boston he and his roommate, Mark Messier, actually agreed they wanted to win one for Wayne. Shades of the Gipper and the Fighting Irish.

"He was so great, we were able to follow on his coattails for years," Kevin told the *Globe*'s Al Strachan later, speaking of Gretzky. "He took a lot of pressure off us. He showed us how to win. In our hearts he's still part of this. I hope we can pass along to the kids on this club what he created for us."

It's not news that Gretzky was the guts of the Oilers for a decade, but perhaps not everybody knows about another side of this remarkable fellow that reflects the kind of person he remained through his breathtaking decade of headlines and almost unceasing attention.

Here he was on an overcast Saturday, he and his tall, lean, blonde wife of one year, Janet Jones, at an annual sports day and celebrity ball game he stages in his old home town to raise money that helps blind people read. It's for the Canadian National Institute for the Blind. And with him was this array of high-profile entertainers he had brought together – John Candy from the movie screen, Jim Kelly from the Buffalo Bills, Gordie Howe from the Hall of Fame, Tug McGraw from the World Series, Paul Coffey from the Stanley Cup, Wayne's pal Alan Thicke from television, tiny Elizabeth Manley from the Winter Olympics medal podium, Russ Courtnall from the terrible Maple Leaf trade that sent the speedy fellow to the Canadiens, and a score or more more.

Wayne had wanted Ben Johnson in this crowd. He said he thought it would be a nice switch for Ben so soon after his appearance before the Dubin Inquiry into sports doping, a Canadian hero everybody dumped on the instant his urine test turned out to contain an anabolic steroid at the Seoul Olympics. Overnight, the world's fastest human went from Our Ben to That Jamaican.

"I think what Ben did was wrong but I thought it would be good for him to be here," Wayne said. "He's been through a lot."

So I asked him why Ben wasn't there since he'd been on Wayne's invited list.

"The corporate sponsors," Wayne said. "See, we draw up a list of the people we'd like to have but the sponsors, especially Labatt's Brewery, have the final say."

Also in Wayne's thoughts that day was seven-year-old Shane McSweeney of Hamilton, a pale little fellow slumped in a wheelchair and wearing a black and silver L.A. Kings jacket and oversize cap on his tiny blond head. The boy's father, Fred McSweeney, was with him, and I asked him about Shane.

"He's terminally ill with cancer," the dad said, looking at Wayne, who had knelt beside Shane's chair and was talking quietly to him. "He's wanted to see Wayne since he first watched him play hockey on television."

Naturally, cameramen swarmed to the scene back of third base as Wayne knelt by the chair. It was the obvious move for a celebrity to make, to chat with a small sick kid. For the big star it's like visiting a hospital while the news cameras roll. But what none of the cameramen and perhaps few others noticed after the ball game was that as people milled on the field getting players' autographs Wayne spotted the McSweeney family leaving the field. He pushed through the crowds and slipped his black fielder's glove to Shane, stuffing it beside him in his chair, then hurried to rejoin Janet and the forest of microphones awaiting them.

You'd rarely catch Wayne out of character. This was something that could be said, too, of the preposterous late owner of the Toronto Maple Leafs, Harold Ballard, who, before he and his blonde-haired companion Yolanda launched the 1990s in a series of magnificent soap operas in hospital corridors and courtrooms, grew sufficiently miffed at the relentless criticism of his hockey team's shabby record that he banned *Globe and Mail* sportswriters from the home rink's press box. So the scribes bought tickets from scalpers, sat in the stands, and then rushed to the nearby apartment of *Globe* writer Bill Houston, computers in hand, to write their stuff and send it to the office on Bill's phone.

In this period I made a rare trip to Detroit for a Leaf game, finished my work in the press balcony in the Joe Louis Arena, and was standing there waiting for Jim Christie, who was covering the game, when here came Harold, closely followed by the general manager of the moment, Gerry McNamara, hustling along the aisle. When Harold drew abreast of me, huffing and puffing, a florid-faced man of 84 then, a full 15 years older than I, he gave me a quick, hostile glance and muttered, "Trent, why don't you get the fuck out? You've got a kisser like a fuckin' prune. You're too old for this." He hadn't paused to deliver this encomium, just muttered it in passing, the lugubrious McNamara in his wake.   Another time, in Boston, I went down to the Leaf room from the press coop to hear the pearls from the little rookie goaltender, Allan Bester, who'd been the game's star. As I turned to return to my work, my eyes locked with Harold's. He gave me a wicked little grin and cackled, "Whyn't you get a fuckin' haircut? You look like a fuckin' violinist."

As the dear old fellow said to me once in his rink with a merry twinkle in his eye, "What the fuck are you bastards gonna write about after I'm gone?"

Which reminds me of the time in 1972 in the Intourist Hotel in Moscow when Team Canada was involved in the first summit series with the Soviets. I was waiting on the sixth floor for the down elevator. When it arrived, out stepped Alan Eagleson, the modern-day Abraham Lincoln, founder of the hockey players' association. Then as now, the Eagle was a restless extrovert, loud and outspoken, impatient and fearless.

"What'd yuh think?" he growled there on the elevator landing. He meant about the game the night before. I was with the *Toronto Star* then, had been in Munich for the Olympic Games so had missed the four games of the Soviet series in Canada. This game the night before was my first. The Russians, who had won two games and lost one and tied one in Canada, won it to take a 3–1–1 lead in the series. I told the Eagle I had been knocked out by the puck control of the Soviets. I said I'd never seen a team pass the puck like that.

"Jesus," he said. "You must be a Communist." The Eagle wasn't fooling around. His thin lips were a straight line and the blue eyes were sizzling behind a pair of silver-framed glasses.

"All I said was the passing knocked me out," I said.

"We lost, you know," he said.

"Yeah, I know we lost."

"We lost, and you're telling me you like their passing."

I said well, yeah, I'd certainly liked their passing.

"Anybody who thinks like you do has to be a bloody Communist."

"What is this?" I said. "I tell you I like their passing and you give me this ideological gobbledygook. What the hell has . . . "

The Eagle was not to be placated.

"Are you calling what I have to say gobbledygook?"

That baffled me. I wasn't talking into an open microphone telling the world that the Canadians were a bunch of creeps; I thought I was answering the man's question, and I remember thinking what a dumb word to be arguing about – gobbledygook.

"Well," I said, "friendship ought to be worth more than that." At which point another elevator arrived and I stepped into it.

A few years later I wrote what I figured was a balanced piece about the Eagle in *Maclean's*, which carried a few warts and a few halos and presented, I thought, a reasonably fair picture of the guy who, as the organizer and absolute boss of the hockey players' union, had dressed the players in top hats and tails. Still, just before the magazine hit the newsstands Jim Proudfoot had a note in his *Toronto Star* column. Something like, "Alan Eagleson is hot over a current article in *Maclean's*. Says it's a hatchet job."

I hadn't had that in mind putting the piece together. I figured Eagleson was reasonable enough to recognize that not every move he made drew universal favour. But, as I discovered in nearly half a century in the toy department, when you're an athletic supporter you meet all kinds.

Such as Reggie Jackson. Upon reflection, I guess Reggie was the most fascinating person I encountered on the sports beat because I never knew which Reggie I was apt to meet. I've sat in restaurants with him when he stopped talking only long enough to swallow and I've been coldly eyed by him as though he figured I was after his wallet. Approaching him, I always advanced warily. Experience taught me that he was a man of infinite moods – pleasant, rude, aloof, jovial, remote, talkative, arrogant, warm, silent.

He was the greatest home run hitter of his time, the most exciting guy up there swinging a bat, even fanning. He played for 20 seasons, ending up at 41 years of age as a designated hitter for the Oakland A's in 1987. He hit 563 homers in his career, sixth on the all-time list back of Hank Aaron, Babe Ruth, Willie Mays, Frank Robinson, and Harmon Killebrew.

Even in his gradual decline he was the most charismatic figure in baseball. On the ball field, everything about him was dramatic. His swing was prodigious, his stance so wide that when he drove himself at the ball his left knee often dug into the dirt. When he swung and struck out there was as emotional a response in the stands as when he connected. On the road when Reggie struck out swinging, the earth shattered, the fans let loose a whoosh and a roar and then shrieked in delight as he stomped to the dugout, face grim.

Like his barrel-bellied predecessor Babe Ruth, Reggie brought a stir of excitement with each visit to the batter's box. As I say, he may have been the only slugger since the Babe who extracted from the crowd as noisy a response when he swung and missed that third strike as when his furious, grunting, untethered and sometimes desperate swipe at the ball knocked it beyond the wall.

But he wasn't plagued by Ruth's undisciplined excesses. Jimmy Breslin once wrote about seeing Ruth come in off the 18th hole of a golf course on a hot humid day and tell the bartender, "Gimme one of them drinks you always make for me, kid," and the bartender put a couple of fistfuls of cracked ice into a big thick mixing glass, building a Tom Collins that had so much gin in it that the other people at the bar started to laugh. The Babe picked up this mixing glass and opened his mouth and there went everything, the gin, the soda, the lemon slice, the cherry, and all the crushed ice in one nonstop gulp.

That wasn't Reggie's style. He loved looking at women, and being with them, and talking about them, but as far as I know his drinking was confined to a couple of post-game beers or several glasses of post-World Series champagne. He was religious, he read his Bible, and he espoused Christianity. I found this out first hand one time in the clubhouse of the California Angels in the Toronto ballpark where I'd gone to see if I could pick up a column talking to Reggie. He knew me by sight and when he was in a congenial mood he'd even call me by name.

This one time he'd apparently learned that my 20-year-old son Casey had been killed in a highway accident a few years earlier and he began talking about the Lord's will and prayer. I told him that since the accident I hadn't had much patience with religion and he told me that this was absolutely the wrong attitude. He sat down in front of his locker, pulled a stool from the next locker for me to sit on, and talked about Christ for a good half-hour. Other news guys were standing around us, wanting to talk baseball with him, but he ignored them completely, giving his entire attention to this topic.

Another interesting side to him was revealed the next day at the ballpark. By coincidence he was coming out of the Angels' room as I was pushing open the door to go in, hoping to find somebody to talk to for a column. Our eyes met. There wasn't a flicker of recognition in his. I said, "Hi, Reggie, how you doin'?" He grunted an unintelligible response, walked on through the Angel dugout, and broke into a flat jog toward the outfield. Reggie was a very unpredictable guy.

I twice had breakfast with him at the Sheraton Centre Hotel downtown where the Angels stayed on their Toronto visits. The first time was in May of 1985 when he came out of the elevator a little past 11:30, the time we'd agreed to meet. He scanned the lobby and his eyes settled on a woman who'd dropped a bill from her wallet. As she bent to pick it up, so did Reggie, but she beat him to it. He gave her a sly grin and pantomimed picking up the bill and handing it to her.

Now she smiled, playing out this little game, and offered him the bill.

"Do you need it?" she asked.

"No, no," he cried, laughing. "Not me, not me." He threw up his hands in a defensive gesture, delighting in this coy foolishness.

As we walked across the lobby heading for a mezzanine breakfast room, people recognized him.

"Hi, Reggie," a guy said. "How're things?"

"Sneakin' by, buddy," Reggie replied. "Sneakin' by."

He eyed people in the lobby as we walked, his glance pausing an extra second or two on the women there. "Say, you've got a lot of good-lookin' women in this town," Reggie said.

When we were seated he said "Hello, Darla," reading the waitress's name-tag. He wanted to know where she was from, how long she'd lived in Toronto, how she liked working here in the Sheraton Centre Hotel. Then he told her he'd like a waffle with syrup, two fried eggs, toast, "and some of your famous Canadian bacon and a small, nice, cold milk to get me started."

While we waited he said he loved baseball but that if he hadn't been a ballplayer he'd have gone into medicine. "I was a biology major in college," he said. Or if not medicine, then working on cars. "I love cars," he said. Anybody who had read anything about him knew he was a collector of antique autos.

"That's right," he said. "I have about 80, four Rolls-Royces, all in their teens."

Recognizing that he was not in the company of a fellow car fancier (or even a fellow millionaire) he explained, "They've all less than 20,000 miles on them." There were three Corniches of vintage 1974, '75, and '76 and a 1966 Silver Cloud 3. Also, Reggie had either seven or eight Mercedes-Benzes, he wasn't sure which, though none was a 450SL convertible. "That's a woman's car," he advised. "Too little. I can't get in 'em."

The next time I had breakfast with him was in early May of 1986 and this time there wasn't much byplay with the waitress, probably because this time it was a waiter. Reggie told him brusquely he'd have fresh-squeezed orange juice, corn flakes with strawberries, three hard-boiled eggs (apparently aware of the evils of high cholesterol, he spooned aside the yolks and ate only the whites), burned toast – "and, look, I mean *burned*," Reggie said – and decaf coffee with sugar.

This time he mentioned that he had been married once but

hadn't been married for 16 years, and he said yes, he liked the company of women and had many women friends. He said he had many business interests, too, holdings in real estate in northern California, and a newly acquired fascination with banking and finance. He also had an acute sense of his achievements, for I said to him at one point that I'd never forget the three home runs he'd hit in succession in the 1978 World Series.

"Nineteen seventy-seven," he said instantly. "It was the sixth game. I hit the first one off Burt Hooten, the second off Elias Sosa, and the last one off the knuckleballer Charlie Hough."

"Actually," he went on, "it was four in a row. In the last game in L.A. I homered my last time up off Don Sutton."

Reggie knew where he stood on the all-time home run table and the runs-batted-in list, too. He said he expected to wind up with 550 or 560 homers and recognized that with a mere five homers more a year over his 20-year baseball life he'd be right there with Willie Mays's 660, third on the all-time list. What completely astonished him, he said, was contemplation of Hank Aaron's 755 career homers. "That's staggering, buddy," he said, eyes wide behind the round, silver-rimmed glasses. "I mean *staggering*, 200 home runs more than me."

I saw him for the last time out in Arizona in the spring of 1989. He had retired after a final season with the Oakland A's in 1987 but the A's manager, Tony LaRussa, had invited him to talk to the A's players about how difficult it is for a team to repeat as pennant winners. The A's had won the American League flag in 1988 and LaRussa was concerned about overconfidence in 1989. So he brought in Reggie, among other former winners, to talk about the hazards of complacency.

When I read in a Phoenix paper that Reggie would be at the A's ballpark I instantly thought, "Oh boy, an easy column; I'll go see my old pal Reggie." I should have known better.

He was at Phoenix Stadium the next morning, all right, in civvies. When I spotted him he was coming from a room under the stands along the first-base line where he'd addressed the players.

"Hi yuh, Reggie," I said, catching up to him as he climbed from the dugout. "What did you tell those guys?"

He didn't break stride or change expression.

"Nuthin' much," he said, stomping off to an adjacent field where the players were assembled in six long rows for calisthenics. He stopped in the middle of the pack and stayed there, watching, off limits to waiting scribes. Whatta guy, my pal Reggie.

Reggie was in Toronto early in the 1990 season, a broadcaster with the California Angels. Milt Dunnell, the longtime *Toronto Star* columnist, told me he'd run into Reggie at the ballpark.

"Hi yuh, Trent," Dunnell reported Reggie saying.

"No, no, you've got the wrong guy," Milt said. "I'm Milt Dunnell."

"Yeah, right," Reggie said. Then he chuckled. "What the hell, Milt," he said, "all you white guys look alike."

Down the road from the A's park in Phoenix was Scottsdale Stadium where the San Francisco Giants could be found, and so could another of baseball's immortals, the Say Hey Kid, Willie Mays. Willie's job with the Giants was listed as special assistant to the owner, Bob Lurie, and to the general manager, Al Rosen, but mostly it appeared that Willie's job consisted of being Willie Mays.

This marvelous outfielder, this complete ballplayer of the 1950s and 1960s, turned 59 in the spring of 1990, a muffin-faced fellow of surprisingly stocky build. I say surprisingly because he did, after all, wallop 660 home runs and he is only 5-foot-10½. You wonder where he got his power, a man who weighed in at a modest 170 in his years at the top. As baseball mortality is measured, Willie became immortal in the first game of the 1954 World Series when the Giants were still a New York team and Willie was the darling of the fans and the favourite of the manager, Leo Durocher. The Giants played the Cleveland Indians in that Series, which opened in their home park, the Polo Grounds.

As a ballpark, the Polo Grounds was a joke, as big a joke as Boston's Fenway Park is today with its ludicrous cement wall and zigzagging outfield fence. The Polo Grounds was a huge rectangle with curved corners similar to those of a race track. The plate was centred at one end of the field so that the foul lines were short and centre field went on forever. Actually, the right-field foul pole was a mere 258 feet from the plate, and the left-field pole 280 feet. Guys would plunk a flyball down the line that would drop over the wall into the seats, and because of the tiny noise of ball meeting bat to lift these pop-fly homers, they were called Chinese home runs. In this setting, straight-away centre ended practically at the Empire State Building, close to 500 feet.

In the opening game, Cleveland slugger Vic Wertz hit a ball almost as far as a ball could possibly be hit in the Polo Grounds, a high shot to centre that sent Mays scurrying with his back to the plate to the farthest reaches. As the ball came down Willie took it over his shoulder in his outstretched palms, still running all out, and people have talked about that catch ever since.

When I spoke to Willie in the Giants' clubhouse in Scottsdale a mere 35 years after his catch he naturally had no recollection of our first conversation. That had been early in the 1962 season after the Giants had jumped to San Francisco when I had been sent by the old *Star Weekly* to do pieces on Willie and three or four other West Coast people.

Willie was not a popular figure out there at that time. The locals resented him. For them, he was a New York interloper usurping the territory of a native son, Joe DiMaggio, who had not only been born and raised in San Francisco but had played for the old Pacific Coast League Seals before going on to the Yankees. Better still, Joe came home every winter to a restaurant that bore his name on Fisherman's Wharf. Anything Willie Mays could do, Joe could do better; that was the prevailing sentiment. Willie had walloped 40 homers in the 1961 season but the only statistic that seemed to matter to the yokels was DiMag's 56-game streak, nobody dwelling on the number of times scorers had ruled a hit on a last-chance hopper that an infielder had sparred with.

The Giants were undertaking their fifth season in 1962 since the move from New York, and even the weather had conspired to sap some of Willie's lustre. By day, the winds of Candlestick Park blew stiffly against the towering flies he hit toward left, home runs in the Polo Grounds, tall outs at the Stick, as fans called their park. By night, the damp chill from the nearby bay often turned all of Candlestick Point, for which the ballpark was named, into a deep-freeze even in midsummer. Yes, Willie had some great days. The most spectacular one the season before was on a hot autumn afternoon when he hit four homers – in Milwaukee.

Adding to Willie's disenchantment, his gorgeous wife Marghuerite had left him after four years of marriage and he was living alone in a three-storey apartment building on Spruce Street, not far from the downtown area. As with so many places in this crowded town, there was no room for landscaping. Willie's building sat flush against the sidewalk.

The Giants' p.r. man Garry Schumacher told me about Willie's low mood: Schumacher was a tall, droll, large-boned former baseball writer for the *New York Journal-American* who had left the ink-stained business to join the Giants while they were still tenants in the Polo Grounds. He set up the interview but to be on the safe side I'd phoned Willie two days prior to my visit to confirm it.

And so at one o'clock I climbed a long winding flight of stairs to see him in his seven-room apartment. He was standing at the top in a pair of rumpled blue linen pyjamas, silently watching me ascend.

"Hi," I said, suddenly seeing him.

"Who're you?" he asked, standing immobile.

I reminded him that I'd called him two days ago about seeing him.

"Okay, okay," he said, turning down a long hall. "I just wanted to know."

I followed him to a red-carpeted sitting room decorated with blue upholstered chairs, mahogany end-tables, pleasant pastoral pictures, and a built-in television set. Willie stretched out on a couch, pulled a blanket over him, and turned to the television screen.

"You watch a lot of TV?" I began, the first of many penetrating questions.

"Yeah. Where am I gonna go? There's no place for me to go. I shoot pool a little and in the winter I play basketball to get the runnin'."

I asked him if he thought he'd be playing better if Leo Durocher hadn't left the Giants. The current manager was the former infield star, Alvin Dark, with whom Garry Schumacher had said Willie got on well, but I'd asked the question badly.

"What do you mean, better?" Willie demanded. "Did somebody tell you somethin'?"

"No, no, nobody said anything," I blubbered. "I only meant that you and Leo got along so well."

"Yeah, that's so," he allowed. "Leo was good for me. He was like a father, you know? He treated me like I was never treated, at the ballpark and away from it. He knew me inside out. I used to be scared when the newspaper guys would crowd around in New York. I didn't know how to answer them, swarms of them. Leo knew I was scared. He said if the guys would ask him the questions he'd answer them and I could okay them." He stared at the television screen, not seeing it, I suspected. Finally Willie said, "That was a long time ago."

"And out here?"

"How do you mean, out here?"

"You know, the booing?"

"Yeah, it bothers me," Willie allowed, throwing off the blanket and climbing to his feet to pace. "Any time a guy gets it in his home town it's bound to affect him. You feel depressed if the best you have in you doesn't come up to what they want."

"Maybe it's partly the DiMaggio business." I told him that Garry Schumacher had said Joe D. was a hard act to follow in San Francisco. Willie responded to this.

"The thing I don't get is that DiMaggio was my idol. I broke in in New York in '51 when Joe owned the town. Why, I thought he was the greatest man ... and now I get booed because he was born here."

Well, as it turned out, the fans eventually came around for Willie. All he had to do was hit 49, 38, 47, and 52 home runs over the next four seasons and he had them in the palm of his hand. He stayed around for a long time, too, and in his 22nd season in the big leagues he was traded by the Giants back to New York, this time with the Mets. In 1973, an eldering dude of 42, he faced the Oakland A's in the World Series, starting the opening game in centre field and appearing in two other games as a pinch hitter. In the second Series game with the score 6–6, Willie banged a 12th-inning run-scoring single that put the Mets in front to stay.

"Never another like him," Red Smith wrote of Willie. "Never in this world."

In 1974 Red brought out a book he chose to call *Strawberries in the Wintertime*, a title that was directed at Willie.

"How come you called it that?" I asked Red this night in the Yankee Stadium catacombs, and he said that Garry Schumacher had been responsible.

In 1951 Willie was batting .477 for Minneapolis, the Giants' farm team in the American Association, when Leo Durocher insisted he be called up, though he was barely 20 years old.

"Garry knew how important Willie could turn out to be for the Giants," Red said. "What I remembered him saying was, 'Willie's the guy who'll have us all eating strawberries in the wintertime.'"

"Garry was right," James T. Farrell said.

"Yeah," tiny Sam Taub said, nodding vigorously. As I recall, he didn't bother removing the heater. We all went upstairs to the press box.

Chapter 2

Shoeless Joe didn't make it to Virden

It is impossible to move any farther from baseball's roots than to climb several leagues toward heaven to a seat under the rim of the SkyDome, Toronto's $600 million ode to excess. This unique architectural creation, with its massive retractable roof panels, is "a masterly piece of conceptual engineering," Paul Goldberger wrote in the *New York Times* a few weeks after the enormous concrete pile was opened in June of 1989. However, at 34 storeys above the emerald carpeting on its floor, it is several eons removed from what everyone for a century considered to be a ballpark.

In a nice ironic twist, this 21st-century creation opened for baseball the week the movie version of W.P. Kinsella's mystical novel, *Shoeless Joe*, began its summer run in theatres across the land. In the movie, which was called *Field of Dreams*, Kevin Costner is moved by an unseen voice to tear down a field of corn higher than his head and carve out a ball field in the middle of Iowa. In one scene, Shoeless Joe Jackson, a gifted outfielder for the Chicago White Sox, some of whose players threw the World Series of 1919, comes back from the grave in his baseball uniform and stares wistfully around him.

"I loved the game," Kinsella had him say at this point in the 1982 novel. "I'd have played for food money.... It was the game, the parks, the smells, the sounds.... There was the chugalug of the tin lizzies in the parking lots, and the hotels with their brass spittoons in the lobbies and brass beds in the rooms. It makes me tingle all over just to talk about it."

In the air-cooled theatre, entranced by a glowing ambiance that was alive all through the film (though conspicuously absent in the heavy-handed book), I was suddenly transported to a time long ago when baseball tournaments spotted the Canadian West, and inevitably my memory of Prairie baseball settled on two of the leading players of their time in the big leagues, the uninhibited Brooklyn outfielder Babe Herman and the hot-tempered pitcher of Connie Mack's old Philadelphia Athletics, Lefty Grove, of whom the cartoonist Bugs Baer once remarked, "That man could throw a lamb chop past a hungry wolf." The Cooperstown Hall of Fame yearbook wrote far less colourfully of Grove but did sum up his 17-year career concisely:

"Lefty Grove is generally considered the greatest left-handed pitcher in American League history. Although he did not reach the majors until the age of 25, he still won 300 games by fashioning eight 20-win seasons. He led the AL in strikeouts seven consecutive seasons. With a temperament as mean as his fastball, he was 31–4 for the 1931 Athletics, compiling a 16-game winning streak."

The two things I remember most about Grove are his temper and his fastball, for along about 1931 or '32 he lined up with an all-star team heading for Japan. The all-stars barnstormed their way west to board a ship for the Pacific crossing, playing exhibitions against local Manitoba teams in Winnipeg and Virden, among other stopovers. God knows how Harry Allen, the station agent in the tiny town of Virden, 50 miles or so west of Brandon, got that whistlestop's name on the all-star itinerary. The team included some of the best players of the era.

Along with Grove and the slugger Babe Herman, there were the stylish Hall of Fame second-baseman Charlie Gehringer;

Washington's first-baseman Joe Judge, a little fellow of 5-foot-
8½ who nonetheless batted a lifetime .298 in 20 big-league
seasons; the Detroit outfielder Heinie Manush; and Boston's
brilliant little shortstop Rabbit Maranville, then nearing the
close of a 23-year career.

All of these stars showed up in Virden and played a pickup
team of area farmers and store clerks, since it was mid-October
and Virden's talented tournament team had been disbanded for
the season.

The day was overcast and cold but this had not dissuaded a
school pal of mine, Hap Fraser, and I from travelling from
Brandon to Virden on railroad passes obtained for us by our
fathers, both of whom were CPR conductors. When we got to
Virden, a couple of 13-year-olds, we spotted the all-stars' railway sleeping car parked on a siding and we climbed aboard to
collect autographs.

I can remember walking along the aisle to Grove's seat as
clearly as though I was confronting Dave Stieb in the Blue Jays'
clubhouse yesterday. Robert Moses Grove, his name was, and
he was staring bleakly from the window at tiny pellets of snow
that were beginning to dapple the empty countryside. He had a
lean hawk-like face with spiky reddish hair parted on the side
and a few freckles across high cheekbones and a sharp beak. I
asked him for his autograph, proffering a little leather-bound
book. He glared at me silently. Then he turned his cold eyes
back to the countryside.

"Beat it!" he rasped.

Other players must have known of Grove's moody nature for
one of them said, "C'mon Bob, write your name. There's only
two of these kids."

Grove turned his icy eyes to the player, who then shook his
head resignedly and pulled me away.

"You can be our batboy, kid," said this player, who turned out
to be Babe Herman.

One day in 1987 not long before Christmas I read in the paper
that Babe had died in California, an old dude of 84. By then he

had shrivelled down to 6-foot-4 and 200 pounds but back when he made me the all-stars' batboy he was easily twice that tall.

Babe's square name was Floyd Caves Herman. He was a tough out in his 13-year career, mainly with the Cubs and the old Brooklyn Dodgers. One year he hit .393 for the Dodgers, accumulated 137 runs batted in, and struck 38 homers. For this he got honourable mention as the National League's most valuable player. He happened to pick the year that New York's first-baseman, Bill Terry, batted .401 and won the MVP award.

A lot of people claimed Babe's life was in danger whenever a flyball approached him in the outfield but this wasn't necessarily so. John Lardner, a great sportswriter of the time, once conceded that Babe might circle a little while closing on a descending baseball but insisted that Babe always got his glove up in time.

Babe's adventures on the bases were never conducted in secret. Once, with runners at first and second, Babe stroked a prodigious wallop off the wall in Ebbets Field, but the runners were uncertain whether the ball would be caught, so held up. There was no indecision in Babe's mind, though, and he set off, head down, to get as far as he could get.

That happened to be third base, where he found himself in the midst of a crowd. There was the Giant third-baseman holding the ball, the Dodger third-base coach looking aghast, Babe looking wide-eyed and puffing, and the other two Brooklyn baserunners, who had decided the ball wouldn't be caught after all and had set sail. Two guys were tagged out and the scorer decided Babe had doubled into a double play.

It was in the wake of this episode that Babe and the boys landed in Virden, including the grouch, Lefty Grove, who worked two innings and wore a farm work-glove on his pitching hand. He fanned six batters in a row, throwing only fastballs, then stomped back to the warmth of the Pullman car. Somebody wrote once in a line that has remained with me that Grove "was a man of surly anger on a long, thin neck." For Babe's part, when he went up to hit he carried a pale yellow bat and in fouling off a pitch cracked the handle. As he returned to the all-stars' bench back of first base to replace it he handed me the cracked bat and said, "Here, kid, you can have this." I had that bat for years and, naturally, I never once took it outdoors.

I was always a little distressed in later years when I'd read stories about Babe and his eccentricity. Perhaps the nature of the Daffy Dodgers placed an exaggerated emphasis on his modest quirks, I reasoned. Once, he complained to a Brooklyn writer about the inaccurate picture being drawn of him. After an earnest discussion, the writer said he'd try to correct the image.

"Gee, that's swell," Babe said. "I knew you'd understand." Whereupon he drew a lighted cigar butt from his pants pocket and strolled toward right field puffing on it.

I mentioned earlier how the Shoeless Joe movie had brought memories of the baseball tournaments that spotted the West. These were annual one-day events in Prairie towns where touring teams and local nines played for cash prizes during the Depression, the tournaments a unique social phenomenon unknown to any other part of Canada.

What was I, twelve? Fourteen? I know I was hooked on sports in this Prairie town of Brandon. I'd go to the *Sun* office where the kindest man, Howard (Krug) Crawford, who had two daughters and for some reason treated me as his only son, welcomed me and let me read the exchanges, the out-of-town newspapers that came into the *Sun* office every day, papers from the big Canadian cities and, with them, the *Chicago Daily News*, the *New York Times*, the *New Orleans Times-Picayune*, and the *New York World-Telegram* that I can remember. The names of the giants who covered sports for the big papers are as clear to me now as my own – John P. Carmichael, whose column was called The Barber Shop in the Chicago paper, and John Drebinger, who covered the Yankees for the famous *Times*, and Joe Williams who wrote the column in the *World-*

Telegram, and that paper's renowned baseball writer, Daniel M. Daniel. I read these people as a divinity student reads the Bible.

Anyway, when I was a kid I saw two of the Chicago White Sox players who were banished for life by the commissioner of baseball for their part in the Black Sox scandal. This came about one summer in the early 1930s when Harry Allen, the CPR station agent who had brought Babe Herman and company to Virden, attracted the two banned players to play tournaments for Virden, whose population couldn't have been more than 2,000. There was the muscled centre-fielder from the White Sox, Hap Felsch, and the lanky shortstop, Swede Risberg. Felsch was a six-footer who had his best season the year after the Black Sox scandal – 14 homers in Chicago's spacious Comiskey Park and 115 runs batted in. That was in 1920; in the 1919 Series he batted .192. He was at his peak, 29 years old, when he was banished and now here he was toiling on an open field in a flat wheat-belt country he'd scarcely known existed.

For his part, Risberg was one of those rangy, long-legged infielders who lives by his glove, not yet 25 years old when he decided to join the dumpers. As for Joe Jackson, I don't know if Harry Allen tried to bring him north of the border but Shoeless Joe never made it. He was older than the other pair, 33 when the baseball commissioner, Kenesaw Mountain Landis, a stern-visaged judge with a shock of snow-white hair, threw the book at him in 1920. That was Joe's 13th season in the big leagues, and he produced a wonderful final year, a .382 average, 121 RBIs, 12 homers, 42 doubles, and 20 *triples*. Ballplayers nowadays would kill for such numbers and their slavering agents would extract an easy $4 million a year. The prevailing notion is that Joe was clean in the Black Sox episode because in that Series he had 12 hits in 32 at bats and six RBIs. Those aren't a crook's numbers.

I must have seen Risberg and Felsch a half-dozen times that summer. My dad always took me to the big tournament in Brandon, and sometimes we'd drive to the ones in other Manitoba towns such as Virden and Neepawa. There were tournaments in Saskatchewan, too – in Delisle and Indian Head and Yorkton, but those places were too far for us to drive to. Most offered $1,000 in prize money, the winning team collecting $500, the second team $300, and the third $200. Fans paid $1 for the day of baseball. These were Depression days, you understand. I remember that the town of Plumas in north-central Manitoba, short of the kind of cash that lured good pitchers, hit upon the idea of donating a 40-acre field of flax to a good right-hander. On a yield of 20 bushels to the acre at a price of around $4 a bushel, the pitcher stood to make something like $3,200 if the crop held up until fall.

Usually four teams were invited to the one-day tournaments. The gates opened at noon when a draw was made and at 12:30 the first two teams drawn played nine innings. At 2:30 the other two teams played and at 4:30 the two losing teams met for third money. The big game of the day, the final between the two winners, began at 6:30, giving a fan four nine-inning games for his buck. It was an era long before television commercials, of course, and without those intrusions and the breathtaking philosophies of windy commentators, games usually were zipped off in less than two hours. Anyway, the flood-lighting of ballparks was unheard of, so the tournament *had* to end in the light God provided.

The fields were often unfenced, the outfields ringed by the parked cars of fans. Balls that rolled under the cars were ground-rule doubles. Infields were scraped bare and bounces were generally true but life was somewhat harsher in the outfields, where ballhawks roamed in buffalo grass and fought off gophers for possession of ground balls.

Even in those Depression years, certainly the early ones, there was a holiday mood on tournament day. The town drunk got a little drunker than usual, the local tough guy picked more fights, the town bootlegger sold more beer and Catawba wine, and the inevitable Chinese café sold more glutinous and sinewy raisin pie. On the main drag, sunburned sports in striped silk shirts and Christie straws were on the lookout for what used to be called flappers.

Tournament day wound up with a dance in the public hall –
often at the top of a creaky flight of outside stairs in a sweaty
cave presided over by a band called the Silver Seven or the
Rhythm Six. In Brandon we'd repair to the Imperial Dance
Gardens at Princess Avenue and Tenth Street, owned and
operated by Jack Jewsbury and featuring trumpet-playing
Johnny Bering and His Orchestra. Not all girls went home with
the guys who brung them. We were a pretty sophisticated
bunch, we Brandonites.

There was one barnstorming crew whose arrival stopped all
traffic, a team of Cuban players run by one Lee Dillage, a guy
with a big cigar who operated out of Fargo, North Dakota. The
ballplayers themselves made a mysterious, exotic sight as they
rolled into town, their swarthy faces peering out between the
curtains of two big Buick touring cars. Their boss headed this
small procession in a yellow Dusenberg roadster as long as a
boxcar, with the muffler cut out, a four-note musical horn
fluting for gangway, and a minimum of two and a maximum of
six sensationally underdressed and overcoiffed blondes packed
around him like excelsior.

Bigger attractions even than Dillage's Cubans at the larger
tournaments were the black teams. This was an era, remember,
before the lords of organized baseball deigned to permit black
guys to mingle with white guys in the big leagues. So accomplished touring teams such as the Kansas City Monarchs, the
Birmingham Stars, the San Francisco Sea Lions, the Muskogee
Cardinals, the Chicago Black Barons, and the San Francisco
Cubs rolled in and out of the Prairie towns.

These teams ran up impressive totals in road miles as well as
base hits. The K.C. Monarchs once played a tournament in
Brandon on a Wednesday, roared across the dusty roads 300
miles overnight to Carman for a tournament on Thursday,
tumbled back into the cars for another 800 miles or so to
Yorkton in northeastern Saskatchewan for Friday, and then on
to Nipawin nearly 400 miles away on Saturday. That was about
1,500 miles in three nights and included seven ball games.
These days you hear millionaire ballplayers in charter aircraft

complaining about five-hour trips to the West Coast, two trips a season.

The team I'll never forget was Gilkerson's Colored Giants, Gilkerson being a dapper little guy in a straw hat and a vest he likely slept in. Gilkerson's Giants toured for so many years in the late 1920s and early 1930s that their players became as popular as the local heroes, who were mostly imports anyway. Such names as Charlie Akers, Pee Wee Dwight, Satchel Paige, and Pee Wee McNair come easily back to me and, while nostalgia might have something to do with it, it seems to me this club owned players more exciting than the modern Toronto Blue Jays and Montreal's Expos, memorable as players such as Rusty Staub, John Mayberry, Rico Carty, and Bill Lee became. Of course, I was a hell of a lot younger and considerably more impressionable then, too.

Charlie Akers, a shortstop, was a grinning, gangling magician with the glove, the idol of the kids who trudged after him on the Brandon streets and cheered his exaggeratedly casual fielding plays at the old Athletic Grounds. Brandon had a first-baseman named Jimmy Currie, a handsome left-hander from North Dakota who, as was not uncommon in those times, had no affection for black guys. He particularly didn't like Charlie Akers, having played against him many times for the Brandon Greys. He carried on a verbal assault on Charlie, and Charlie responded in an indirect but highly effective way. Whenever Currie grounded to short with the bases empty Charlie would scoop up the ball, flip it to the second-baseman, who would pivot and throw out the hustling Currie on an imaginary double play. Akers, meanwhile, would grin and cry in a high shrill voice, "Let 'im run awhile, brothah."

Gilkerson's Colored Giants had a little guy in centre field named Pee Wee McNair who could outrun an antelope. I adopted his name one summer and had my mother stitch the name Pee Wee on the back of my baseball sweater (we wore V-neck pullovers). The team's catcher, a big, strong, drawling youngster from Georgia named Quincy Troupe, whom I can remember following along Princess Avenue and down Tenth

Street to the Olympia Café to get his autograph, once told a story about the astonishing ground-covering skills of McNair. The story appeared in the *Brandon Sun* under the byline of Krug Crawford, the sports editor (and managing editor and news editor and city editor, as well, on that 12-page paper).

"In a game last week in Delisle, a guy whaled the ball a mile," Troupe told Crawford. "He flew past first base and tore towards second. He steamed past second and rushed towards third. He rounded third full tilt and then the third-base coach threw up his hands. 'Whoa, man, that's far enough,' he said. The runner looked around, wide eyed, and cried, 'What happened, what happened?' And the third-base coach said, 'McNair just caught the ball.'"

But the most fabulous tourist (there's no other word) was Satchel Paige, the pitcher who eventually, at the age of 42 going on 62, was allowed into the big leagues with the white guys. That was in 1948 with the Cleveland Indians, whose owner, Bill Veeck, had introduced the first black guy, Larry Doby, to the American League. Veeck brought in Doby not long after Jackie Robinson made his debut in Brooklyn in 1947 following a season with the Montreal Royals.

A skinny, loose-jointed, deadpan guy of 6-foot-4, Satch often was called the greatest pitcher in baseball. In the 1930s he performed in post-season exhibitions against barnstorming major-leaguers. He sometimes outpitched the great fireballer, Bob Feller, and sometimes Dizzy Dean when Ol' Diz was in his prime and backed by teammates such as Jimmy Foxx, Al Simmons, and Lou Gehrig. Bill Veeck had a chapter on Satch in his autobiography *Veeck as in Wreck*. He recalled seeing him beat Dizzy Dean in California in 1934 after the Cardinals had beaten Detroit in the World Series. The game went 13 innings and Satch won, 1–0.

"Satchel Paige is a skinny Paul Bunyan, born to be everybody's most memorable character," Veeck said in the book. "For 20 years, he pitched every day of the year, night and day, summer and winter, following the cry of the wild dollar all over the United States, the Caribbean and South America, a different city every day, a different team every night. He pitched in the fancy big-league parks and he pitched in scrubby sandlots in such small towns as Lost Woman, North Dakota. He barnstormed against all-star big-league teams, greater himself than the greatest stars, and he pitched his guaranteed three innings against sandlotters, a giant among pygmies.

"Completely uneducated, he picked up a tremendous range of knowledge in his travels. Satch can hold forth, with equal ease, on baseball, dictators or mules. 'Ah've majored in geography, transportation and people,' Satch likes to say. 'Ah been a travelin' man.' When Satch got on the train – the times he made the train – he would always sit alone. Pretty soon the whole team would be gathered around, listening to him spin his yarns. Satch doesn't hold conversations, he holds court."

Satch, born Leroy Robert Paige, started only 25 games in the five seasons he performed in the big leagues. He pitched during two seasons for Cleveland and three more with the St. Louis Browns in the early 1950s. He worked three innings for the Kansas City A's in 1965 and then gave it up. By then he was 59, give or take.

As a tournament player in the West, Paige never went hungry. His windmill windup, his smoke-trailing fastball, and a stratospheric blooper pitch attracted fans wherever he appeared, enabling him to pretty well name his own ticket. The summer I saw him in the 1930s he was pitching for a touring team from Bismarck, North Dakota, whose owner supplied him with a cream-coloured Cadillac convertible in which he did his own travelling to tournaments. Paige was asked once if he thought he could win in the big leagues.

"Plate's same size," he replied civilly.

Satch received a few perks but it wasn't an era of pampered pitchers. It wasn't deemed extraordinary that he sometimes pitched two games at a one-day tournament and was ready to amble to the mound for a couple of innings of relief if the need arose. Back then, pitching coaches weren't sitting in the dugouts counting pitches, ready to hop out to the mound for a consultation once 120 pitches had been clicked off, ready to relieve the poor devil out there if he confessed he was weary. For one thing, nobody had pitching coaches.

It wasn't just the barnstormers who worked overtime; big-league pitchers toiled long hours, too. Warren Spahn, who pitched for 20 seasons for the Braves of both Boston and Milwaukee in the 1940s, '50s, and '60s, worked more than 250 innings 16 times and twice topped 300 innings. In Fergie Jenkins's first four seasons with the Cubs in the late 1960s, he produced more than 300 innings each time. By contrast, in 1988 the Blue Jays' workhorse, to use that word, was elderly Mike Flanagan who toiled 211 innings. The only other pitcher to work more than 200 was Dave Stieb at 207. And just three Expos bettered 200 – Dennis Martinez with 235, Kevin Gross at 231, and Bryn Smith at 198 (well, almost 200).

Spahn, for one, thinks the workload borne by current pitchers is meagre enough to be ridiculous. One early evening he turned up in the press lounge at the Toronto dome for a Blue Jays game on the eve of an old-timers' exhibition. The conversation turned to modern-day pitchers and Spahn, by then 68 and still taking an occasional turn in the old-timers' tussles, grunted his displeasure. "They're so damned lazy," said Spahnie, as everyone called him. "They won't work."

Also, they are coddled. "You get to the sixth or seventh inning and the manager goes out there worried to death that the starter has gone far enough and he brings in a reliever. But look how many relievers lose games. They blow all kinds of ball games, yet the managers keep taking out the starters. They coddle them."

The Cy Young Award is the one every pitcher yearns to win; it means he's his league's top hand. Yet if modern pitchers studied old Cy's workload they'd faint. In five of his first six seasons with the Cleveland Nationals, Cy topped *400* innings, and in seven of the next eight he pitched between 325 and 390. The *Baseball Encyclopedia* records that in his 22 years in the big leagues, Cy Young pitched 7,356 innings. That figure is completely meaningless until you realize that it averages out to 334 innings per season.

Spahn was no Cy Young but he did top 265 innings 13 times and he won 363 games. He wasn't that big, either, an even six-footer and 175 pounds. But he loved to work.

"I used to go out to the outfield between starts and throw the ball like an outfielder," he said this evening at the ballpark, wolfing down spareribs and boiled potatoes and salad.

What did he mean, I wondered, "like an outfielder."

"Oh, you know, not lobbing it back to the guy hitting fungoes, but rifling it in like you were making a play at the plate. I used to throw it in hard like that, pretending I was nailing a guy sliding in."

He never had a sore arm and he brooked no kind thoughts for the person, whoever it was, who began the modern practice of counting a pitcher's pitches or the one who felt young pitchers could ruin their arms by pitching too much too early in their baseball lives. "They used to say the reason I lasted was because I didn't pitch much until I was 25. Hell, I was in the army was the reason I wasn't pitchin' and anyway I was pitchin' in there."

Unlike most modern ballplayers who are often impatient with the hard-thinking scribes (in Toronto they showed more patience when the TV interviewer Fergie Olver buttonholed them – Fergie carried American $50 bills stuck in his belt with which he lured the millionaires for a couple of questions on camera), Spahn was never chary with his time or his opinions. It was his conviction that modern pitchers do not pitch often enough. He said he used to pitch every chance he got. "The second day after a start I'd throw batting practice and I loved it," he grumbled. "You ever see a starting pitcher throw BP these days?"

Then he was struck by a new thought.

"The guy I roomed with, Paul Waner, and another outfielder, John Cooney, they'd take a fungo bat and lay it down 10 feet inside the foul line away out in the outfield and then in BP they'd see who could land the most balls between the bat and the foul line. I mean, that's a two-base hit out there in the corner every time. You ever see guys doin' something like that now. No, they're all tryin' to knock BP home runs."

Chattering away, age 68, full of vigour and opinions, Spahn was a non-stop talker once he cleared his throat. It pleased him that the classic piece of doggerel, Spahn and Sain and pray for rain, became part of baseball lore.

"A Boston writer came up with it," he said this night. "It was 1948, and Vern Bickford and Bill Voiselle had had good years for us, but they were hurt late in the season. There were a lot of rainouts and off days, so Johnny Sain and I were doing most of the pitching and the club got to the World Series. Amazing how many people remember. Even little kids will come up to me and say, Spahn and Sain and pray for rain. It's one of baseball's few colloquialisms, like Tinkers to Evers to Chance. It has a ring to it. I didn't have that good a year that time but I came on pretty good late in the year. Even so, Sain should get the credit. I mean, what if his name had been Vuckovich?"

Or if it had been a dry fall.

Chapter 3

Everything is different on grawse

A person can grow all dewy-eyed over Wimbledon because more often than not it's raining. Everybody sits there at Centre Court blinking and wiping as the drops land on a large, tent-like tarpaulin that droops a few feet above the court in an inverted V.

Wimbledon is wondrous in its tradition but it is mighty slow to change its habits. I got to four Wimbledons and at each one I wondered why, with all the dough they bring in at the gate, they didn't put a retractable roof over half a dozen courts, and especially the Centre Court, so that the big sellout crowds would have something to contemplate during the rain delays besides the fascinating sight of drops of water forming pools of water on top of tarpaulins.

Wimbledon celebrated its centenary in 1977 but it wasn't until 1987 that the tournament committee permitted ball girls to join ball boys in fetching tennis balls for the players at Centre Court. And it was only one year earlier that the committee accepted (with great reluctance, one assumes) the use of yellow tennis balls, the flight of which is easier to follow than that of the once traditional white tennis balls.

As it happened, I was there that day in 1986 when the yellow balls made their inaugural appearance at the cathedral of tennis, but they were by no means the only surprise for the regulars. Quite as remarkable, it wasn't raining at 2 p.m. There is a long tradition at Wimbledon that on opening day it rains at 2 p.m., which is the starting time for the Centre Court's opening match. Early arrivals who watch the players on the outside courts assemble at 12:30 for the day's first matches out there, but at Centre Court the gentry are given time to digest lunch properly. Until then people with reserved seats walk about the grounds quite dry, admiring the strawberries, watching the matches on the outback, and making such comments as "Oh, I say," or "Jolly good shot, Trevor."

But the instant they feel a raindrop they know that it is 2 p.m. and time for the big match at Centre Court and they hurry to their seats for the rain delay that precedes the opening serve. Similarly, when the tournament's chief referee feels the first raindrop, he climbs into his high chair and says in his careful way, "Quiet please, ladies and gentlemen. Thank you. Linesmen ready? Players ready? Play." Then he says, "Ah, by jove. Well, shall we wait a few moments, ladies and gentlemen?" And there begins the afternoon's first rain delay. However, as I say, on this opening day of 1986 there was the remarkable fact that the sun was high and shining and play began and the rain didn't arrive until 2:45.

Still, there was the matter of the yellow balls. What a body blow their sanction surely was to many of the 375 people who constitute the total membership of the All-England Lawn Tennis and Croquet Club, 300 men and 75 of the other sex. For them, tradition matters. The grand shrine of tennis had long stood firm as the last bastion of the white tennis ball, and the feeling of most of the 375 members was that if the white ball was good enough when Fred Perry struck it and won in 1934, 1935, and 1936, why wasn't the white ball good enough now?

Here is how one of them phrased his objection:

"If you take a yellow ball and play on grass you pick up green grass stains, and do you have any idea what yellow and green together make?"

Not pausing for a reply, he supplied his own.

"Well, I shall tell you: blue. In the name of being modern, should we play with bloody blue balls?"

The first Wimbledon I went to was the 1977 centenary (the way the English say centenary, it comes out cen-*teen*-ary), the one that marked the second of Bjorn Borg's record five straight titles. It also marked the maiden appearance of an 18-year-old kid from New York, John McEnroe. I remember him so well in the semifinal almost knocking out the grandstanding Jimmy Connors, who, along with Ilie Nastase, the pest of Bucharest, was refining his remarkable skill at being a jerk.

Of course, there was only one Nastase. Who knows what it was about his crude antics and brutal language that so fascinated Connors that he became practically his clone for so many years? In 1977 Nastase played Borg and as early as the second point of the first game he was into his act. The baseline judge called Nastase's long forehand shot out and the rogue of Romania went into his pat routine of staring at the linesman, hands on hips, then approaching the umpire's chair at midcourt and appealing there. The umpire just shook his head.

So after losing that opening game at love and while the players were changing ends, Nastase walked past the umpire again, carrying a tennis ball in his right hand and his racquet in his left. As he drew abreast of the chair he zipped the ball, in the manner of a guy tossing a dart, between the legs of the seated umpire.

"Did Nastase toss that ball where he appeared to toss that ball?" a newshound asked the umpire after the match.

"He most certainly did," said the ump with an embarrassed little smile.

That same day, in the quarterfinals, McEnroe knocked out the No. 13 seed, the Australian Phil Dent. By this time, he was drawing all sorts of attention because he'd arrived in England, unknown, to play in the Wimbledon junior event. Then he went into the qualifying round for the main draw and won three qualifying matches to get into the field of 128 starters, and he just kept beating people until there he was in the semis.

On the court he was earnest and intense, none of the ranting that later became a trademark. He wore a red bandana around his head to keep wild curly hair out of the way, and afterwards when he turned up for the mandatory meeting with the news people he wore a faded red Marlboro cigarette T-shirt, old blue jeans, and battered sneakers. The scribes wondered if he felt intimidated by the forthcoming match against Connors, back then a top player.

"I don't think much about who I'm playing," McEnroe said in an offhand way. "I never heard of half of them. I'm getting used to Wimbledon because I've been on almost every court except the Centre one. As for Connors, geez, I don't think I can beat him. I'm just gonna go out there and do the best I can and if it turns out that I win I'll probably drop dead on the court."

He broke into a sudden hysterical laugh, either at the prospect of beating Connors or lying out there dead on Centre Court – or maybe both. No, he didn't beat Connors, not that year, but soon he owned him. Soon he owned everybody and hardly anybody could stand his childishness.

During subsequent Wimbledons the thing that struck me was how much the players and officials spoke about the grass courts. I wrote a piece in the *Globe and Mail* about this, about how a great deal of time was occupied in serious discussion of the ball's erratic bounce on the grass, so different from the bounce on the clay of the Roland Garros Stadium in Paris and the painted hard stuff of New York's nuthouse at Flushing Meadows. I mentioned that everybody called the Wimbledon surface "grawse." They'd say, "Oh, Chrissie's service is much stronger on grawse." Or they'd say, "Steffi's forehand is devastating on grawse."

Well, that's okay, that's how English people talk. But the talkers were inconsistent. Like, they didn't call Pat Cash Pat Cawsh. You didn't catch them saying, "Pat Cawsh is strong on grawse." No, they'd call Cash Cash. They'd say, "Pat Cash is strong on grawse."

Even the marvelous nonpareil of tennis announcers – no, not Bud Collins, for God's sake – called Cash Cash and grass grawse. I mean Dan Maskell, who this year, 1990, made his 62nd appearance at Wimbledon. He was there away back in the days when the French Musketeers – Rene Lacoste, Henri Cochet, Jean Borotra, and Jacques Brugnon – and the American wizard Bill Tilden were dominating the game.

Dan Maskell works for the BBC but the geniuses who run the networks in the U.S. and Canada would run him off the air over here. That is because he keeps assuming that the people tuning in are not complete idiots. If a guy serves an ace Dan doesn't jump out of the broadcast booth advising the poor devils watching at home that this is probably the hardest-hit ace in the history of the Slazenger LTA official ball. He doesn't even say it's an ace; he doesn't say anything. He has this revolutionary notion that since *he* can see that it's an ace anybody watching at home can see that it's an ace.

When I was at Wimbledon in 1988 a story going the rounds related that Dan Maskell and the BBC cameras were watching Ivan Lendl fuming on the court. The former Czech star was grimacing, swiping his racquet at the worn grawse, stomping to the umpire's chair complaining about a call.

In the broadcast booth Maskell let the camera do the work. He had nothing to say until finally, after a long period of silence while Lendl stormed, he noted, "Not a very happy man."

Dan is a warm, suave, white-haired gentleman now 82 and going strong the last I heard. He looks a little like John Gielgud. At age 14 he was a ball boy at the Queen's Club in London and later, encouraged by his father, he became a tennis teacher and eventually the club pro at the Queen's Club. He was hired by the BBC in the early 1950s "to help fill the void between matches," as he phrased it in typical understatement.

Sometimes Dan grows a trifle lyrical in his descriptions. Rallies are occasionally "gorgeous" and he's been known to say of some overhead smashes that they're "glorious." One day I heard him say when Lendl whistled a topspin streak past Mark Woodforde at the net that the shot was "an absolute blissful pass."

Even so, what do you require on your tennis telecasts, a blissful pass or Bud Collins falling down the stairs?

It is difficult to let one's mind resurrect the scene at Wimbledon without another legendary figure inching into the picture, a mighty hard figure to miss, one that rose 6-foot-4 above the grawse and was crowned by an egg-shaped, bald head. All of this belonged to Ted Tinling, whose absence from the 1990 renewal at the tennis shrine was truly conspicuous. Two months earlier, closing on his 80th birthday, Ted Tinling died in Cambridge, England, after a lengthy period of failing health.

Ted was a commanding person – to look at and to listen to. He wore a diamond in the lobe of his left ear and clothes that resembled a sunset in Antigua. One afternoon in 1988, after seeing him in the press dining lounge over three or four Wimbledons, I decided I'd like to write a piece about him. He sat alone at a table in the press dining area, a brightly lit cafeteria, having a cup of tea and reading Rex Bellamy's daily tennis article in *The Times*. I asked him if I might join him. I had already carefully written in my notebook his garb for the day – a red-and-white checked shirt with a green-and-white checked collar, a tie of navy blue, a double-breasted jacket of navy blue with gold buttons, and cream trousers and white shoes. His elongated face was the colour of a vine-ripened beefsteak tomato. He said, "By all means, old boy. Sit down."

Ted Tinling was a fashion designer and tennis buff who created the most famous pair of women's panties in the history of global sports, the lace-trimmed ones for Gussie Moran that didn't bother the Wimbledon establishment any more than the explosion of a nuclear device might have. The question I asked him first concerned that highly attractive woman who was known as Gorgeous Gussie. What year did he design those pants of hers and had he been contemplating doing so for long?

"It was 1949," he replied briskly, a tanned, brusque fellow then 78. "No, there was not a long period of incubation. I wanted something for her for Wimbledon, and it simply seemed lace was the answer."

"Why did you do it?" I said.

"Why? Because everything the players were wearing was dull. Dull, dull, dull."

Teddy began working at Wimbledon in 1927, first as an umpire, then counting the day's gate receipts at night. But the uproar of Gussie's panties relegated him to the role of uninvited guest, and it wasn't until 1981 that he was invited back. In the meantime he continued designing women's tennis clothes and was well enough connected that it wasn't necessary for him to join a queue outside the gates in order to attend. He shared with the announcer Dan Maskell an abiding love for tennis. "Remarkable place, this," he said once to John Feinstein, who works for the daily sports newspaper, the *National*, in the U.S. "There are no three words in the English language that give me more pleasure than getting into a car in the morning and saying, 'To Wimbledon then.' As long as I can do that, life is worth living."

Until Teddy came along with Gussie's pantaloons the evolution of women's apparel was appalling. People who have taken the London Underground to the matches will recall that there's a Barclay's bank directly across the street from the tube station, Southfields, that serves the tennis complex. All during the 1988 tournament, just inside the bank's front door, there was a nonstop, closed-circuit film of the legendary Suzanne Lenglen in action in the early 1920s. She was a most athletic, even balletic figure performing on Wimbledon's Centre Court, shooting one leg at a 90-degree angle as she floated to hit a high forehand. But she was dressed like one of Shakespeare's witches in *Macbeth*. Her ankle-length, pleated skirt clung to her extended limb, and her ballooning blouse was buttoned at the wrist. Ted Tinling did everyone an enormous favour when he got the women players into short shorts and shorter skirts. By jove, much easier for mobility, old chap. Especially on grawse.

Speaking of which, grass in now a unique feature at Wimbledon among the four Grand Slam sites. Once, the Australian Open in Melbourne and the U.S. Open at Forest Hills were also played on the natural stuff, but not any more. Even so, even though the switch to this tricky, scuffed surface requires a big adjustment by the players, Wimbledon is still the centrepiece of tennis. Partly, no doubt, this is because Wimbledon has been anointed by royalty and partly because of its long tradition. Most days there is a royal personage seated under a wide green and mauve tapestry at one end of Centre Court, the royal box. The Duke and Duchess of Kent are there almost daily, for they are the tournament's patrons and always make the presentations to the winners of the men's and women's singles titles. Princess Diana attends three or four times during the fortnight, as does her sister-in-law, the flamboyant Fergie, the Duchess of York.

The royal box accommodates 75 or 80 guests each afternoon, half a dozen long rows of wide, comfortable, padded chairs located next to a section of wooden benches that affords the lowly scribes an excellent sightline of the court. Next to the scribes, in turn, is a section for friends and relatives of the contestants and a daily clutch of visiting celebrities, such as former tennis greats Fred Perry, Evonne Goolagong, or Tracy Austin, and film stars Brigitte Bardot, perhaps, or Dyan Cannon. The fascinating aspect of this arrangement is that between games while the players are toweling off, the scribes have their heads turned to the right to see who are in the celebrity section, the celebrity heads are turned to the left to peer past the scribes at the royals, and the royals are staring straight ahead, giving everybody what Damon Runyon used to call the big ignore.

For two weeks, little else gets front-page attention in the London dailies, and one of the two BBC television channels carries each day's play in entirety, plus a one-hour wrapup of highlights at 10 o'clock each night. Tournament tickets are hard to get and scalpers collect outrageous prices. A friend of mine, book publisher Avie Bennett, relates that in June of 1989 he was in London on business and was hopeful of spending a day at Wimbledon. A well-connected friend of his said he thought he might be able to get a ticket for Avie for 1,000 pounds. Avie suddenly remembered a previous engagement.

Still, in some fashion, tens of thousands of people make their way through Wimbledon's iron gates each afternoon. Long,

long lines stretch along Church Road outside the main gates inching slowly forward to buy standing-room space. The queue stretches two and three abreast for at least two miles, winding for half a mile along the sidewalk on Church Road and then twisting off into the vast rolling lands of Wimbledon Park, bending around in the distance like a giant question mark. Crowds are there rain or shine, and sometimes in withering and unaccustomed English heat.

I recall one such day during the 1986 tournament when the papers allowed the weather to share front-page space with tennis and had everybody rushing off to the coastal beaches to escape winds drifting north from the Sahara Desert. "By mid-afternoon, roads to the South and West were in the grip of stifling jams," reported the tabloid *Daily Mail*.

The temperature was either 92 or 86 (over there in the heart of the Commonwealth, nobody bothers with Celsius). The tabloid *Sun* cried "92!" in its tallest type. The sedate *Times*, under the small heading, Warm Weather Will Continue, said 86. In the *Sun*, a picture of British tennis player Jo Durie appeared beside the "92!" She was fully dressed, causing a sensation among *Sun* readers exposed for the first time to a picture of a woman wearing clothes above the waist.

When the gates opened the waiting thousands slowly squeezed through narrow entrances. The announced attendance was 39,090. Wimbledon, by its own count, seats 26,005 including temporary bleachers and small benches beside some of the outer courts. Obviously, then, many thousands had no hope of watching tennis that day, so once inside they sat under umbrellas at outdoor bars and watched the hordes pushing past the ivy-adorned, dark-green stadium, in hope of finding standing room beside an outside court or moving beyond the stadium to a treeless picnic area.

There, little kids romped and young grownups lay on blankets on yellowed burned-out grass, exposing their pale English pelts to this unusual day's unrelenting sun. Around them there was a carnival atmosphere of outdoor commerce – a long rectangular Food Village where half-chickens slowly turned on spits, weiners sizzled, fish and chips bubbled, and people in booths sold gin-and-tonic mixes, film, sandwiches, pastries, nuts, and beer. And beyond, there was a post office and a parcel-checking window and a souvenir stand and a carousel-shaped sporting-goods shop and a huge tent under which little kids whaled a plastic tennis ball with a plastic racquet and another huge tent packed with people milling for Wimbledon-crested sports clothes in the shrine's colours, green and mauve – sweaters, shorts, windbreakers, shirts, sweatshirts, socks, visors, and tote bags. Indeed, out in the vast picnic area there was just about everything a tennis fan could possibly want except this one thing: tennis.

On the courts in the late 1980s Boris Becker was the game's dominant figure, a warm, earnest, big-boned German who, at 17 in 1985, was the youngest Wimbledon winner ever. He repeated this triumph in 1986, lost in 1987 to a tall, skinny Australian, Peter Doohan, in a stunning second-round upset, lost in the final to Sweden's Stefan Edberg in 1988, regained his eminence by crushing Edberg in straight sets in the 1989 final, and, when they met in the final for the third straight time in 1990, lost by 6–4 in the fifth set.

Becker was at the top of his game when he won for the third time but I liked him best after Doohan shocked him and everyone else in 1987. Tennis is among the best organized of all the sports in making its heroes available to the press for interviews (it shares this distinction with golf). After big matches the players are delivered to podiums in large secluded rooms where they answer the questions of the assembled word-mongers.

On this day when Becker was beaten by Doohan he replied to a number of crepe-laden queries in a forthright fashion. ("Is this your most disappointing defeat ever?" "No, I've lost other tough matches." "Have there been other matches where you've been this bad?" "I didn't play so badly as he played well. That second set was like magic. Every time he would guess where I was going to put the ball he would be right.") And then, as the dark questions continued, Boris made a comment of his own.

"Look, I tried my best and I lost," he said. "I'm human, I cannot play good every day. But there was no war, no one was killed. It was just a tennis match."

Not too many athletes have their heads in so mature a perspective. And as Boris also said that day, "I am not immortal and I am not even 20 years old yet, so I have many more chances."

Indeed, he was back in the Wimbledon final the following year and the year after that. In 1988, getting there without the loss of a set, he somehow managed to fall to Stefan Edberg, but a year later, when he met the stylish Swede again, his brutally hard serve guided him past Edberg in straight sets for his third Wimbledon title in five years.

Entering the 1990s the red-headed Boris was the game's dominant player, very effective on grass where every ball stays lower than on other surfaces and where, as a tournament wears along, bounces are often unpredictable on the chewed-up sod. Still, his crushing serve was becoming a crashing bore. The example of his power was threatening to turn men's singles into a one-shot sport. When he and the hard-serving Edberg were on the court there were few rallies and little deftness, just violent service winners or smoked volleys off hapless service returns. There were few delicate drop shots. What there was was this: boom, boom, boom, boom.

However, in Boris's encounters with the scribes he was still the level-headed, earnest, and responsive fellow who had faced them after the loss to Doohan. There was no trace of false modesty but a ready acceptance of the evidence that on grass he could likely beat anybody alive, including Edberg most days.

At 19 Becker's personality was developed eons beyond McEnroe's at 29. The game's *enfant terrible* went into a self-imposed six-month exile in 1986. He and his actress wife Tatum O'Neal had a son that summer and then in the autumn he essayed a comeback, saying that fatherhood and other responsibilities had given him a new look at himself from which he'd prospered. No more Mr. Bad Guy.

"I was out of hand," he told scribes assembled for the U.S.

Open. "I was going in a direction that wasn't beneficial to tennis. I'm talking about every match I played. I had become resentful of everything. Yeah, there's no question things were going in a bad direction."

Big Mac can be charming when he's introspective, sitting on a dais with a microphone all to himself, answering questions from us mortals with our quills. He talks with earnestness, brow furrowed and pale face drawn. But as soon as he's back on the court some inner force takes over and he turns sour and petulent, questioning every close call, insulting umpires and fans, sometimes cursing himself.

"His tennis is merely miraculous. He is smart and often more honest and aware than most athletes of his level," the bright young New York columnist Mike Lupica wrote of him. "But he will not stop being a churlish nuisance. He will not stop doing things that would get him beat up on the street. He thinks it is his right to scream at officials in front of 20,000 people. It is not his right. It is lousy, miserable behavior."

The last time McEnroe won one of the Grand Slam tournaments – Wimbledon and the French, Australian, and U.S. Opens – was 1984 when he won at both Wimbledon and Flushing Meadow (he has never won at Paris or Melbourne), when he was considerably shorter in the tooth than in 1990 when he turned 32. Will he ever come back? "No," said the stern-visaged Ion Tiriac, the former Romanian Davis Cupper who is Boris Becker's manager. "Once you fall from the top in this business you do not climb back up." Closer to home, Arthur Ashe, once Big Mac's Davis Cup captain, concurred. "Tiriac is probably right."

One player, impassive as a stretch of wallpaper on and off the court, may nonetheless have found particular relish in handling McEnroe in the late 1980s. This was the world's No. 1 player, Ivan Lendl, who had won finals everywhere except at Wimbledon. A decade ago when Ivan was just getting going and Big Mac had arrived, they turned up in Maple Leaf Gardens for a midwinter tournament. Following an early-round victory Mac sat still for the usual post-match press scrum, during which he was asked his thoughts on this new silent kid from Czechoslovakia.

"You got me. Who is he?" said the Big Mac. "So many of these guys come and go I can't place him."

Pretty soon, Mac was seeing more of Lendl than his ego needed. Ivan won that Toronto tournament, only his second North American victory (he'd scored at Houston a couple of weeks earlier). One of his great wins came three years later when he met McEnroe in the 1984 French final. The latter won the first two sets 6–3 and 6–2, seemingly headed for his first French title, but Ivan came off the red clay in the next three sets and won them by 6–4, 7–5, 7–5. Indeed, through the whole decade of the eighties Lendl was the game's dominant player, never worse than third in world ranking from 1981 on and No. 1 in '85, '86, '87, and '89.

Even so, poor Ivan, nobody loved him. He was the best tennis player on earth (though not on grawse) but his crowd appeal approached zero. It wasn't that anybody disliked him particularly; it was simply that he was a hard man to feel anything for. As Gertrude Stein once said in a different context, "There is no there there." Having an emotional reaction to Ivan was like having an affair with wallboard. His on-court demeanour was what did him in with the fans. He'd never acknowledge the folks. McEnroe would snarl at them, curse them, give them a finger, but at least he acknowledged them. Not Ivan. He was concerned only with the matter at hand. Sometimes he'd react to a bad call but mostly he was absorbed with his current predicament. Everything was between Ivan and the round yellow ball, point after point, set after set, match after match. He never laughed.

That was on the court. Off the court Ivan seemed to spend a lot of time going to the bank. By the end of the decade he'd won $15 million. That was just his winnings. There were all those endorsements on the shirts he wore, the racquets he swung, the shoes he tied on his big feet.

The scribes didn't love him any more than the fans did, especially the Brits during Wimbledon. "He won yesterday with an impressive contempt," a guy wrote in the *Daily Mail* (the *Dylie Mile*) during the 1988 tournament. Another grumped, "His victories and his failures seem always to be achieved from the midst of a thunderous sulk." The gentleman from *The Times* huffed, "McEnroe does not invariably make friends but he certainly makes the most passionate enemies. Lendl cannot even do that."

But Ivan wasn't all robot. He sat on the dais in front of the rows of deep thinkers after a very difficult five-set squeaker with Tim Mayotte in which he prevailed by 9–7 in the fifth, and showed real emotion. "I don't think you can have a tighter match and get through it," he said, rubbing a thick green towel across his dripping beak and chin. "If it had been any tougher I would have lost. It gets just so tight; your eyes are tired, your feet are tired, your hand is tired." He laughed shortly. "And you're *nervous*."

He looked out across the sea of faces focused on him. Sweat popped onto his forehead again and he ran the towel across his dripping head.

"It helps to win such a close match, especially with 90 per cent of you guys saying I'd lose. Since I got here I have been chopped up for everything. I've been chopped up for not smiling, for not wanting to have pictures taken with my girl friend. I've been chopped up for beating my opponent too easily in the first round, for not having enough sting in my volleys in the second round, and advised that I move crummy. So I just don't read it any more. I just get my *Herald-Tribune* and read the baseball scores and the politics."

It's only in the recent years of enormous purses in tennis that the players have been put under such scrutiny. Once, it truly was a gentlemen's game with only an occasional extrovert to break the serenity. Just before World War Two there emerged an agreeable little braggart named Bobby Riggs, a con man extraordinaire and a mighty hard guy to forget. Bobby talked a great game but he was capable of playing a clever one, too. Actually, Riggs surfaced twice on the world's tennis stage, once in 1939 when he won everything in sight at Wimbledon, and once in 1973 in a crazy battle of the sexes with Billie Jean King when, in a phrase he pounded relentlessly, he was 55 years old with one foot in the grave.

Chances are, Riggs in his prime could not have stood up to the Becker of 1990, but he wasn't bad. "Riggs did everything right," a noted American analyst of style, Julius Heldman, observed one time of the stocky fellow. "He was undoubtedly the cagiest player of all time. More than any other player, he exemplified the champion's will to win."

Riggs stopped growing at a half-inch under five-eight, a hustler, a non-conformist, a fast talker on the rise when he reached Wimbledon in 1939 (later that year he won the U.S. Open and repeated in 1941). One of his first stops in London was a betting shop on Fleet Street. As he wrote later in his autobiography, *Court Hustler*, the conversation began like this:

"What are the odds on this fellow Riggs winning the Wimbledon singles?"

"Let's see. 'Ere now 'e's three to one."

"Three to one! It's his first Wimbledon. He ought to be twice that."

"No, 'e's No. 1 in the U.S. Three to one's quite sufficient."

So Riggs bet a hundred pounds on himself, a pound being worth about $5 back then.

Craving more action, he wanted to know what odds the bookie would lay against Riggs winning the men's doubles if he won the singles and parlayed his bet.

"Six to one."

"Six to one! But Riggs and Elwood Cooke lost the French to two old guys, Borotra and Brugnon."

The bookie yawned. "Six to one," he repeated.

"Okay, okay, but what if Riggs gets lucky, wins the singles, wins the doubles, and I go ahead and parlay the bundle on him and Alice Marble in the mixed?"

"For a bet like that, 12 to one."

"Oh come on."

"As I say, 12 to one."

"All right, all right."

And Riggs laid down his hundred pounds.

He zipped through the early singles rounds, then met his doubles partner Cooke in the final. After three sets he trailed, two to one.

Enter the spectre of his hundred-pound bet.

"I've always believed the incentive of the parlay made the difference," Riggs wrote in *Court Hustler*. "That was enough to spur me into taking the last two sets."

Next, he and Cooke beat England's Charlie Hare and Frank Wilde in the doubles, and following that triumph he teamed with Alice Marble and beat the British pair of Wilde and Nancy Brown for the mixed title. Come Monday morning and Riggs was off to Fleet Street to lay his hands on 21,600 English pounds. That converted to about $108,000 American back then, maybe a million-dollar bet nowadays.

Some 34 years later, in 1973, Riggs was back in the news, a central figure in the emerging women's liberation movement, a non-stop male chauvinist pig, in the phrase of the day. One afternoon that September, working for the *Toronto Star*, I caught up to him at the Westside Racquet Club in Beverly Hills, a not particularly pretentious club nestled in the midst of the movie colony. Its eight hard courts were painted a brilliant green with white lines, and the clubhouse was California Spanish, flat-roofed and sprawling, with pools and patios and saunas and bars.

Riggs, the super hustler, was there to practise for a wildly hyped match with Billie Jean King scheduled for the Houston Astrodome in the fall of 1973. Billie Jean had taken the burgeoning women's movement to the tennis courts, proclaiming that the women's game was every bit as entertaining as the men's and therefore deserving of purses on a parity with theirs. The 55-year-old Riggs (with one foot in the grave) had stumbled back into the public consciousness in a challenge match in which he'd beaten Margaret Court, who with Billie Jean dominated women's tennis. King, in turn, had agreed to take him on to defend women's honour, or at least to make a buck for both of them.

The timing was perfect and the match caught on. Tennis buffs everywhere made bets on it; even people who knew diddly-squat about tennis were drawn to this hugely ballyhooed Battle of the Sexes. "I happened to arrive on the scene at the right time," Riggs proclaimed this day at the Los Angeles club. "The women's lib thing is here and there's nostalgia around now. I'm an old guy 55 years of age with one foot in the grave but I'm the right guy at the right time in the right place."

Wearing a crooked grin and ad-libbing anything that popped into his greying old head, Riggs showed up on tiny screens and in Sunday supplements. He never stopped talking, loud and clear except for the s's. The s's came out as sh's because, as someone remarked at the time, "There'sh more teeth than there'sh room for" in the amiable kisser of this little guy in hornrims, strutting and preening and playing his unexpected windfall to its hilt. Answering questions that nobody asked, he'd cry, "You're wondering what I've got against women's lib? Nothing. It's just that I'm pro men's lib. I've been married twice and divorced twice so I've escaped twice. But this Billie Jean is playin' for a cause, for all those women who want to keep guys from playin' poker on Friday night and goin' fishin' on the weekend, all the young guys just gettin' married. I'll win for us guys."

The match in the Astrodome drew the largest crowd that ever sat in on a game of tennis – more than 34,000 in the indoor dome. Millions more were peering at the screens at home. And the spectacle was pure hokum as Riggs and Billie Jean arrived on separate curtained litters carried by half-naked slaves. An hour or so later Riggs departed on his shield. Billie Jean flailed him in three straight sets.

Chapter 4

An athletic supporter is born

The way I see it, I became a sports fan 10 days after I turned eight. I clearly remember sitting in Lowell Hyde's house on 13th Street in Brandon and listening to the squeaky, crackling radio broadcast of the first Dempsey-Tunney fight, the one in which Gene Tunney, who was called the Fighting Marine, scored a big upset in the rain in Philadelphia, winning the title from the brutal Manassa Mauler, Jack Dempsey. That was on September 23, 1926. I had turned eight on the 13th and the following week Lowell Hyde's father let me strap the earphones of his newly acquired crystal set across my head and actually hear a man give a blow-by-blow account of this battle for the heavyweight championship of the world.

I don't know whether the World Series was broadcast that autumn for we had no radio at our house that early. But I remember my dad taking me by the hand down Tenth Street below Rosser Avenue, the main stem, to the *Sun*, where we stood outside the newspaper's three-storey brick building and watched a man emerge from the front door every 15 minutes or so, climb a stepladder to a bulletin board above the first-floor windows, and in a small neat hand paint each half-inning's runs on a sheet of white paper pasted to the board. When he'd climb down, if the Yankees had scored a run people would ask, "Did the Babe get a homer?" One afternoon during a one-sided win by the Yankees he came out wide-eyed late in the game after the Babe had already hit two homers and told us, "He did it again!"

Old-time fans still recall the seventh game of the 1926 Series as the one in which Grover Cleveland Alexander – Ol' Pete, he was called – came out of the Cardinal bullpen with the game on the line. He needed a shave and wore the pained expression of a man suffering a nagging hangover, a worn right-hander of 39 who'd already won two Series games, and now here he was unexpectedly called upon by the St. Louis manager, Rogers Hornsby, to protect a 3–2 lead. The bases were full of Yankees, there were two out in the seventh inning, and the batter was the rookie slugger Tony Lazzeri, who had been second only to Ruth himself as the American League's runs-batted-in leader that season. Ol' Pete, hangover and all, struck him out. Then he set down the Yankees in the eighth and ninth for the Cardinals first World Series victory.

It was partly because of that ball game that I eventually became a sports writer. Another reason was the young woman who taught music in Park School, Helen Bennest. She later married a Brandon hockey player, Jimmy Creighton, who played for the Detroit Olympics in the old International League. In a game against the Windsor Bulldogs Creighton was severely injured, a broken pelvic bone. While he mended in a hospital a scribe from the *Windsor Star*, Gillis Purcell, visited him to do a feature story. There, Purcell met Helen Bennest, visiting her love, and they became good friends.

Creighton's injury slowed his progress in hockey. He married Helen, played minor-league hockey in Boston, Philadelphia, and Kansas City, and eventually settled in Brandon as an insurance agent and became a good one. Later on he was a success as a hockey coach with the Brandon Wheat Kings juniors. Meantime, Gillis Purcell left the *Windsor Star*, joined the Canadian Press, and rose rapidly in this country's national wire service to become CP's feared and hard-driving general manager. But over the years, any time he visited CP bureaus in western Canada, he usually managed to drop in on his friends the Creightons in Brandon. My own notion is that he was sweet on the lovely Helen. For her part, Helen kept telling Purcell about this kid in her music class who possessed a stupefying amount of sports trivia.

"Gil, you must keep an eye on this boy," she told him more than once. "He knows the batting averages of all the baseball players. He can tell you how many home runs Babe Ruth hit in his whole life. And Jim says he knows all about hockey, too."

Once, in October of 1934, Purcell visited Brandon and Helen telephoned my home, asking me to come over (I know it was October of 1934 because the World Series was on and Detroit was playing the Cardinals). "Gil, this is the fellow I've often told you about," she said to Purcell.

He extended his hand, a stocky man who parted his hair in the middle and wore glasses. I shook his hand, not having the faintest notion who he was or why I was there.

"Helen tells me you're a sports fan," he said. "Do you think the Cardinals can handle the Tigers?"

"Yes," I said, taking this very earnestly. "I expect Dizzy Dean will be as good for them in this Series as Grover Cleveland Alexander was in 1926. Dean won 30 games this year, you know."

No question about it, I was steeped in useless information. Every fall and spring I'd go to the Tip Top Tailors store on Rosser Avenue and get outdated style books, large slick-paper catalogues of men's suits and coats. There were spring and summer style books and there were fall and winter style books. I'd get one every six months as it became outdated and I'd fill each with pictures and writeups from the sports pages of newspapers that Krug Crawford would let me have at the *Sun* – Army-Notre Dame football games in Yankee Stadium, Joe DiMaggio kneeling in the on-deck circle, Donald Budge and Baron Gottfried von Cramm after Budge won the U.S. tennis title, a cartoon of Satchel Paige under the heading, "Colored Race Produces Another Great Athlete," little Mel Ott, the

Giants outfielder, cocking his right leg before taking his cut, Chuck Conacher signing autographs for a swarm of kids, a panel showing Carl Hubbell's motion for his celebrated screwball.

Almost anybody who played a sport was my hero. One time I went to Winnipeg to visit a young friend of mine who'd moved there from Brandon and I tore off to the softball game at Wesley Park where the Uneedas were playing the YMHA. I got the autographs of the two pitchers, Googs Hindle of the Uneedas and Harry Broverman of the Y. This was maybe sixty years ago but I still remember Hindle, a big blond fellow with chubby cheeks, looking startled when I asked him to sign my book. I doubt if he'd ever been asked for his autograph before.

This fascination with sports must have been some sort of escape for me. I was an only child growing up in a one-bedroom apartment, sleeping on a pull-out couch in the living room. I was raised by a father who was away a lot and a mother who was the oldest girl in a family of 10 children. My father, Homer Frayne, went west to Brandon from Smiths Falls, Ontario, around 1910 and worked on CPR freight trains as a brakeman and later, when his seniority dictated, as a conductor. He married Ella Trent in August of 1916. It would have been all right with her if they had had no children because she had been compelled to leave school at 13 and help her mother care for her enormous brood. Even today I can hear my mother mutter, as she did many times, "If I never again see a washboard it will be far too soon." She'd had her fill of taking care of kids.

They named me Trent Gardiner Frayne, for her surname and for the maiden name of my father's mother, Frances Gardiner. When I was a baby, my mother started calling me Billy, the name her best friend Jessie Neale gave *her* son born at about the same time. Bill Frayne I remained for 25 years, known in Brandon, which had a passion for nicknames, as Biff, for my initials, B.F. When I was a reporter on the *Globe and Mail* the managing editor, Bob Farquharson, decided that the byline Bill Frayne wasn't sufficiently dignified for Canada's national newspaper. He looked up the personnel files and learned that my real name was Trent, and changed my byline. Ever since, I've had to explain over and over why I have two names.

When I was a boy in Brandon, we were poor in the way that most of the people we knew were poor in those days, but my mother was ingenious at stretching our income and we were never hungry. I remember, for instance, that she used to add bread cubes to stretch a pan of fried potatoes. For years I thought that was the way you cooked fried potatoes.

What saw us through the Depression in the 1930s was the fact my father had enough seniority on the railroad to keep his job. Through the 1920s, though, he was often on the spareboard, meaning that he didn't work regularly. In these lean periods he kept us eating by playing poker in all-night sessions that sometimes lasted three and four days. My mother detested his absences. She fretted and stewed aloud, while I kept a discreet silence. I was sympathetic but I didn't know what to do to help her.

My parents were oddly matched. My dad was tall, blue-eyed, and outgoing, and he loved a good discussion about politics. Like many westerners of his time he came mighty close to being a Communist. He rose in the Brotherhood of Railway Trainmen to become the local chairman and I can remember him talking by the hour on the telephone in our apartment trying to settle railway disputes. He had a nice sense of humour and he was a good singer, too, with a true tenor voice. He could sing harmony as though he belonged to the Mills Brothers.

Along with this he was a gregarious, charming man who loved sitting around with other railroaders in the hotel beer parlors swapping tales. In those days there were no women's beer rooms and, anyway, my mother was never a drinker. Many times when I was about eight or 10 she'd prepare a meal and then she and I would sit far past the dinner hour waiting for him to show. Sometimes when her patience was exhausted she'd take me in the family Plymouth to look for him in his various haunts, the Cecil Hotel on Tenth Street, the Prince Edward

Hotel and the Beaubier Hotel on Princess Avenue. She'd wait outside in the car, sending me into the beverage room to fetch him. I didn't like it any more than he did.

My mother didn't have much humour and took almost everything literally. She was short, full breasted, determined, and fiercely concerned about appearances. To her, there was no calamity to compare with the neighbours finding out that everything in her marriage wasn't serene. She loved her husband and her only child. She was fastidious and neat. She prized cleanliness, order, and the proprieties, and she sent me to Sunday School in the Methodist church every Sunday, where I sang in the choir until I was 13 and my voice changed. I went from boy soprano to boy basketball player overnight.

Some kids raised by oddly matched parents hide away and become readers – I suspect television serves that purpose for them these days – but I found my outlet in sports. Though I was never the biggest kid on the block I was wiry and determined and I had enough natural co-ordination that I could pick up the fundamental moves of hockey and baseball and tennis and basketball. I don't remember there being many coaches around but I learned the technique of games by buying how-to books. I learned the fundamentals of tennis from a booklet by Wilmer Allison, a U.S. Davis Cup player, and basketball's shooting technique from Nat Holman, an early New York Knick, if I remember correctly. Because of my size, I suppose, I had to pay more attention to the science of the games than bigger kids did, so I avidly followed the careers of sports greats and read every sports book I could find.

I played baseball and softball all summer when I wasn't on the clay courts of the Brandon Normal School playing tennis. In winter, it was basketball at the Y or hockey on the rink in Doc Bigelow's backyard. Doc Bigelow – Dr. W.A. Bigelow, who was the founder of the country's first medical clinic – had two boys, Bill and Dan, who grew up to be doctors, Bill a world renowned pioneer in deep-freeze vascular surgery at the Toronto General Hospital. Bill's square name is Wilfred but Brandon was an astonishing town for nicknames, and a name like Wilfred had no chance. Among the kids who played hockey in the Bigelow backyard were Bryant (Sonny) Warren, Harry (Hab) Fraser, Gordon (Gite) Wright, and me, Biff. Gite had two brothers, Puss and Custy, whose parents had named them Bruce and Russell. Other kids I used to run with were the August brothers, Nuts and Simp. Simp's square name was Howard and Nuts's name was Paul.

Not to forget Don (Boom) Cannon, Glen (Suds) Sutherland, Pat (Fuzz) Petrucci, Victor (Shad) Ames, Albert (Gunner) Cross, Jack (Killer) Keppel, Edgar (Boy) Mann, Gordon (Gob) Kirk, Harry (Ham) Mummery and his brother Charles (Chub), Douglas (Dude) Robertson and his brother Gordon (Gig) and, no relative of theirs, John (Joker) Robertson. Earlier I mentioned Lowell Hyde, at whose home I listened to the Dempsey-Tunney fight on a crystal set; actually, Lowell's name was Zero in honour of his French mark in Grade Seven. Leslie Gratton was called Weiner because his father was a butcher, but I can't recall why Cecil Moore was called Mink (we were too young for the one you may be thinking of).

As I grew I was sometimes on teams that won trophies but it bothered me that the *Brandon Sun* never printed accounts of these mighty triumphs. I was about 15 when, late one afternoon at the Y during a school basketball tournament, I encountered Krug Crawford, the *Sun*'s editor. He was a friendly, kind man, always considerate of young people, so I summoned the nerve to complain to him that results of these kids' games rarely made it to his paper.

"Well, son," he said patiently, "I simply have too many other things to worry about. But if you were to send the results in to me, why I'd make sure they got in."

That suited me, I'll tell you, especially if I happened to score four or five baskets or pick up a couple of basehits or score a straight-set win (I could already see the headline: Frayne Victorious in Straight Sets).

So I began to send him brief reports of our games and he'd run them in the next day's *Sun*, introducing the scores with a few paragraphs of summary. I studied his style and after a while

I began to write the paragraphs myself. He made a lot of changes in the beginning but I was anxious to learn and soon my stuff was appearing pretty much as I'd written it (even when Frayne went scoreless).

One day when the Brandon juvenile hockey team was playing Dauphin in the provincial playdowns, the exhilarating moment arrived when Krug asked me if it would be all right with my parents if I went to the Saturday night game in the Brandon Arena and covered it for the *Sun*.

After that I covered games regularly for Krug while I was going to high school. The *Sun* was an afternoon paper, appearing around five o'clock, but I had to write my copy before I went to school in the morning. I'd set the alarm for 5 a.m. and go into the bathroom and close the door to avoid waking my parents. I'd perch on the throne, next to which was a small radiator with a wooden cover where my mother would pile towels and facecloths. I'd move them off and use the radiator cover for a desk. I'd write my piece with a thick black pencil on copy paper Krug had supplied, hike down to the *Sun* and drop it through the letter slot, then continue on to school.

To augment the family's fluctuating income, I worked after school. One job was a *Winnipeg Tribune* paper route, 60 customers on 13th Street. I made six cents a paper, a weekly income of $3.60 out of which I paid my mother $2.50 for board and room. The buck-ten that I kept made me about 75 cents richer than any of my pals who didn't have jobs.

One October day in 1932 I read in the *Trib* that Jimmy Foxx, the home run star of the Philadelphia A's, had been released from the hospital in Winnipeg and would be leaving the next day to join a team of touring major-leaguers in Calgary. Foxx, who had hit 58 homers that season, had been struck on the head by a pitched ball in an exhibition in Winnipeg.

The next day at 12:55 I was on the CPR station platform at Tenth and Pacific Avenue when the westbound train pulled in. I studied the passengers strolling the platform during the train's 10-minute stop and knew instantly that a big-chested, round-faced, tanned guy in a grey tweed suit was Jimmy Foxx.

"Who do you think will win the World Series, Mr. Foxx?" I asked, extending my autograph book opened to a fresh page.

"Oh, the Yankees won't have much trouble," he said, signing. He looked down at me and grinned. "They beat *us*, you know."

For the next day's paper I wrote three paragraphs on Jimmy Foxx's prediction, and sure enough the Yankees destroyed the Cubs in the World Series. That was the Series in which Babe Ruth may or may not have pointed to the centre-field bleachers in Wrigley Field before delivering a home run to the spot he'd indicated. Years later Red Smith said that for three days following this incident nobody wrote or mentioned that Ruth had pointed before hitting the homer. Then somebody did, and as the days turned into weeks and the weeks into months and years the legend grew that the Babe had called his shot. "I was there and if he pointed it must have been when I blinked," Red told a bunch of us one night in the Royal York Hotel.

My autograph book also acquired the names of one of the last Canadian Olympic hockey teams to win a gold medal, the Winnipegs of 1932. Once, when the world was a great deal younger, Canada never lost an Olympic hockey game. Never, never, never. But now in 1990 it's nearly a quarter of a century since the land of the game's birthplace has won an Olympic medal – a bronze in 1968 at Grenoble, France.

Long, long ago it was difficult for Canadian players to hide their chuckles when the first Olympic medals were distributed for hockey. That was in 1920 at Antwerp when for inscrutable reasons the Belgian Summer Games people decided to stage competitions in figure skating, speed-skating, and ice hockey in late spring prior to their Olympic program.

Upon receiving an invitation for Canada to play there, Canadian officials, already heavily involved in the Allan Cup senior final in Toronto, had no idea who to send to Antwerp. But when the Winnipeg Falcons beat the Toronto Eatons and won the national championship they were hurriedly shanghaied for the trip. Each player on the skimpy roster of nine was handed $25 for mad money and a spare toothbrush (you could buy a Tip

Top Tailors made-to-measure suit for $27 back then) and all were hustled out of Union Station on an eastbound train for Saint John, New Brunswick. There, they boarded the Royal Merchant Ship *Grampian* for the Atlantic crossing. In Belgium they had no difficulty destroying Czechoslovakia 15-1 and Sweden 12-1, but in the process their brains grew inflated and they barely staggered past the United States in their final game, 2-0.

Four years later, the Toronto Granites went to the newly created Winter Olympic Games at Chamonix, France. They were bracketed with Sweden, Czechoslovakia, and Switzerland in the preliminary round and survived with three victories and an aggregate score of 85-0. Yes, *eighty-five* to zip. They won the final round, somewhat more modestly, and brought home gold medals.

In 1928 hockey was still an Olympic lark for Canada, this time in St. Moritz in the Swiss Alps when the Varsity Grads from Toronto thoroughly enjoyed the outing. Billy Hewitt, father of young Foster, who would become the game's peerless broadcaster, was the team's manager. The coach was the outspoken Conn Smythe, but he did not make the overseas trip. He was already involved in the purchase of the Toronto St. Pats, the team he had renamed the Maple Leafs in February of 1927. Three Plaxton brothers, Hugh, Herb, and Roger, played on this team, as did another pair of brothers, Frank and Joe Sullivan, the latter the goaltender.

In later years I got to know Joe Sullivan quite well. After hockey he became an orolaryngologist and since I owned a perforated eardrum, the legacy of a five-week bout with scarlet fever when I was six, he became my ear doctor. Joe, who later was appointed to the Senate, was a short, bald, opinionated arch-conservative who during my visits to his chair didn't just empty my ears of wax but also filled them with tales of his three shutouts at St. Moritz in the final Olympic round – 11-0 over Sweden, 14-0 over Britain, and 13-0 over Switzerland.

"It was a delight," he cackled once, peering into my head through a silver reflector strapped to his bald pate. "The puck was at the other end of the rink for such lengthy periods that I'd skate to the sideboards and chat with the spectators."

But within four years victories became much more difficult to achieve and in 1932 Canada barely made off with the gold medal when a red-sweatered crew called the Winnipegs journeyed to Lake Placid in upstate New York for the Winter Games. It definitely wasn't easy. The 'Pegs nudged the United States by 2–1, then beat Germany 4–1 and Poland 9–0. But in the final round Canada had a terrible time with the Americans. They were trailing by 2–1 when, with only 33 seconds to play, Romeo Rivers scored for Canada to force overtime. A tie was required for a Canadian victory celebration and a tie was what the team got following three scoreless ten-minute overtime periods.

Then the 'Pegs returned home to resume their Manitoba senior league commitments and when the schedule brought them to Brandon I was at the train station to greet them at 12:55 with my autograph book, 14 years old, a Grade Nine student at Earl Oxford Junior High, a figure of sartorial elegance in a black mock-leather jacket, heavy woollen jodhpurs (or breeks, as we called them in Brandon), calf-high moccasins, and an aviator helmet.

But the players were quickly hustled a block south on Tenth Street, past the *Sun* building, to the Olympia Café at Rosser in the heart of the downtown area (that's where the town stoplight was, at Rosser and Tenth) for their lunch. I was in their wake, book in hand.

"Here, let's see that," a player said. He thumbed through it, looking at the scrawled names I'd collected of local stars.

Suddenly my eye caught the clock above the cash register at the front of the Olympia – 25 minutes to two! I was late for school. I told the player I had to have my book.

"What's your teacher's name?" he asked, and when I told him he began to write:

"Dear Miss Ross,

"Please excuse Bill for being late for school as he was showing us his autograph book."

He signed his name, Alston (Stoney) Wise, and passed the book to the other players for their names under his – Hack Simpson, Bill Cockburn, Vic Lindquist, Romeo Rivers, Walter Monson, Ken Moore, Gus Rivers, Spunk Duncanson, Tic Garbutt, Hughie Sutherland – Canada's gold medal champions.

Miss Ross – her name was Jean – took the book home to show to her friends and then brought it back a couple of days later. I still have it, a little book I got from my mother for Christmas in 1931 when I was 13.

By 19 I was working for the Canadian Press in Winnipeg, my music teacher's nudging apparently having made an impression on Gillis Purcell in Toronto. One day at noon in the spring of 1938 I came home from Brandon College (it's Brandon University now) for my lunch and Mom handed me an envelope bearing the letterhead of the CP's Winnipeg bureau. In it was a one-paragraph note signed by Frank Turner, the bureau chief there.

"Your application for the position of junior night editor has been approved. You will receive $18 a week. Kindly reply at your early convenience."

Now the confusing elements about this letter were that I hadn't the faintest idea what a junior night editor was, I had never heard of Frank Turner, and most interesting of all I had never made an application to the Canadian Press. This had to be the hand of Gil Purcell.

My only contact with Purcell, apart from the time Helen Creighton introduced us, was a note maybe 10 years later asking me if I'd like to write a feature story for CP about a man named George Tackaberry who fashioned hand-made hockey boots in Brandon. I knew of Mr. Tackaberry's little shop at 39 Ninth Street just above Rosser. I also knew that Tackaberry boots, called Tacks, were the finest money could buy and, with CCM skates attached, were worn by the vast majority of players in the National Hockey League.

I had no idea how to handle a feature story but I had an idea how to pursue Purcell's request. I went to see Mrs. McNaughton, who was the nurse for my dentist, Dr. William Jones, and whose son John was the Brandon correspondent for the *Winnipeg Tribune*. Did Mrs. McNaughton think John would help me with this assignment, I wondered. Well, Mrs. McNaughton said, employing a mother's wisdom, we could ask John.

So tall, lanky John McNaughton, a quiet fellow in his midtwenties, took the information I'd gathered during a conversation with George Tackaberry and put it together in feature-story form and I mailed it off to Purcell. A few weeks later I got a cheque for $10 from the CP office in Toronto and that was the last I heard of the Tackaberry piece or of Gil Purcell or of the CP itself until this letter arrived from Frank Turner.

Meanwhile, after graduating from Brandon Collegiate in the spring of 1936, a couple of my pals, Glen Sutherland and Gob Kirk, planned to go to Brandon College in the fall (back then the school was a Baptist college affiliated with McMaster University of Hamilton). My folks didn't have tuition money for me in the Depression years but I knew from Krug Crawford that the *Sun* had carried several advertisements for the college on credit in those desperate times. So I asked Krug if the *Sun* would write off my college tuition against part of the college's debt in exchange for the sports coverage I was doing for Krug. The paper okayed the proposition and, come to think of it, so did the Wheat City Business College where I stayed long enough to learn to type with eight fingers.

As part of the *Sun* arrangement I spent one great summer at the Clear Lake holiday resort in Riding Mountain National Park, sixty miles north of Brandon, as the Clear Lake correspondent. I covered tennis and golf tournaments and wrote little features about the people who ran stores or owned cottages, and every Sunday I'd write a column of social notes about the people who had driven up from Brandon for the weekend. "Dr. Bud McDiarmid and his wife, Ann, are here for the annual Clear Lake golf tournament," I'd write. Or "Austin Boyd and Leona Cunningham were weekend visitors here in the park. Austin caught a four-pound pike."

Needless to say, Bud and Ann didn't care one way or another

if their names were included in my sparkling stuff, but one day Krug phoned to say it might be a good idea if I left the names of unmarried couples such as Austin and Leona out of my social notes. "They were on the sneak," Krug chuckled.

Before I took off for Winnipeg I wrote a note to Scott Young, a young fellow working at the *Free Press* whom I'd met during the hockey playoffs, asking him if he knew of a good boarding house where I could hang my hat. He wrote back that he was moving into a new place himself and why didn't I join him.

The $18 a week I was to get from CP was $6 a week more than I was making in a job I had in Brandon where I had become the Standard Brands company's representative in charge of the distribution of Fleischmann's yeast, Chase & Sanborn coffee, and Tender Leaf Tea. The company provided me with a bicycle and a suitcase-sized container into which 24 one-pound packages of baker's yeast fitted perfectly.

I pedalled yeast to the city's half-dozen bakeries and I also made twice-a-week calls to retail grocery stores that handled yeast-cake cubes. Also, I handled orders for coffee and tea and forwarded them to the Winnipeg office each week along with the billing for the week's yeast sales. This was a great job in the summer but nowadays when I think of those Manitoba winters I shudder. I delivered yeast on the company bicycle between classes at Brandon College, sometimes in 30-below-zero weather. I wore a suit of woollen underwear with long arms and long legs and over that a pair of waist-high longjohns. I wore a flannel shirt, a sweater, and a hip-length navy-blue woollen jacket with an imitation beaver collar. I wore a lined cap and earmuffs and woollen gloves inside leather mitts. I wore felt boots over woollen socks. In storms or strong wind I wore a woollen scarf wrapped around my face.

Well, all right, the clothing kept me warm. But part way through my yeast deliveries it would be time for a class at Brandon College. I'd lean the bike against a wall at the school (I don't remember ever locking it) and carry my suitcase of yeast into class where steam would be sizzling inside the long radiators under the windows. I'd pull off 30 or 40 layers of clothes, listen to a bewildering (for me) 50-minute lecture on political economy, which for reasons utterly foreign to me now was my major, climb back into 30 or 40 layers of clothes, and finish delivering the day's yeast.

In that winter of 1938, my third year at Brandon College, I was spending far too much time pedalling yeast cakes and playing basketball and writing for Krug to earn a college degree in the foreseeable future. For this reason, and for the fact that unemployment was ravaging Canada in the bleak eighth year of the Great Depression, I was incredibly lucky to get the job offer from Purcell via his Winnipeg bureau chief Frank Turner. I left school in April for Winnipeg where I moved in with Scott Young at 301 Assiniboine Avenue at the foot of Donald Street and began working nights 5 p.m to 1 a.m. at the CP bureau in the Free Press building.

A sweet old absent-minded woman named Mrs. Shore ran the house where Young and I shared a room. She persistently showed people seeking accommodation through the house in mid-morning when Young and I, being night workers, were sleeping, and invariably in her dreamy way she'd open the door of our room before realizing we were there.

One day around 11 a.m. we heard her coming with a couple of prospective roomers as we sleepily eyed one another across the room.

"Goddammit, this is too much," Young grumbled.

He threw back the sheets and lay on his back, naked, eyes closed, feigning sleep.

Enter Mrs. Shore, followed by two old biddies clucking over the climb to our attic aerie.

"And, here . . . " began Mrs. Shore, and then all three emitted shrieks, spotting the bare Young, and after that we had no trouble with Mrs. Shore and her prospective guests.

A couple of months later, accommodation became available half a block north at 55 Donald Street, a castle of a place of red brick and white pillars and large turrets and a solarium with a piano and several divans, and we grabbed it. Scott joined Ed McNally, the editorial-page cartoonist at the *Free Press*, and I roomed with Jack Wells, the sports broadcaster for CKRC, who, widely known as Cactus Jack, later became the most beloved broadcaster in the West.

As far as boarding houses go, this was Nirvana for me, three floors of large bright rooms occupied by a dozen or more business people in their mid- and late twenties. The man whose work I admired above all others, Ralph Allen, the *Winnipeg Tribune* sports columnist, roomed with a sportswriter from the *Free Press*, Cam McKenzie, who later became the managing editor of the *Saskatoon Star-Phoenix*. Two *Tribune* photographers, Gordon Aikman and Bruce Watson, lived there, and so did Jack Andre, the *Tribune*'s top feature writer. Jack arrived in the newsroom one night just before midnight, ashen-faced and shaken. He had just come from Headingly jail, a dozen miles west of Winnipeg, where he'd witnessed a hanging, and he had to sit down and write about it. He was so upset he was scarcely able to type.

"I can't stand seeing people hurt," Jack told us the next night in the large dining hall in the basement at 55. Five years later, a lieutenant in a Winnipeg regiment, Jack was killed wading ashore in the Normandy landings.

Among the non-newspaper residents were Birdeen Lawrence and her sister, Dorothy, dental nurses in downtown offices who'd arrived in Winnipeg from a small Saskatchewan town, a pair of beauties who charmed all of us residents. My ex-roomie, Scott, and Ralph Allen were particularly taken with Birdeen, and their rivalry ended only when Ralph accepted a *Globe and Mail* offer, took Birdeen by the hand into the solarium at 55, and sat her down on the piano stool where she'd led many a raucous Saturday-night singsong. "Look here, Bird, I'm leaving for Toronto," he growled. "We're getting married and you're coming with me. Okay?"

Or, anyway, that's how Birdeen remembered his proposal years later, telling me about it one afternoon after we'd played one of our annual rounds at the Thornhill Golf Club where she was a member.

By the time Ralph left for Toronto in December of 1938 I'd

spent eight months at CP. We had a mail service that compelled some unlucky soul to burrow through piles of western newspapers seeking out timeless local news items that could be assembled and run off a Gestetner copying machine and mailed to papers across the West. I was usually the unlucky soul. Similarly, I dug out sports squibs from western papers, assembled them, and once a week sent out a column called Western Sports Corral. I covered occasional junior hockey playoffs in the Amphitheatre rink, too, but in truth, far from being a junior night editor, whatever that was, I was an unglorified office boy.

One night I was sitting on a streetcar with Herb Manning, a *Tribune* sportswriter, on our way from the Amph after a game.

"Allen is leaving for Toronto and I'll be writing his column at the *Trib*," Herb said. "If you're interested in my job, I'll pass the word."

By a timely coincidence I had been in the CP office early on the preceding Sunday afternoon when no one had yet arrived for work. Frank Turner's door was open so I poked through his filing cabinet under the letter F – as in Frayne. There was a note there from GP, as everyone called the boss, Gil Purcell, advising Turner that if the new man, Frayne, wasn't working out, Turner was under no obligation to retain his services.

Accordingly, it was with a certain alacrity that I advised Manning that I would be delighted to accept his proposal.

A couple of days later he called me.

"The boss says okay," Manning said.

Which is how I became a full-fledged, 100 per cent sportswriter with a fat raise – all the way up to 20 bucks a week.

Chapter 5

Women athletes I have known

There are still people who think women have no serious place in sports. How they can think this way – with someone who can crush a tennis ball crosscourt as Steffi Graf does or float serenely over a crossbar as Debbie Brill does or knock a golf ball a mile down the middle as Jan Stephenson does or who can do what any number of other women do under stress in tough competition – boggles the mind.

Still, women have had a hard time making the point that many things men can do they can do in just as entertaining a way, and they probably didn't really begin to make people aware of it until the early 1970s. That was when Billie Jean King made herself the apostle of a campaign to boost the purses in women's tennis closer to men's on the grounds that their box-office attractiveness was every bit as powerful.

It's my notion that in games where women excel, particularly in golf and tennis, they provide an even better spectacle than men, or at least one that the average fan can better relate to. The male pros serve tennis balls so hard and drive golf balls so far that their skill is as meaningless to the average player watching them as that of a pilot bringing in a Boeing 747. Guys complain that women's tennis grows boring when a couple of baseliners begin trading endless moonballs, but this is in no way more monotonous than watching Boris Becker and Ivan Lendl whoosh service aces at one other through a long hot afternoon. Watching Becker serve is like watching a guy fire a rifle. Bang! He's pulled the trigger. So what? And when the British Columbia golf-ball basher, Dave Barr, hits a drive that purrs off toward heaven at 120 miles an hour before sinking gently into the middle of the fairway 275 yards away, weekend golfers in the gallery might as well be watching heart surgery for all the mechanics of the shot mean to them.

But with women, reality emerges. Tests show that a man's swing is, on average, one second faster than a woman's. On impact with the ball a male pro's club head has reached 120 mph, which is some 30 mph faster than the average female pro swings her stick. Men usually outdrive women by 30 to 40 yards and the ball gets there quicker.

As I say, though, the extra speed and distance are lost on the weekend players in the gallery, and watching someone such as the British Columbia star Dawn Coe use a nicely balanced swing and perfect timing to loft a golf ball 235 yards and more or seeing Victoria-born Helen Kelesi, with an explosive grunt, drill an overhead smash against the baseline, average players can relate to their own games and marvel at the technique of these skilful women.

The very nature of some sports, though, is such that sex has got to raise its delicious head. For close to two decades, keeping in mind the indisputable fact that it's not how a woman athlete *looks* but how she *performs*, it was still mighty hard to escape the notion that if the willowy high-jumper Debbie Brill never cleared another crossbar you could still watch her all day long.

Debbie Brill was something. I think back to the Canadian Olympic trials at Quebec City in midsummer of 1976 and the image that jumps to mind is of Debbie Brill. There she is, maybe 20 yards from the crossbar, calmly eyeing it, one foot slightly ahead of the other, teetering slowly, back and forth, back and forth, long legs bare and smooth and tanned, twin cynosures.

Suddenly she stops this slow teetering and in a quick high bound she has launched her approach to the crossbar, never taking her eyes from it, swerving to her right in the last couple of long strides to reach the bar almost parallel to it, and then vaulting herself six and a half feet into the air and rolling head first and upside down over the bar, lifting her lissome legs at the last instant to clear the bar, then landing on the back of her neck on the big red air pillow at the base of the bar.

Now of course there are athletes and there are athletes. There is Paul Coffey, a bird in flight, and there is Mario Lemieux, a cruise ship docking. There is Tim Raines, who can overtake any batted ball, and there is George Bell, for whom the most routine of fly balls is an adventure. So what I'm saying about Debbie Brill's legs is not so much that they're sex symbols as that they're part of this poetry in motion she shares with Paul Coffey and Tim Raines. The slim smooth legs are part of the costume of her game. Coffey's work clothes are the dumb blunt trappings of hockey and Raines's are the shrunk knickers of baseball. Brill's – and most women's – game calls for muscular freedom, which means a suit of pure unsullied pelt.

Accordingly, sensuality is a bigger part of women's sports than men's, more pronounced in some of the Olympic events than in the other games in which women are attracting the multitudes. When the tennis people began saying, "You've come a long way, baby," they were talking about the new big money and the new big crowds, not the fact the costumes had grown starkly abbreviated. Women golfers started bringing in crowds in the mid-1970s but their get-up had little to do with it. Even now, 15 years later, there's still a certain decorum about the clothes women golfers wear – long shorts and proper blouses. But the tennis tourists favour fetching short, short skirts that give them full freedom of movement and invariably show off their silk-clad bottoms.

Even more so, most of the Olympic sports reveal the human form in all its grace and shape. Men get down to the essentials in track and field apparel, too, but it goes without saying that most women are far more graceful and therefore more compelling to look at than men. Tower diving is the closest thing to high-jumping in this area, maybe more so. When a curved and captivating figure belonging to someone such as the tiny three-metre gold-medal winner of the 1984 Olympics, Quebec City's Sylvie Bernier, or such as Vancouver's 1976 Canadian champion, Terri York – when one of these young women stood up there above the water getting her concentration together, a solitary silhouette etched against the sky, who'd claim that sexuality wasn't part of women's athletics?

And great women. The last time I saw Debbie Brill she was blowing the froth off a beer in the press lounge at the Commonwealth Games in 1986 in Edinburgh. She was laughing and casual and aware. She wore a grey silk shirt, had a pair of red-and-black striped pants, calf length, hugging her long legs, and had a black sweater tied around her waist, clinging upside down to her behind. She had been invited to chat with news people on the day before her event. She sipped the beer while she talked, standing relaxed and smiling, and after 20 minutes or so she set down the plastic container and departed. There was still a little beer left. It had really been just a social prop.

I talked to her just before Christmas of 1988, by phone from Toronto to her houseboat on the Fraser River close to Vancouver where she lived then with her seven-year-old son, Neil. Since 1972 at the Munich Olympics, a 19-year-old kid, she had been travelling the world high-jumping for Canada, but in 1988 she didn't make it to the Summer Olympics in Seoul so I'd called her, wondering what she was up to and what happened that she'd missed the games.

She said that she had trained hard that summer for the Olympic trials, a two-day event, and that she was "really, really fit." But for years she'd had a chronic knee problem and this time it *wouldn't* get better. "As the trials came closer I realized I couldn't possibly jump two days in a row," Debbie said. "So late in June I decided I'd have to give it up."

By then she was 35, still a free spirit, but resigned to the knowledge her international jumping days were over. She had become a coach at Simon Fraser University and was taking a psychology course there, too.

Debbie Brill was one of the all-time all-timers wearing the maple leaf in competition. At 17 and 18 she had won gold medals at the 1970 Commonwealth Games and the 1971 Pan-Am Games. At 19 she was eighth at the Munich Olympics and over the next three years she had improved enough that in 1975 she was ranked fourth in the world.

I like to remember her in Brisbane in 1982 when she outjumped the defending Commonwealth Games champion, Katrina Gibbs, under a hot Australian sun (it was October and summer was coming) and won the high-jump gold for Canada. That day I sat for a while with Greg Ray, the father of Debbie's little boy. He was looking after the baby while Debbie competed and had a bottle of milk and a pacifier and a bag of extra diapers stacked on the seat of Neil's stroller. We sat in one end of the stands watching Debbie go for her medal and behind us were a bunch of noisy fans waving a Canadian flag. When Debbie won she came jogging from the high-jump pit to the grandstand railing where Greg handed Neil to her, and she trotted off with the contented little boy to show him to her teammates. Neil was just past a year old at the time, a little guy with dark brown eyes like his mom's and blond hair like his dad's.

Debbie and Greg met in 1972 when he was living in Maple Ridge, outside Vancouver, and she lived in Garibaldi, 10 miles away. She hadn't done as well as she'd hoped in the Munich Olympics and one night soon after she got back she dropped into a pub in Maple Ridge because, as she remembered later, "my feet hurt and I was thirsty." After a while this guy alone at a nearby table asked her if she'd mind if he sat with her.

"That was it," Greg said to me this day in the Brisbane stands. "We've been sort of together ever since. I mean, we're in love and all but we don't like living together for long periods. Right now I have a house and Debbie has her houseboat, about five minutes away. We have joint custody of Neil."

For a while after they met they lived in Greg's house and so did Kate Schmidt, an American javelin thrower, who taught Greg to cook. When he was looking after Neil he fed him omelets, mostly, although Greg said little Neil also liked peas and beans. Other times Debbie took Neil with her. That summer of 1982 she'd taken him to Europe when she'd competed in Yugoslavia and Italy.

"I know people most of the places I go," Debbie told me once, explaining Neil's sitter arrangement. "There's usually somebody who can look after him when I'm competing. When I'm not, he's with me, eating what I eat – steak, chicken, peas, carrots." She laughed, thinking about Neil's diet back then.

She and Greg decided to have Neil when Canada pulled out of the Moscow Olympics in 1980. She had worked hard preparing for the Games so when the Canadian government made its pointless statement about Soviet involvement in Afghanistan she and a couple of hundred other athletes were suddenly grounded.

"We took advantage of the Olympic situation," Greg said in Brisbane. "She became pregnant. Anyway, we felt it was time."

In some ways, it must be said, Debbie's life plays like an afternoon soap opera. By late December of 1989, for instance, she and Greg were living four doors apart in Burnaby, near Vancouver, and Debbie was about to give birth to a baby girl, whom she called Katie Rose, but who wasn't Greg's baby. No, Katie Rose's daddy was Debbie's new companion, Doug Coleman, a medical doctor, and Greg was living close by to maintain a family connection for eight-year-old Neil and, for that matter, for the new-born Katie, too, with Doug's help.

Obviously, Debbie at 36 was still her own person, as she'd been during her years as a world-class performer, one who'd likely have made her own emancipation without benefit of Billie Jean King's pioneering in the early 1970s. Not that either of them has eliminated sexism in women's sports, by any means. Even now in the 1990s most men spend as much time studying the physical attributes of women athletes as their technical skills, even among scribes who ought to know better. The way the hard-thinking scriveners interview the highly attractive Jan Stephenson, say, bears very little resemblance to the way they handle the highly attractive Curtis Strange, golf champions both.

For instance, when Curtis was seated before a clutch of thinkers following his victory in the 1989 Canadian Open, none of the following questions was posed:

(a) "Did you try modelling before you went on the golf tour?"

(b) "What about your marriage? You're travelling alone, aren't you?"

(c) "Is it true you've had offers from Hollywood?"

But these were three of the penetrating posers that worked their way into a press scrum with the Australian Jan Stephenson at Toronto's St. George's golf club one early summer afternoon in the mid-1980s when she was hustled into town, all the way from Tokyo, to stimulate publicity for the women's Canadian Open. Sessions of this nature are staged every year for the men and women pros of golf and tennis – a star plays an exhibition, has lunch with the steely-eyed scribes, and fields their questions for the nightly television news and the next day's papers.

Women follow paths just as harrowing as those of the globe-trotting males and arrive looking fresh and cheerful to fulfil the appointments. On the day Stephenson beguiled the newshounds, she arrived in a frilly cotton dress, white with a pale blue trim, silk stockings, and spike pumps, hastily explaining that she'd left Tokyo a mere day and a half earlier, and to get here on time had a police escort from the golf course to the Tokyo airport, flown Tokyo to Honolulu, Honolulu to Phoenix, Phoenix to Dallas, Dallas to Toronto, and felt so discombobulated from all the air travel and time changes that she'd bought the dress the instant she lay eyes upon it in a shop in the downtown Harbour Castle Hotel. By the damnedest coincidence various scribes observed that the dress happened to accent her large, firm-looking breasts. (Would a green Masters jacket have embellished Curtis Strange's bum?)

Jan began attracting attention in sexy poses soon after she started winning regularly on the North American circuit. Tournament promoters were delighted with the attention the exposure was drawing to women's golf. In 1983 when she was at the peak of her game and closing on age 32 she posed "a la Marilyn Monroe," as the golf tour's annual player guide was pleased to term it, for a widely circulated poster bearing the caption "Come Play a Round With Me." Most of the women pros were highly critical of the poster, insisting they wanted to be recognized for their skill as golf players, even as men were.

Out on the fairways Jan was an arresting figure, too, with a long, smooth, carefully timed backswing and full, unhurried follow-through. Once, in the 54-hole Mary Kay Classic in Dallas, she had rounds of 65, 69, and 64 for an implausible 198 total that included 20 birdies – an assault on par that few men could match. By 1990, after 15 years on the North American circuit, she'd won 19 tournaments and had accumulated more than $2 million in purses.

And this day in Toronto, sitting through the inescapable post-luncheon speeches by the sponsors, she offered more than a nicely tailored bodice. As they spoke, she quietly borrowed a pen (from me; I was seated next to her) and jotted down the names the sponsors mentioned. When time came for her to speak she especially thanked committee volunteers who'd organized various phases of the tournament, mentioning each by name without reference to the notes she'd taken, and then she turned to Jocelyn Bourassa, a former tour golfer from Quebec and a member of the tournament committee, and thanked her – in French.

As I remember it, hardly anyone paid attention to women's sports until the early 1970s when Billie Jean King began stomping around for an improvement in tennis purses. Before that, there'd be a flurry of interest each summer when Wimbledon rolled around, followed by the U.S. nationals at Forest Hills, but apart from them and an occasional spectacular outburst by someone such as the immortal Mildred (Babe) Didrickson Zaharias, who could run and jump and play basketball and golf and who died at age 42 of cancer, women who pursued sports seemed a little, well, odd.

Of course, there were the figure skaters, such as Ottawa's Barbara Ann Scott, who won an Olympic gold and lasting fame at St. Moritz in 1948, and the skiers, such as the freckled and perpetually smiling Nancy Greene, who could conquer a mountain as fast as anyone in the world in the 1960s, but these triumphs were brief explosions, bursting spectacularly and disappearing as suddenly.

In team sports, though, it was a different matter. There, a group of women basketball players, the Edmonton Grads, outshone absolutely everybody. Even today their mastery of their game overshadows the dominance of all other teams, even the three giants, the Montreal Canadiens in hockey, the New York Yankees in baseball, and the Boston Celtics in basketball, teams whose names became synonymous with their games. But for a quarter of a century the Grads' record was just short of unbelievable. Back in 1965 Peter Gzowski and I collaborated on a book called *Great Canadian Sports Stories*, a collection in which I did a piece on the Grads. The following two paragraphs from that book might sum up their dominance:

"From 1915 to 1940 the Grads beat everybody everywhere. They beat American champions in any city you care to name from San Francisco to New York, and they beat European teams from any city you care to mispronounce from Bobaix to Lille to Rheims to Douai, and from London to Paris to Rome, too. They shaded that bunch in Lille by 61 to 1, and the ladies they caught up with in London must have wandered in from a week in Soho: the Grads' edge there was 100 to 2. In 25 years of utter destruction the Grads played 522 games, facing all comers, and won 502.

"The Grads played entire seasons without defeat. Once, they compiled a winning streak of 147 games; another time it was 78. During their quarter-century of eminence they lost the provincial championship only once (to the University of Alberta in 1921) and never lost a game in 21 Western Canada finals. They won the Canadian championship when it was established in 1922 and were never beaten in a national series thereafter, winning 29 games and losing two. They won 138 of 152 games against American opponents. They went to the Olympic Games four times – to Paris in 1924, to Amsterdam in 1928, to Los Angeles in 1932 and to Berlin in 1936 – played 27 games, won 27, and scored 1,863 points to their opponents' 297. Any arguments?"

Still, none of their staggering successes or the victories of assorted skiers and skaters had a lasting influence on the games these people played. I can think of only one woman who managed that. Billie Jean King revolutionized professional sports for women. She put money in women's pockets, hundreds of women and millions of dollars. In a sense, Billie Jean got for women athletes what Jackie Robinson got for black ballplayers – acceptance.

She dominated women's tennis for a decade as a player but where she became a world figure was in the aforementioned comic charade enacted by Bobby Riggs and her in 1973 in the Houston Astrodome when millions of television viewers plus 34,000 people in the flesh assembled to see if she could handle the waddling 55-year-old male chauvinist. In retrospect, the impact of that weird match seems ludicrous but at the time it was of vast significance, somehow grasping international attention and in the end getting women's tennis – and by extension women's pro golf, too – the acceptance Billie Jean had been striving for.

The stage was set for the bizarre matchup in an earlier challenge match that year in which the irrepressible Riggs had demoralized the tall and oh-so-earnest Margaret Court – psyched her out, as they say – at a time when she was the reigning queen of the U.S., the Australian, and the French Open championships (Billie Jean blocked her bid for a Grand Slam by winning Wimbledon that summer). Riggs proclaimed to anyone who came within earshot that women's tennis was a joke.

Billie Jean was returning from a tournament in Tokyo when she learned of the rout of Margaret Court. She had wanted to avoid matches of this nature on the grounds that no good and a lot of bad could come of a young woman playing an old guy, and

Riggs had proved her point. So she accepted his challenge and somehow the match grasped the fancy of millions of people, tennis fans and otherwise, a sort of battle of the sexes in which even delivery boys and office girls became caught up and made bets.

The weeks leading to the match packed more hype and ballyhoo than heavyweight championship fights usually generate, most of it inspired by the non-stop-talking Riggs but part of it subtly assisted by Billie Jean. She was holed up in an opulent South Carolina outpost called Hilton Head Island to which I was dispatched by the *Toronto Star* to prepare a feature on what the promoters naturally were billing as the greatest male-female confrontation since Delilah took the shears to Samson. At Hilton Head Billie Jean was surrounded by the Atlantic Ocean, forests of live oak and palmetto, one husband, one secretary, one agent, one public-relations firm, three doctors, and an occasional breakthrough of sanity.

Shielded by all of these forces except sanity, she was a mysterious figure during the week before the Riggs match. On the one hand she kept appearing publicly in a tennis confection being taped by ABC television for future exposure, and on the other hand she kept rushing off to her chambers with an attack of at least the vapours, refusing to talk to any of us minions of the press.

For two days she was reported in medical bulletins to be suffering from stomach flu, then a vague virus, then something called hypoglycemia, which is a sugar deficiency in the blood, the opposite of diabetes. Lurking over every medical bulletin was the possibility that King's illness might cause postponement of the Riggs affair. No sooner was this possibility explored than here would come Billie Jean from her bungalow amid the Spanish moss and she'd tear around the tennis court in vigorous assault and then rush back to her cottage, speaking to no one.

One evening after three days of this, I knocked on her door and asked a young woman who answered if I could talk to Billie Jean for a few moments. It was a new approach; until then we'd been dealing through the p.r. firm. "I'm down here all the way from Canada," I whimpered. "I won't take long."

Before the woman could respond a voice called loudly from within, "My God, it's Canada, all right. Listen to that accent."

It was Billie Jean, suddenly giving audience to two of us standing there, a guy from the *Philadelphia Inquirer* named Stan Hochman and me. She was seated on a divan, a far more feminine-looking woman off the court than on it. (A couple of years later Joe Hyams wrote a piece about her in *Playboy* magazine in which he noted that off the court "she is soft, feminine, sexy – despite the glasses, a broad beam and a flat chest." Hyams, a guy married to the chesty movie actress Elke Sommer, used to write a movie column in the old *New York Herald-Tribune*. He wrote in *Playboy* that whenever he saw Billie Jean she reminded him of the beautiful Grace Kelly, "who had equally unimpressive vital statistics but was all woman – no question about it.")

Well, anyway, there on Hilton Head Island Billie Jean said that Bobby Riggs and vast numbers of insecure men had misconstrued the arguments she'd been advancing on behalf of women's tennis. "Technically, women play a sounder game because we're not as strong physically. Things they can do with a flick of the wrist we have to do with technique and execution. What men do with power we do with finesse and dexterity. With us, everything has to be a little surer. But the attraction of this match is that it's man against woman. Americans love fads. I hear people are betting like crazy, dumb little his-her bets. That adds something extra."

Psychologically, Billie Jean had a far greater burden in her match with Riggs than he was carrying. For him, what was there to lose? ("I'm a 55-year-old man with one foot in the grave.") Physically, at 30 she was probably a little past her peak as a player but, even so, Riggs was no match for her when they got to Houston. Her concentration was impenetrable amid the hoopla and she showed none of the nervous hesitancy that had been Margaret Court's downfall a few months earlier. Billie

Jean's easy victory was icing on the cake for her argument that women played the game as entertainingly as men.

After Riggs, Billie Jean continued to dominate her rivals on the women's tour for a few more years, and won her sixth Wimbledon singles title in 1975. She was ultimately slowed by knee injuries that required surgery on three occasions but she had made her point. By then, women's purses were on a par with men's at most of the big tournaments and new favourites were exciting the crowds, particularly Chris Evert and Martina Navratilova, each a little more than a decade younger than Billie Jean, a pair of players who so dominated the women's field over the next 15 years that it seemed they must have played each other a thousand times.

At first, Evert dominated the chubby, dark-haired Czechoslovakian, who threatened to eat the junk-food emporiums out of business when she first arrived on this side of the Atlantic. But a quality that helped make her a great player, along with tenacity and desire, was discipline. When, at 17, she defected, she was cut off from home, family, and friends and was rootless and confused. She became the junk-food queen of the known galaxy, the kid McDonald's and Wendy's and Burger King live for. She kept herself stuffed with enough French fries, pancakes, hot dogs, hamburgers, potato chips, and doughnuts to get her weight to 172 pounds. On the court she was the terrible-tempered Ms. Bang, and she would sob on the sidelines after defeats.

Then she met the 1974 U.S. women's golf champion, Sandra Haynie, who had retired to represent pro athletes in business. She encouraged the bulging Czech to control her weight and her emotions. In time Martina became an exercise and health-food zealot, dyed her hair blonde, put on rimless glasses, and grew into one of the great serve-and-volley players, who won a record ninth singles title at Wimbledon in July of 1990. Still, no matter how successful she became, she remained surprisingly insecure. I remember mentioning to her one afternoon at the tennis centre on Toronto's York University campus (the women's and men's championships are played in alternating years there and at Montreal's Jarry Park) that the trouble with women's tennis was that she and Evert were too good for the rest of the women.

"There's no suspense," I said airily. "Everybody knows you'll be playing her in the final."

"Is that so?" she said harshly. "I'm glad you're so damned sure. I'm not."

That day, seated under a beach umbrella, she was composed, trim, and fit, that famed left arm of hers muscled and veined. She wore a pale blue cotton T-shirt and short white shorts over smooth tanned thighs. With this casualness, there were gold earrings and gold-and-diamond necklace, bracelet, and wide ring on her right hand. Stringy pale-yellow hair lay flat. Her answers were straightforward and informative, yet there was an underlying watchfulness. I never had the feeling I was getting beyond the impassive mask.

Evert, for her part, always seemed icily confident. American crowds loved Chrissie, as she came to be known, because she was a winner and because she was an American (that's all most Americans require). She broke onto the national scene as a poker-faced, tight-lipped kid of 16 in pigtails, relentlessly pursued by camera crews and magazine writers and autograph seekers at Forest Hills at the 1971 U.S. Open. She reached the semifinals that year against Billie Jean. She lost, but for the next 18 years she hugged the baseline and slammed her ground strokes deep to the corners and ran her opponents until they damned nearly dropped.

Some people, including me, found her ungenerous. One year at the Toronto Lawn Club she partnered her sister Jeanne, three years younger, in women's doubles. Jeanne was never the player Chris was, shorter of stature and tubby. Chris showed no patience with her, turning from the net frequently when Jeanne was serving to hiss instructions, her face contorted, or snapping at her if Jeanne missed an overhead or miscued on a volley.

Then there was a Sunday afternoon in April of 1983 when Chrissie played the rake-thin Carling Bassett, the wealthy Torontonian, in what may have been the best match Carling ever played. She was a child of 15 then, 105 pounds with these two long blonde braids bouncing down her back, and the match was the final in a pine-dappled retreat for rich folks called Amelia Island Plantation on Florida's northeast coast. Carling was the sensation of the tournament that spring. She beat Eva Pfaff in three sets, sixth-seeded Virginia Ruzici in two, third-seeded Bettina Bunge in three, and in the semifinal Kathy Rinaldi, the No. 5 seed, in two sets. That put her in against Florida's own Chrissie in the final.

I was working at the *Toronto Sun* back then, whose publisher, Doug Creighton, phoned me at home early on the Sunday morning of the final and said I ought to go down there. Creighton was a close friend of Carling's grandfather, John Bassett, who had been the publisher of the old *Toronto Telegram* when Creighton worked there as a police reporter, sports editor, and managing editor, a man of easy charm and long damp lunches who found his true niche when he and two other reporters, Peter Worthington and Don Hunt, got the money together to start the delightfully crazy tabloid *Sun* when Bassett folded the *Tely*. All three of them became millionaires (Bassett already was one) and the great thing about them for a working newspaperman was that all of them came from the editorial side rather than the business side of newspapers (publishers from the business side look only at the bottom line; they might as well be selling shoes).

Anyway, off I went to Jacksonville that morning, rented a car at the airport, and drove to the Amelia Island Plantation where Carling took on Evert. It was a terrific match. Chrissie coasted easily through the first set at 6–3 and had a 2–0 lead in the second. It appeared Creighton had blown the *Sun*'s money on a routine Evert outing, but then Carling began laying into her crosscourt forehand and started slamming her two-fisted back-hand into the corners, often leaping at the ball, both feet off the ground, and first thing you know she has won eight games in a row, meaning, of course, that she owned the second set at 6–2 and was up 2–0 in the decisive third.

At which point Chris got her own thudding ground strokes in order, used occasional deadly drop shots to upset the young

Canadian's timing, and after eight more games they were locked at 5–5.

Whereupon the seasoned Evert showed a champion's composure and pulled out the last two games.

Afterwards, though, sitting at a high table to talk to news people, Chris got a lot of mileage out of the word but.

As in:

"Carling played really well, but . . . "

"She was better than I anticipated she'd be, but . . . "

"Yeah, Carling should make out fine on the tour, but . . . "

In this post-win setting, much of the questioning understandably related to the newcomer to the big time, the wide-eyed sensation of the week, so naive back then. I remember her face when she'd been asked if she still felt in awe of Evert. She was speechless for long moments, brown eyes wide and round, befitting a 15-year-old.

"Oh, my gosh, *yes!*" she blurted finally. "I mean, um, *of course!*"

So now here was the old champ being asked to assess the ingenuous newcomer, and saying with a certain hesitancy that yes, um, Carling has the makings, all right.

"But I thought Kathy Rinaldi had them, too," she added thoughtfully. "And then there's Tracy Austin. I mean, her injuries and her other interests. You never know, do you?"

Well, Chris, how do you think young Carling will do on the tour?

"Oh, she should do great. I saw her play doubles at the French. I'm not surprised by her success today. I mean, she played real well in the French."

Long pause.

"But it will be a matter of the players getting used to her game, too. We haven't seen much of her so we don't know much about her weaknesses."

But she handled the pressure pretty well today, don't you think, Chris?

"Oh, yeah, of course."

Thoughtful pause.

"But the pressure was all on me today. I mean, what was

working for her was that for a 15-year-old to beat me would be big press, right, big exposure."

And so on.

Carling, ranked No. 98 in the world that April day, climbed in the ensuing 11 months to No. 20, and once again, in March of 1984, here she was playing Evert in a Florida outpost called Palm Beach Gardens, a semifinal matchup. Once again Carling was set aside by the queen of clay, this time at 6–3, 6–3. In spite of this she felt her game was a whole lot better, and I asked her in what aspect.

"Oh, my forehand is much stronger, I'm more consistent, I come up to the net more, and my serve is better," she said in her high, baby-like voice.

She had dropped a comical line on the eve of the match, saying she didn't figure her success a year earlier at Amelia Island against Chrissie was bothering Evert much. "Oh, I know that Chris is very confident, that clay is her turf, that she likes the new graphite racquet she's using. I know she isn't . . . sweating bricks."

So after the match it was natural to ask Evert the difference between the Bassett she'd played at Amelia and the one she'd handled this time. Grim-lipped Chrissie considered her reply.

"She wasn't hitting the ball as hard then. She had a little more meat on her bones; she's lost 10 or 12 pounds. But so much has been made of that match. I don't think I played that well there. I played sloppy tennis but nobody seemed to ask my side of it."

Sure they had. I had. She was ungenerous then, too.

Carling wasn't overjoyed to learn of Evert's comment on her weight.

"I'm up to 108," said the blonde matchstick. "I'm 5-foot-6. Well, I'm 5-foot-5, if you must know. I was 5-foot-4 a year ago. Right now I'm really growing. Right this instant I can feel it in my bones."

"Is growing okay?"

"Well, 5-7 is," she replied, a tiny frown arriving on her tanned, unlined, concerned, 16-year-old face. "But that's it. You can't date small guys if you grow more than 5-7."

So maybe over the next couple of years she dated small guys, but then she ran into Robert Seguso, a 180-pound, round-faced hulk of 6-foot-3 from Minneapolis who, with Ken Flack, became one of the world's best doubles players. Carling and Bobby were married in Toronto in September of 1987 and when they had a child Carling's tennis career petered out.

Just about then Steffi Graf was becoming a new and exciting force in the women's firmament. On the brink of her 18th birthday she stopped Martina Navratilova in the French final. A few weeks later I vividly recall *hearing* her the morning of the day she played Martina for the Wimbledon title, July 4, 1987.

It was an unexpectedly soft, warm, cloudless morning in southwest London. I rode the tube out early, leaving the train at the Southfields station where a sedate sign on one of the light standards says, Alite Here for Wimbledon Tennis, and I walked the mile or so along tree-lined Church Road to the courts. The gates weren't to open for another hour but already the sidewalk was alive with long, long lines of patient fans three and four deep. I could walk past because my pass took me through the press gate on this lovely sunny morning.

Inside the grounds and moving along the flagstone walk between the looming vine-covered green wall of the Centre Court stadium and the outside courts I could hear the çrisp *thonk-thonk* of a tennis ball being thoroughly massaged out on Court 8, and I wondered who the two guys might be who were walloping the ball so strenuously at 10 o'clock in the morning. And, grateful that I could while away time sitting in the sun and watching this distant and anonymous pair blister the ball, I strolled between courts out to Court 8.

Now close enough, I could plainly see that one of these bounding sluggers was Steffi, her shoulder-length, honey-coloured hair pulled into a short ponytail, her legs and arms and face a sandy tan, blue eyes, a generous beak, and a crosscourt forehand to cloud men's minds. And what energy.

She was exchanging line drives with a lean, red-haired Australian, Mark Woodforde, a tour player she'd engaged because he was left-handed, as was her opponent that afternoon, Navratilova, the defending champion. Martina was seeking her eighth Wimbledon singles title, one that would equal Helen Wills Moody's record of long ago.

It wasn't simply that Steffi was exchanging low, whistling shots with Woodforde, shots that sizzled mere inches above the net cord; it was what she was doing between shots that caught my attention most. All through the long rallies she'd bounce, once, twice, three times, waiting for the return shot. And between bounces she'd shuffle her feet the way a fighter does working the speed bag. Watching those feet and that bounce, I thought of whistling "Sweet Georgia Brown," the song the Harlem Globetrotters frolic to when they put on a ball-bouncing show.

Earlier in the tournament as Steffi worked her way through the draw, she'd shown an expressive personality and even a quiet turn of humour (I say "even" because on the court, as tennis fans know so well, her expression never changes). One afternoon, facing the assembled descendants of Shakespeare in the interview room, a guy had said, when somebody asked if her half of the draw worried her, "You don't worry who you play, do you? You'd play anybody." She'd stared at him, perhaps considering whether her answer might appear immodest, and then said, "Yes, anybody." Her face changed. "You!" she cried.

However, impressive as she'd been that morning rallying with Woodforde the Australian, Steffi was hung out to dry in the afternoon by one particular weapon in Navratilova's assortment: the left-handed sliced serve to Steffi's backhand, especially when Martina served from the left-hand, or ad, court. There, she took Steffi wide with a twisting bounce that had her helpless and frustrated. It was like watching the Chinese water torture, each biting serve another drop of torment for Steffi. In spite of her work with Woodforde, Steffi couldn't find a way to cope with Martina's delivery and Martina was relentless with it.

"I didn't have to go for big serves," Martina told us riff-raff of the printed page afterwards. "It seemed that my spin bothered her more than the pace on the serve, which enabled me to get a high percentage of my first serves in. In fact, with some second serves she had a harder time timing it than my first serves. So I just kept saying, 'Let's see what she'll do with another serve to her backhand.'"

Thus, Martina won her eighth Wimbledon that day but it would be a long hot summer before she'd again find a Graf area to exploit, if ever. Steffi went home to Bruehl, the little West German town near Heidelberg where she was born and where her father, the stern, dark-haired Peter Graf, runs a tennis school. The word at Wimbledon a year later was that Peter Graf had uncovered an obscure left-handed junior in the boondocks of Germany with a serve like Navratilova's and he was hired to lay endless serves against Steffi's backhand until she could whack them back in her sleep (also while wide awake).

And this she did in the '88 final and again in '89. Instead of blocking back Martina's serves or pushing them with her backhand, she began to drill the ball, giving the shot a full backswing and follow-through, the sort of thing she'd been doing in burying lesser mortals.

And, arguably, entering the 1990s, Steffi Graf had emerged as the best women's tennis player of all time, surely the hardest hitter, although a whole new galaxy of adolescent knockouts was emerging. Foremost were the girl with the biggest grunt in the game, 16-year-old Monica Seles of Yugoslavia, the 14-year-old American hope, Jennifer Capriati, and a square-set little bouncing ball from Spain, Arantxa Sanchez-Vicario, who at 17 had become the youngest player to win the women's singles title in the French Open by beating Steffi in the 1989 final. Then Seles displaced her a year later at 16, upsetting the same Steffi, who by then had grown into an old lady of 21. The 1990s were sure to produce a whole new set of faces to make people forget the dominance of Martina and Chrissie that had once seemed endless.

Chapter 6

The Splendid Splinter and Joe D.

Ralph Allen went to the *Globe and Mail* in the autumn of 1938 and that created an opening in the *Winnipeg Tribune*'s sports department. Herb Manning took over Ralph's column, called One Man's Opinion, and this night Herb and I were sitting in one of Winnipeg's big iron yellow streetcars trundling along Portage Avenue from the Amphitheatre rink when Herb said, "How'd you like to be a full-time sportswriter?"

As I've said, the money was outstanding. It wasn't every day that $20 loomed on the horizon. So I leaped at the opportunity. Within three years I had climbed to $22 but, even so, I hadn't thought of buying a Mercedes-Benz. Then I struck it rich at *Maclean's* magazine. I mailed them a story on Turk Broda, the goaltender for the Toronto Maple Leafs, a guy I'd known when we were kids growing up in Brandon. The piece turned out to be what the magazine world called "a keeper." It was my first sale outside of newspapers and I got $75, nearly four weeks' pay at the *Trib*.

Emboldened (and flush) I approached the *Tribune* managing editor's office and, finding him there, entered the sanctum of Fred O'Malley. I told him I'd been offered $25 a week by the

Regina Leader-Post, which I hadn't but I thought maybe in his desperation to retain my pen O'Malley would offer me twenty-six.

He was a scrawny little guy with spiky white hair and a cock eye and he peered at me owlishly through silver-rimmed spectacles before replying. "If I were you," he said at length. "I'd take it."

Checkmated, I babbled something to the effect that Winnipeg was a much better town to work in and fled from his sanctum.

I have run on at some length here about the scanty amounts of money available to a hard-striving youth in the newspaper game but, really, relatively speaking, the income wasn't all that meagre. In 1941 in Winnipeg I was paying $10 a week for my large comfortable room *and* meals. I had breakfast when I got up around noon, the evening meal with the rest of the boarders at six o'clock, and then a lunch was prepared for me that I could either take to the office or eat when I got home around 2 a.m.

And, by 1990 standards, the cost of living was hilarious. Men's broadcloth shirts cost 89 cents or three for $2.50 at Eaton's. You could buy a cloth coat with a fur collar for $8.44 at the Hudson's Bay department store. Coffee was a nickel at Child's restaurant on Portage Avenue, 15 cents if you had a hamburger with it. In October that year the Garrick Theatre was showing Clark Gable, Spencer Tracy, Claudette Colbert, and Hedy Lamarr in *Boom Town* (show daily at 9:30 a.m., 25 cents to 1 p.m.).

A current-model Ford four-door with a heater, defroster, and built-in radio cost $925, not that I could afford an outlay so grand, and Tip Top Tailors was offering men's made-to-measure suits at $27.50. For women, Eaton's ran a full-page ad shouting: "Here's Our Answer to the Clamour for a coat 'to slip on over everything.' Soft wool and rayon woven into a herringbone design, dyed in versatile beige and belted into youthful smartness. The price? $22.95."

At the Safeway market a boneless rib roast was 31 cents a pound, pot roast 16 cents a pound, leg of veal 17 cents a pound, and leg of lamb 24 cents a pound. Choice peas at 10 cents a tin, wax beans 8 cents a tin, fresh eggs grade A medium at 36 cents a dozen.

Really, then, on my $22 a week in Winnipeg and my $10-a-week room and board, I had $12 to blow, week after week. On top of that, there was my $75 windfall from *Maclean's* and, with it, I asked the *Trib* sports editor Johnny Buss to accredit me for the 1941 World Series between the Yankees and the Brooklyn Dodgers. Then I hit the Canadian National Railways p.r. man Bruce Boreham for a return railway pass to Toronto (the railways usually accommodated newspaper people back then). In Toronto I spent $25 on a one-way Trans-Canada Airlines ticket to New York for the experience of airline travel (I rode the bus and smoked Camel cigarettes back to Toronto for the return trip home).

A couple of days before the World Series opener I read in my favourite New York paper, the *World-Telegram*, that Ted Williams, a tall, skinny kid of 22 who was batting .399 for the Boston Red Sox, would close out the season in a Sunday doubleheader with the Philadelphia Athletics. He was seeking to become the first player to bat .400 since Bill Terry of the Giants hit .401 in 1930. So I took a train to Philadelphia on Sunday morning and bought a grandstand seat behind the plate in Shibe Park. It cost $1.25. I debated whether to buy a box seat at $2.50 but decided to hoard my wealth.

This was Williams's third season with the Red Sox and the papers were already calling him Ted the Thumper and the Splendid Splinter because he was putting up remarkable numbers. As a 19-year-old rookie he had batted .327 with 31 homers and an improbable 145 runs batted in, and now here he was with this .399 average and 36 home runs.

Years later, when the Red Sox second-baseman Bobby Doerr became the first batting coach for the Toronto Blue Jays, he enlivened many a conversation for me with tales of Ted Williams's matchless skill at the plate. I asked him once about that Sunday afternoon in Shibe Park when Williams, who had been Bobby's roommate on road trips, went for the magic number.

"You know, the thing I remember most was how quiet things were," Bobby said. "These days, if somebody was close to .400 there'd be televison cameras and newspapermen everywhere. It would be a circus. Of course, there was no television then but, even so, that day in Philadelphia I don't recall anything unusual, just a couple of teams finishing out the year. Ted got four hits in the first game to climb well over .400 and our manager, Joe Cronin, told him he could sit out the second game if he wanted to. But there was no way he'd do a thing like that. Not Ted."

For my part, I suspect an unseen hand is in operation at certain times in sports – the hand that pushes a line drive a couple of inches outside the foul line, the hand that sends a puck clanging off a goalpost, the hand that twists a long field goal inches wide.

And this day. Ted Williams banged six hits in eight at-bats in the two games, boosting his average seven points to .406. On one, the A's first-baseman, Dick Siebert, was holding a runner close and Williams shot a ground ball through Siebert's normal fielding position into right field. On another, the bases were empty and Williams drilled another ground shot a couple of inches inside the first-base bag past the diving Siebert, who'd been playing his normal position. And on a third the A's second-baseman, Benny McCoy, broke for the bag on a hit-and-run play and Williams smashed the ball through the hole McCoy had deserted (don't ask me why the second-baseman was covering the bag with a left-hand pull hitter at the plate; maybe that's partly why the A's were a cellar ball club back then).

Anyway, there you have three of Ted's six hits. Each had been crushed but all could have been outs in different circumstances – the unseen hand. Of course, as any baseball fan will tell you, those things even up. Chances are, earlier that week Williams had blistered three balls directly at somebody for outs.

In his memoir, *My Turn at Bat*, written with John Underwood, Williams says that when he went to the batter's box for the first time the Philadelphia catcher, Frankie Hayes, told him Connie Mack, the A's elderly owner and manager, had instructed his pitchers to bear down hard on Williams; they weren't to make a gift of the .400 average.

Still, old Connie Mack wasn't sending any potential Cy Young Award winners to face Ted that afternoon, either. The pitcher in the first game was Toronto-born Dick Fowler, then 20, a 6-foot-5 right-hander who had been extracted from the Toronto Maple Leaf farm team late in the season and was making only his third big-league start (subsequently Dick endured 10 seasons with the lacklustre A's and now is in the Canadian Baseball Hall of Fame).

Williams got his day's first hit off Fowler in the first inning, a single, and in the third he sent a home run off Dick over Shibe Park's tall right-field fence, a long, high blast. This park was named for Ben Shibe, a manufacturer of baseballs, who owned the A's when the park was built in 1909. For a quarter of a century the fence in right field had been 12 feet high, which was low enough to invite competition from neighbouring property owners, who built bleachers on their rooftops and sold tickets to the ball games. But in 1935 a light went on on Ben Shibe's veranda and he had the wall raised to 50 feet, shutting down the competition outside. It was over this 50-foot barrier that Williams stroked his 37th home run that season.

When Ted came to the plate in the fifth inning, Manager Mack had already permitted his rookie right-hander to shower early and replaced him with a left-hander named Porter Vaughan, whose lifetime record in two seasons with the A's was two wins and 11 losses. Williams tagged this guy for two more hits.

Impetuous, emotional, and proud, Ted declined to sit out the second game to protect a batting average now safely above .400. He galloped out to left field when the A's came to bat in the bottom of the first inning, and as he stood out there, hands on hips, I turned in surprise to the Red Sox pitcher, the once peerless Robert Moses Grove, the man who'd scorched my ears 10 years earlier in the Pullman car in a little Manitoba town.

Groves, as Connie Mack used to call him, had spent nine seasons with the A's until 1933, when Mack traded him to the Red Sox. By 1941 he was completing his 17th season as a big-league pitcher and though most of his skills had waned (he was 41 years old) he had won his 300th game that summer. Now, as it turned out, he was starting for the final time in his big-league life.

If I had blinked I'd have missed him. The A's knocked him out with five runs in the first inning, locking up the game early. But most of the fans stayed until the end anyway to watch Williams finish off his remarkable season. First time up he drove a ball through the infield for his day's fifth hit. Next, he lashed a one-hopper to second that Benny McCoy couldn't handle. The official scorer decided McCoy should have made the play and charged him with an error.

Still, Ted wasn't through. In the seventh inning he hit a rising liner toward right-centre that rocketed over Benny McCoy's head and kept climbing. The ball slammed into the mouth of a loudspeaker attached to that 50-foot wall (the way I see it in my mind's eye, the wall is a dull beige in colour and there is a sudden loud *squ-awk* as the ball smacked into the horn) and Ted pulled into second with a double. Nobody has hit .400 since.

"I don't recall any big celebration," Bobby Doerr said one sunny morning years later in Florida. He was leaning against the stucco wall of the Blue Jays' old clubhouse along the right-field foul line at the Grant Field training base. "We were all glad for Ted but we just packed our bags and got out of there. Our season was over."

Doerr was connected with the Blue Jays through the first dozen years of their existence. It was a wrench for him to leave Oregon where he and his wife Monica had settled in the off-season back when he was still a Red Sox player. He was addicted to hunting and fishing, and both were ideal for him in Oregon. But he worked diligently with the young Blue Jay hitters at spring training and joined the team several times during the season to check up on their progress.

He was – and no doubt has remained – a lovely man, soft-spoken and gentlemanly, square-set with snow-white hair and expressive blue eyes in darkly tanned features. David Halberstam writes in *Summer of '49* that Bobby was the most popular member of the Red Sox in his 14 seasons in Boston, "and possibly the most popular baseball player of his era. He was so modest and his disposition so gentle that his colleagues often described him as 'sweet.' He was the kind of man other men might have envied had they not liked him so much."

Doerr's quiet way more than balanced the manners of his roommate, the terrible-tempered Mr. Williams, a guy who refused steadfastly to doff his chapeau to the clamouring fans after knocking any of his hundreds of homers far into the night in Fenway. Once when the fans grew particularly delirious, demanding that he emerge from the dugout and acknowledge their worshipful ways, he appeared. Cap firmly in place atop his curly brown locks, he jogged up a couple of dugout steps – and spat.

But this irascible fellow, the most passionate hitter in baseball, remained one of Bobby Doerr's closest friends. Even 30 years after they left the Red Sox Bobby would raise the Williams name a couple of times a day around the Blue Jay batting cage. His sentences would begin, "Well, Ted Williams always maintained that . . . "

Bobby would fold his arms along a bar at the back of the cage, rest his chin on the backs of his hands, and watch the batters at work – Ernie Whitt, Lloyd Moseby, Willie Upshaw, and the rest – quietly advising them to take a level swing at the ball, not to uppercut it.

"Stroke down on the ball. Lay the bat on it the way you'd lay an axe against a tree. That'll put underspin on the ball, make it float and rise toward the fence. Uppercutting gives the ball topspin, makes it dive."

One morning Doerr was chatting with Peter Bavasi at the Dunedin training base and Bavasi, the first Blue Jay president, wondered aloud if Williams might be persuaded to talk to the players.

"Well, I'll call him and ask him," said the agreeable batting coach. "It ought to be an inspirational thing for the younger fellows."

The unpredictable Williams, who was not far away in Winter Haven giving helpful hints to the Red Sox, agreed to oblige his old teammate, and the Blue Jay players arrayed themselves in two tight rows, like teams having a group picture taken, to hear the great man. Ted handed a bat to John Mayberry, the jolly, moon-faced first-baseman, for illustrative purposes.

"What you have to do if you're hitting for distance," Williams said, adjusting the bat and Mayberry's stance, "is uppercut the ball slightly."

There were nervous coughs and a few titters and then everybody, led by Doerr, burst into laughter.

"I suspected it would happen that way," Bobby chuckled later. "All through our years in Boston, Ted and I argued that point. I used to say to him, and I feel the same now, '*You* can do it, Ted, but most of us can't.' The problem is, a hitter has to be so fine and so precise his way. There was only one Ted Williams."

And only one Bobby Doerr. He and his idol appeared in only one World Series and, in it, Doerr far outshone Williams. That was in 1946, the year both came back from the armed services. Doerr missed all of 1945 and Williams, a navy flier, was gone for 1943, '44, and '45. Remarkably, Ted batted .342 with 38 homers in his first year back, but in the seven-game World Series against the Cardinals he got only five hits in 25 at-bats, all singles, for a .200 average.

For his part Doerr got nine hits, including a homer and a double, leading both teams in number of hits and batting .409. He did it in spite of missing one game and part of another because of migraine headaches.

This was the Series decided in St. Louis in the seventh game when the delightfully named Enos (Country) Slaughter fled all the way from first base to the plate with the winning run on Harry Walker's single. With the score tied 3–3, Slaughter's single opened the Cardinal eighth. Two batters were retired and then Walker put the ball into left-centre field. Johnny Pesky, the Boston shortstop, ran out to take the cut-off throw and turned briefly to see if Walker was trying for second base. He knew Slaughter had sped to third but nobody gave him a warning cry that Slaughter had wheeled nonstop for home. By the time Pesky spotted him and threw to the plate Slaughter was in there.

Some people rise to the occasion in the heat of World Series exposure, some people don't. Boston newspaper columnists, ignored or scorned as parasites by the strong-willed Williams, turned mercilessly on him early in his career. Dave Egan, a columnist for the Hearst tabloid, the *Record*, wrote scandalously of Williams, referred to him sometimes as "the inventor of the automatic choke," and often cited the player's dismal handiwork in the 1946 World Series as illustration. Still, since the Red Sox got into only one Series during Williams's 19 seasons with them, it seems unfair to hold up one appearance as an accurate barometer. Certainly, Bobby Doerr didn't, but others wondered.

In 1946 when the Toronto Huskies were charter members of the National Basketball Association (they were buried in red ink and lasted one season), a former baseball star for the Yankees, Red Rolfe, was hired to coach them. Rolfe had been a basketball and baseball player at Dartmouth and basketball coach at Yale and had been the Yankee third-baseman for 10 years in the 1930s and early 1940s. When he arrived in Toronto to coach pro basketball the scribes wanted to talk to him about only one thing, baseball. I remember once after a Huskies practice in Maple Leaf Gardens asking him something about the six World Series he'd played in. Rolfe was a quiet-spoken man with the pale complexion of most fiery-haired people, and he might have been referring to Williams when he observed that for the players as well as for the fans there was a different aura about those autumn games.

"When you play in the World Series you feel a challenge, and that makes one of two things happen," he said. "You either rise above your normal game or you're constricted by the pressure and don't play as well as you can."

When Rolfe mentioned this I thought back to that Series I'd gone to on my holiday from the *Winnipeg Tribune*. There was an incident then that I felt illustrated what Rolfe was getting at, an incident involving Joe DiMaggio.

The Series had begun in Yankee Stadium on Wednesday and Thursday afternoons following Ted Williams's big Sunday doubleheader in Shibe Park. The favoured Yankees won the opening game by 3–2 and the Dodgers evened matters by the same score on Thursday. To permit the teams time to make their way from Yankee Stadium in the Bronx to Ebbets Field in Brooklyn, a distance of maybe 10 miles, Friday was an off day, designated for travel. Baseball does things like that, even today.

Fat Freddie Fitzsimmons, 41 years old, pitched the third game for the Dodgers, the first in crazy old Ebbets Field. I had a seat in the auxiliary press box on the roof of the second deck that paralleled the right-field foul line. Two-by-four boards simulated desks for us deep-thinkers along the rooftop and a long white canvas awning was stretched above our heads to ward off rain and passing aircraft. My seat was alongside the foul pole, side by side with one occupied by Elmer Dulmage, who worked for the Canadian Press wire service in its New York bureau.

Fat Freddie held the Yankees to four singles over the first seven innings. On his final pitch of the seventh in a scoreless game he was struck on the kneecap by a line drive by the Yankee first-baseman, Johnny Sturm. You could hear the crack of the ball whacking the bone away up in my seat on the roof. The Brooklyn shortstop, Pee Wee Reese, retrieved the ball and threw out Sturm to end the inning but Fitzsimmons was too badly bruised to continue.

So Brooklyn sent another chubby right-hander, Hugh Casey, to pitch the eighth and the Yankees got successive singles from

Red Rolfe and Tommy Henrich to put runners on first and third. Joe DiMaggio singled to score Rolfe, Charley Keller singled to score Henrich, and the Yankees won the game 2–1.

Now came the fourth game, one that is remembered to this day by fans whenever the conversation turns on World Series gaffes. It is a Sunday afternoon and the seats in the old park are filled by 33,813 bottoms, including one belonging to the guy in the front row of the second deck back of third base who immortalized the Dodgers as the Brooklyn Bums. This was back in the 1930s when the Dodgers couldn't lick their lips. The grumbling fans constantly berated the ballplayers, crying "Ya bum ya" among other imprecations for every miscue.

Then one afternoon there was a flock of errors. The Dodgers fumbled so frequently that even the Phillies smothered them. In exasperation, the fan in the upper deck in left field climbed slowly to his feet and delivered a blanket condemnation.

"*Yez bums yez!*"

From that day forward the Brooklyn nine was celebrated everywhere as the Bums, or Dem Bums, and immortalized in the *World-Telegram* by the cartoonist, Willard Mullin, as an old dude in a battered top hat, a patched swallowtail coat, baggy striped pants, worn shoes and spats, and wearing a dead cigar butt in his happy-go-lucky kisser.

The inventive fan may have been the one who earned an anonymous immortality during a brief period when the veteran pitcher Waite Hoyt found himself in a Dodger uniform. In his 21-year career Hoyt hadn't missed many stops and then he became an admired television announcer (he didn't talk much) for the Cincinnati Reds.

But after pitching in six World Series in the 1920s with the Yankees of Babe Ruth's vintage, Hoyt drifted until 1937 when he joined the Dodgers. One afternoon at Ebbets Field he was felled by a line drive and lay writhing next to the mound. It was not just an ordinary injury. He didn't struggle slowly to his feet and hobble to the dugout. The team's trainer scurried from the dugout and knelt beside him and a hush filled the stands.

Then in the stillness there arose a solitary voice as the pitcher lay there. "Geez, Hurt's hoit."

But now in this fourth Series game the legions were assembled to hail their pennant-winning Bums, and heading into the ninth inning the Dodgers were grimly holding a 4–3 lead. Hugh Casey was again on the mound. He had gone into the game in the fifth inning with the Yankees threatening and had yielded only one hit through to the ninth. He got the first two batters and had only Tommy Henrich between him and a 4–3 victory. The count went to three balls and two strikes and Casey fired his toughest pitch of the day, a sinking curveball that fooled Henrich, who swung and missed. The Series was tied.

But wait.

From my rooftop perch I could see the ball bouncing swiftly toward the stands back of the plate. I thought Henrich had fouled it off. Yet Henrich was running to first base and Mickey Owen, the Dodger catcher, had hurled off his mask and was chasing the skittering ball. Henrich hadn't fouled off the pitch; he'd swung and missed, and the diving ball had eluded Mickey Owen, too.

Now DiMaggio stepped in, feet set wide apart, bat cocked high behind his right ear. He walloped Casey's first pitch on a line over shortstop into left field, sending Henrich to second.

And this was the moment I was to think of five years later listening to Red Rolfe in Maple Leaf Gardens. DiMaggio, after lashing the liner into left field, had slammed his bat angrily to the ground as he set off for first base, obviously upset that in this dramatic situation, his team one run down, he'd delivered *only* a single; he hadn't tied the game with an extra-base hit or won it with a homer.

As it turned out, it didn't matter. The burly Charley Keller drove the ball high against the right-field wall just below Elmer Dulmage and me, scoring Henrich and DiMaggio. Next, catcher Bill Dickey got a base on balls as Casey continued to flounder. And with the Dodger manager Leo Durocher still not injecting a new reliever, Yankee second-baseman Joe Gordon laced a double into the left-centre field gap. That scored Keller and Dickey, and the Dodgers once again had snatched defeat from the jaws of victory. The next afternoon the Yankees won again, and the Series was over.

Had this been Joe DiMaggio's only World Series a case could be made that he, too, had not delivered his best work, failing almost as notably as Williams in Ted's only Series. DiMag got five hits in 19 at-bats, all singles, for a .263 average and one run batted in. But, unlike Williams, Joe had *10* World Series in which to accumulate eight home runs and 30 runs batted in, enough production to silence any newshound seeking controversy.

In my time as an ink-stained wretch I attended 14 World Series and never saw an outfielder approach the grace and style of Joe DiMaggio. And in the years of watching the Toronto Blue Jays and their American League rivals, beginning with the Blue Jays' inception in 1977, I can't think of anyone with Joe's fluidity. When this guy chased a fly ball you could think of sea gulls swooping. I doubt that he ever made a *spectacular* catch; his timing was so remarkable that even on balls hit deep in the gaps, especially in left-centre in Yankee Stadium, he seemed to overtake the ball in the long, loping strides of an Olympic mile runner. At the end he'd reach up casually and let the ball catch up to his glove rather than vice versa.

There was a ball he took from Pete Reiser, a stocky Dodger switch hitter batting left. Joe played him toward right because Reiser was a good pull hitter. But this time he got an outside pitch and shot it into the cavernous depths of left-centre. In that unhurried way of his DiMaggio floated to his right, running hard, his instinct aiming him at the precise spot where he and the ball would intersect. The fence out there, before the park was renovated in the early 1980s, was 457 feet away, and not far short of it Joe reached up and took down the ball as a man might pluck an apple from a low tree.

By 1947 I was freelancing in magazines and the father of two-year-old Jill, the first of four children spawned by my wife, June

Callwood, and me. I'd left the *Winnipeg Tribune* in 1942 and spent three years on the news side at the Toronto *Globe and Mail*. The freelancing was made considerably easier by the fact June, whom I'd met on the *Globe*, also was selling freelance stuff to magazines.

At any rate, in that autumn of 1947 my father, a staunch baseball fan, had wanted for years to see at least one World Series before he grew too old to appreciate it. I was able to get press accreditation for both of us. Johnny Buss at the *Tribune* in Winnipeg applied on my dad's behalf, and Bobby Hewitson, the sports editor of the *Toronto Telegram*, agreed to sponsor an application for me. It was an era when Canadian newspapers rarely staffed the Series. Even today, apart from a flood of reporters from the three Toronto dailies and a trickle from Montreal, Canadian papers usually rely on the wire services for coverage.

So in late September my father and I set off on the overnight train for New York, picked up our credentials the following morning at the Biltmore Hotel, the Series headquarters, and settled into the barely endurable life of World Series scribes: lavish complimentary breakfasts, bus service between the hotel to the press gates, lunch and drinks in the press lounges at the ballparks, seats in the press boxes, and dinner back at the hotel in the evening.

Two incidents jump instantly to mind whenever I think of the '47 Series, one an inspired line by Red Smith in the *New York Herald-Tribune* after the fourth game, and the other my own monumental intemperance during the sixth. In the fourth game, in Brooklyn, Yankee right-hander Floyd Bevens almost pitched a quite astonishing no-hit game. Bevens, who had won only seven games and lost 13 that year, was wild but stingy, issuing 10 walks but getting the ball over in critical moments. Entering the bottom of the ninth he had a 2–1 lead but had given up no hits. He got the leadoff Dodger, walked Carl Furillo, and fanned the third batter. So he was one out away from the first no-hitter in World Series history, though he'd allowed a run.

Now a spare outfielder, Al Gionfriddo, running for Furillo,

stole second base, setting up the key managerial move of the inning. The Yankee manager, Bucky Harris, decided to give an intentional walk to Pete Reiser, a questionable move since it put the winning run at first base.

So with two out and two on, Bevens faced pinch-hitter Cookie Lavagetto. He threw a ball and then he delivered the game's final pitch. Lavagetto laced the ball on a line against the fence in right-centre and both runners scored. For a change the Yankees had snatched defeat from the jaws of victory. And that night, rushing from the hotel to get an early edition of the *Herald-Trib*, I read this final paragraph in Red Smith's column:

"The unhappiest man in Brooklyn is sitting up here now in the far end of the press box. The *v* on his typewriter is broken. He can't write either Lavagetto or Bevens."

The sixth game, on a Sunday, was back in Yankee Stadium. My father and I got out there early to have a drink and a bite and to listen to the baseball geniuses dissect the Series. The Yankees were leading by three games to two and with Allie Reynolds pitching the feeling was they'd wrap it up. Reynolds had won 19 games during the season and was the team's ace.

My father and I drank a couple of scotches before our lunch and near one o'clock headed for our seats for the 1:05 start. To our surprise the stands were only partly filled and there wasn't the excited hum that precedes the first pitch. Even the press seats were sparsely occupied.

And then a guy looking up from the Underwood on which he was writing an early piece cleared the mystery. New York state law forbade a start prior to 2:05 on Sundays. So we went back to the press lounge and had another scotch ... and another ... and ...

By 2:05 my eyebrows were floating as I returned to my seat. On the field below there were two players at every position – two guys batting, two catching, two pitching, and a whole blur of guys in the distant outfield. I had to close one eye to get the field and its occupants into focus. By the sixth inning my stomach was in full rebellion and I fled to the men's room.

By then the Dodgers had gone ahead by 8–5 with four runs

in the sixth. In the bottom half the Yankees had the tying run at the plate when I made my run for the men's room. The tying run was Joe DiMaggio, stepping in to face Brooklyn left-hander Joe Hatten with runners at second and third. It had been a good year for Joe, batting .315 with 20 homers and 97 runs batted in, and he'd delivered Series home runs in the third and fifth games.

Facing Hatten, he bid for a third homer, the one that would deadlock this game at 8–8. The papers next day agreed his long blast to left-centre had the home-run look climbing toward the rows of fans out there. But back in the fifth inning the regular Dodger left-fielder, Gene Hermanski, had been set down for a pinch-hitter, and now the outfielder was Al Gionfriddo, 5-foot-6 and 165 pounds, a journeyman who had put in two seasons plus with Pittsburgh and then was traded to the Bums. He'd been in only 37 games.

Now here he was legging it deep toward a low wire fence and finally, desperately, apparently making a last-second lunge at DiMaggio's drive, getting it in the glove on his right hand and hanging on. I say apparently for I saw none of it. At the moment that Gionfriddo was making his stunning catch I was seeing nothing of anything in the men's washroom.

My dad raved about the catch on the overnight train home to Toronto and, once there, nobody asked me about the Bevens bid for a no-hitter, nothing about Cookie Lavagetto's last-minute heroics, nothing about Al Gionfriddo's key theft of second base – nothing, indeed, about that thrilling fourth game whatever. All I encountered were wide-eyed exclamations over Gionfriddo's catch.

"Oh, wonderful," I kept saying. "Yeah, marvelous." "Yep, you're right; one of the great catches. No question."

I have been going to lunch on Gionfriddo's catch for years. Indeed, for decades. I always say, "Yes, I was there the day he did it." I was, too.

Chapter 7

Wayne & Mario & the Rocket
& Gordie

It is not a closely guarded secret that the most celebrated hockey player of the 1980s was Wayne Gretzky, the national treasure dealt off to Los Angeles by the meat-packer owner of the Edmonton Oilers, Peter Pocklington, who, unimpeded by sentiment or passion, may have mistaken him for a side of pork. In nine of the decade's 10 seasons Gretzky won the Hart Trophy as the National Hockey League's most valuable player and set scoring records undreamed of by ordinary mortals.

However, just short of this astonishing player's ordainment as a saint, along came the towering Mario Lemieux from Montreal, in St-Henri in the West End, as it is called, threatening to replace Gretzky as the most accomplished player on God's tiny footstool. In 1988 the huge young centre of the Pittsburgh Penguins unseated Wayne as the Hart Trophy winner and in both 1988 and 1989 displaced him as the scoring champion. Wayne the Wizard was back in the spring of 1990, aided by Lemieux's chronic back problem that forced him out of the last two months of the season.

Until this development, there had been launched a growing controversy, perhaps inevitable: who was better, Lemieux or

Gretzky? It was the sort of head-to-head comparison that had livened up the firmament 40 years earlier when Gordie Howe and Rocket Richard were bound together in a similar dispute.

The first time I saw Mario Lemieux I figured I'd gone to the wrong rink. Mario had scored a million points, give or take an assist, for the Laval Voisin of the Quebec junior league and in the spring of 1984 here he was in Kitchener, Ontario, in the Memorial Cup final. Once, the Memorial Cup final was a great hockey spectacle. It pitted the 20-years-and-under champions of the West against their counterparts in the East for the national championship, and it was not uncommon for teams to attract capacity throngs to Maple Leaf Gardens when the Winnipeg Monarchs, say, met Toronto St. Mike's or the Oshawa Generals took on the Edmonton E.A.C.s in a best-of-seven-game final.

Nowadays the Memorial Cup is a four-team week-long round-robin tournament between the western Canada champions, the Ontario champions, the Quebec champions, and the host city's local heroes, the latter to provide balance and, more than that, a home-town gate attraction. This time, when Lemieux led his Laval teammates into Kitchener, it was to oppose the Kamloops Oilers, the Ottawa 67s, and the local Kitchener Rangers.

As I say, I thought I'd misread the address because the heralded Lemieux was a bafflement. With that rapturous reputation of his – in 70 league games he'd scored 133 goals and 149 assists and had maintained that pace in the Quebec playoffs – he turned out to be a rather disjointed giant of 6-foot-4 and 200 pounds gliding serenely about the ice. When he had the puck he cruised with long, powerful strides but when he lost it he turned about in sweeping, preoccupied semicircles. When he headed to the bench for a rest he eased up approaching the boards and sat disinterestedly. His shot flew swift as a speeding bullet but there was no evidence that if he were to meet a Voisin defenceman on the street he'd recognize him. Mario operated strictly between the rival team's goal and the centre red line.

Even so, that winter there'd been talk of few other junior

players, so between periods I looked for Billy Taylor. Billy Taylor was a scout for the Pittsburgh Penguins, the last-place NHL team, whose sole consolation was that their hopeless position assured them of first choice in the forthcoming draft of amateur players. It was widely known that Eddie Johnston, Pittsburgh's general manager, was determined to pick Lemieux, rejecting numerous offers from other teams of veteran players for his No. 1 draft position.

Indeed, relieving the dreariness of his longest winter, Johnston, whom everybody calls E.J., often hurried to his native Montreal to watch this scoring star of junior hockey, born and raised in St-Henri, E.J.'s own boyhood neighbourhood. On one such pilgrimage he was joined by scout Albert Mandanici, who had told the *Gazette*'s Tim Burke that Lemieux "is the one guy I see with the talent to catch up to Gretzky." Which prompted Burke, when he encountered Eddie Johnston, to wonder what it would take to pry loose Pittsburgh's draft status in a swap with Les Canadiens. Johnston was appalled by the notion, but recovered quickly enough.

"Up front, a million dollars in a suitcase," sighed E.J. "Plus $200,000 a year for the rest of my life."

Even so, in light of what Lemieux showed during Memorial Cup week in Kitchener, I was happy to spot Billy Taylor in the crowd during the intermission.

"Billy, an off period for Mario, perhaps?" I asked, groping for a diplomatic way to put it.

"Why no, that's him," Billy said, face impassive.

"H-m-m. Have you seen E.J. lately?"

"Sure I've seen him. He's fine."

"He still likes this fellow?"

Billy remained steadfast.

"Loves him."

Billy's lugubrious mien suggested he shared my notion that Mario's immortality was still somewhat questionable, but he declined to discuss the implied heresy and at one point said in his quiet way, "When the time comes, the kid'll be there."

Billy died suddenly at 71 in June of 1990. He had helped the

Toronto Maple Leafs to a Stanley Cup win in the spring of 1942, the nifty little centre for Sweeney Schriner and Lorne Carr. He was from that era when the Memorial Cup crowds were large and thunderous. In 1938, for instance, Wally Stanowski led the St. Boniface Seals from Manitoba to shade Billy's Oshawa Generals, each game a sellout. Similarly, a year later the E.A.C.s from Edmonton were Oshawa's rivals in a series that belonged solely to Billy.

He got nine points in the first game and followed that with five goals in the next one. Whereupon the Edmonton strategists came up with a revolutionary counter: they sent one player, Elmer Kreller, to shadow Taylor with instructions to keep the Oshawa stick-handling wizard company wherever he went. It was a new concept, one man to cover one man, and highly effective. Once, Billy stood beside his own net while his teammates buzzed Edmonton's at the other end of the rink. Kreller stood there, too.

"I drew a blank that night and we lost, 4–1," Billy recalled this time in Kitchener. " 'Hey,' I said to him at one point, 'I'm going to take a leak. You comin'?' He didn't even smile."

"What happened?" I asked. "Did you lose the series?"

"You're kidding, I trust," smiled Billy Taylor. "Next game, I shadowed one of their guys. With Kreller shadowing me, it meant there were two Edmonton guys and me, so we always had a man open. They had to scrap it."

Later that night I encountered Wayne Parrish, a tall, gentle fellow who later became the sports editor of the *Toronto Sun*, and mentioned that the heralded Lemieux looked awesome all right, all right.

"Oh, maybe," Wayne conceded. "But he'll help Pittsburgh."

"Hey, come on," I said. "He won't make Pittsburgh for a while yet."

"Sure he will," Wayne said. "I'd bet he'll get at least 40 goals there next season."

"Twenty bucks!" I cried, fearful Wayne would escape.

He nodded, grinning.

Boy, had Wayne found a mark. The following season, at age

19 and wearing the Penguin yellow-and-black, Mario scored 43 goals, got an even 100 points, and was voted the year's top NHL rookie.

Indeed, he alone kept the team *in* Pittsburgh, a town grown weary of Penguin failure. In Mario's first season there, attendance at the 16,033-seat Civic Arena, a lovely building on a height of ground downtown, increased 46 per cent, from an average of 6,800 to more than 10,000. The next year the average climbed another 18 per cent to just under 12,000 and by the late 1980s it was the rare game that didn't sell out. All of which prompted the Penguin marketing director to observe that Lemieux was totally responsible. "Without him," said Paul Steigerwald, "the team doesn't improve and the fans don't come out. He's meant everything to this organization."

And in Edmonton, Oiler coach Glen Sather, who had watched Wayne Gretzky fill the Northlands Coliseum for nearly a decade, shared Steigerwald's heady assessment. "Without Lemieux, they pack up the team and move to another city," Sather said.

Mario grew better and better, a soft-spoken fellow who had taken Berlitz courses in English while playing for Laval to hasten his relationship with increasing numbers of non-Quebec scribes whose brains were, of course, taxed only by English. To help Mario grow comfortable in Pittsburgh, E.J. Johnston got him settled with a local family, Nancy and Tom Mathews and their three grown sons.

"I just felt it was important for him to have a home base to work from, people he could lean on," Johnston said once. As a player, the Penguin general manager had shared goaltending duties with Gerry Cheevers on two Stanley Cup winners in Boston and had helped nurture a shy, 18-year-old defenceman named Bobby Orr. After Boston, E.J. played goal for Toronto, Chicago, and St. Louis in a 16-year career, a square-set, earnest guy of universal popularity. In those 16 seasons his nose was broken seven times, he picked up 175 stitches in his *face*, and once almost lost an ear lobe when it was sliced by a careening puck in the era before masks.

For years, every time I saw E.J. or phoned him I apologized to him. Back in the spring of 1974 the Bruins had shipped him to Toronto in exchange for Jacques Plante at a time when the *Toronto Star* harboured notions of producing a new weekly magazine. Assigned to oversee the task was a loud, red-faced Australian named Ted Bolwell, who put together a dummy of the magazine with which to test potential advertisers. At the time, I was working in the *Star*'s Insight section writing features, and Bolwell dragooned me to do a piece on injuries to goaltenders for his mock-up. He wanted to illustrate it with a series of pictures of Johnston, getting an artist to paint red welts and black stitches and purple contusions and green abrasions on the various segments of E.J.'s anatomy that had been assaulted over the years.

"*You* ask Johnston," Bolwell beamed one morning. "He'll be glad to get the publicity when the magazine comes out."

So after I'd interviewed the Leaf goaltender I told him about the request to paint his many injuries. (Once during a practice in his Boston days he almost died in the Massachusetts General Hospital after being felled by a slapshot by Bobby Orr. "They kept taking me to the operating room in case a blood clot at the back of my head moved and they had to drill a hole," E.J. had told me. "My weight went from 194 to 155 in the first week.") Seeking to persuade him to sit still for the pictures I promised him the artist wouldn't take long doing the job in the *Star*'s art department and I assured him that the photography would be brief, too. Reluctantly, I'm sure, he agreed and I drove him from the Gardens to the *Star* building on the harbourfront.

He undressed to his shorts and stood while the artist went to work. On and on he painted as time ticked away, and then a couple of photographers came along, setting their lights interminably and studying various angles from which to take their pictures, all of it standard cameraman procedure. Then they shot roll upon roll of film, one in colour, the other in black and white. It was dark when they finished and I couldn't think of anything to say to E.J. as I drove him back to his car at the Gardens. Quite understandably, he sat in sullen silence.

And then, long after I'd written my piece and the photographers had printed their rolls of film, the *Star* decided that the response of the advertisers wasn't sufficiently encouraging to warrant the launching of a new magazine.

E.J. was good about it when I told him. "Okay, okay," he said, "but at least let me have some of the pictures to show the family."

"Oh sure, no problem," I replied airily.

Little did I know that in the lengthy interim between the picture session and the decision to abandon the projected weekly, the prints, negatives, and transparencies had somehow been misplaced. The art department thought the library had them, the library was sure they'd never been filed there, and none of Bolwell's staff had a clue. I tried off and on for months to trace them without success, so in subsequent years whenever I called Eddie Johnston, somewhere in the conversation I'd feel this compulsion to tell him I was sorry about those damned pictures.

And it became necessary to call E.J. frequently after he retired as a goaltender because he turned to coaching, first in the Chicago organization and later with the Penguins for three years in the early 1980s. Then Pittsburgh made him its general manager and through four tough seasons he slowly found the parts to make the team competitive. A key move was hanging in to land Lemieux, although as someone remarked at the time, anyone who would miss Mario would miss Marilyn Monroe (geez, I'd have missed *Marilyn Monroe*?). Still, a lot of teams hounded E.J., proffering good seasoned players to the moribund Penguins, so the temptation must sometimes have been great for him to exchange patience for immediacy. Then later, when the Penguins added the elegant Paul Coffey, they began a slow improvement.

The break came when Coffey declined to report to the Edmonton Oilers in the autumn of 1987 after aiding them in three of their four Stanley Cup triumphs. He thought he was worth more to the team than his boss Sather did. Coffey is no Bobby Orr but he is an eyeful whirling out of his own end with the puck, relieving the pressure, leading a charge. "I've never seen a guy who can skate like that," the smooth little centre for the New York Islanders, Pat LaFontaine, said once.

"I needed that type of player, a guy who could lug the puck," E.J. said in one of those phone calls after I'd mumbled my speech about the lost pictures. "Getting him was hard grinding. I was on the phone to Sather for weeks trying to put together a deal that would satisfy him. How many calls? Oh, a hundred maybe; maybe more. I called every day for three weeks near the end, sometimes 20 calls a day as the situation kept changing."

But finally he got his man and, joined in Pittsburgh, Coffey and Lemieux made a tandem not unlike the one E.J. had known in Boston, the one that had Orr leading the Bruin charge and Phil Esposito finishing it off in the goalmouth. In those days Espo was renowned as the game's foremost garbage collector, parking his busy elbows and large behind in front of the net, rooting around for loose pucks and netting a record 76 goals in the 1970-71 season.

Accordingly, with Lemieux and Coffey, the Penguins finally made a modest move in the spring of 1988, reaching the playoffs for the first time in six seasons. They hammered the New York Rangers in four straight games before succumbing to Philadelphia in the division final. E.J.'s reward was a trifle disconcerting, however; he was fired. Well, not precisely fired. He was demoted to assistant general manager and spent most of his time scouting the boondocks for prospects.

But in the spring of 1989 he was rescued by the Hartford Whalers, who made him their vice-president and general manager. Of course, with the Whalers, E.J. didn't have a Lemieux or a Gretzky to carry the load those players shouldered in Pittsburgh and in Edmonton. With the Oilers, Gretzky's impact was almost immediate once he made the jump from junior ranks to the pros at a tender 17.

I didn't see him as a junior, though everybody was hearing about him during the winter of 1977-78 when, as a scrawny 16-year-old, he played for Sault Ste. Marie and scored 70 goals in 64 games and averaged two points a game in the playoffs. Even so, how could you take him seriously, a kid of 16 as wide as a rake handle? Certainly, Johnny Bassett didn't when the late Johnny owned the Toronto Toros in the World Hockey Association. Wayne was terrifying the juniors about the time that Bassett was discovering that kindly old H. Ballard was skinning the Toros alive for use of Maple Leaf Gardens. The rent alone was $750,000, and that was a dozen years ago. In addition, the warm-hearted philanthropist retained the concessions, and he shunted the Toros and visiting WHA teams into tiny, inadequate dressing rooms in his rink.

One night, moments before a Toro game, the benevolent proprietor noticed that a padded strip of canvas that covered the Maple Leaf bench was occupied by behinds belonging to the Toros. Old H. sent a lackey to retrieve the canvas padding and let the Toros sit on the hard bare bench.

Bassett stood this lunacy for one season, during which he also laid out $100,000 to build a quite luxurious dressing room for his team (a room, by the way, that now serves NHL teams coming in to play the Maple Leafs). One year was enough for Bassett; he moved his team to Alabama where they became the Birmingham Bulls. While they were there Gus Badali, a player agent, called Bassett and told him his client, Gretzky, was ready to turn pro and that he, Bassett, could have first crack at the boy wonder.

One pauses to ponder what might have happened in the fairyland world of Wayne Gretzky had Bassett said yes. Would there have been the Edmonton Oiler dynasty? Would anybody have known of the greed of Peter Pocklington? Or cared? Would Wayne the Wizard have turned Los Angeles into a hockey town, presenting all sorts of opportunities for the game in the far western reaches? Would he have met and married the lovely Janet, the L.A. actress, and lived happily ever after (so far, anyway)?

Instead of saying yes when Badali called, however, Bassett said no. He later claimed he'd turned down the Wizard because he had already signed five junior players for $50,000 each and because Badali wanted more than that for the flaxen-haired stringbean. Anyway, Johnny laughed in an infectious way he had, he'd already blown a bundle as a foil for Ballard and, while Gretzky was a talented kid, he *was* only 17 playing amid peers; who knew how he'd perform in the boisterous WHA?

So Badali sold his client to Nelson Skalbania, who owned the WHA's Indianapolis Racers, and after a mere eight games, during which Wayne picked up three goals and three assists, Skalbania sold his contract to Pocklington in Edmonton. Wayne turned 18 halfway through the season but was still mature enough to become an instant hit, the WHA's rookie of the year. Then the Oilers, along with the Quebec Nordiques, Hartford, and the Winnipeg Jets, joined the NHL for the 1979-80 season and Wayne just kept soaring.

The first time I remember seeing him to talk to was in his third NHL season when his phenomenal scoring skills were carrying him toward records thought unassailable in so brief a period, such as Phil Esposito's single-season mark of 76 goals. Phil had required 80 games with a Stanley Cup-bound team to get the job done; now here was the upstart from the *expansionist* Oilers closing on the record in his 64th game. It was in Buffalo and Phil was there the night he did it. Espo had retired following the 1979-80 season, his 17th in the NHL, and wanted to be on hand if this mark of his was eclipsed.

To that point Gretzky's output had been astonishing. One night he scored five times against Philadelphia to reach the 50-goal milestone in 39 games. Now here he was on March 3 with a month left on the schedule and already seeking his 77th goal. As I drove over from Toronto my mind reflected on the furore that had accompanied Rocket Richard's feat of 50 goals in 50 games, a season goal-scoring mark that had stood for 15 years until Boom Boom Geoffrion and Bobby Hull equalled it in the early 1960s.

Newshounds turned up in Buffalo's Memorial Auditorium at noon when the Oilers skated out the kinks for that night's game. Afterwards Gretzky sat still for a barrage of questions. The attention he was getting had left him unfazed. He said earnestly that the way hockey had evolved made goal-scoring much less difficult than it had been in the old six-team league. Before he left, sweating heavily but patient, he actually thanked everybody for their interest. Greying scribes, accustomed to pursuing the Dave Stiebs and Thurman Munsons of the world, shook their tired old heads in wonder.

There were 16,433 paying fans in Buffalo's renovated Aud when the game began and for the longest time it appeared that the Sabres's own scoring star, Gilbert Perreault, rather than Wayne the Wizard, was going to be the night's hero. With less than seven minutes to play in a 3–3 tie the kid everybody had come to see had been blanked by the Buffalo goaltender, Don Edwards. Meantime the stylish Perreault had scored all of Buffalo's goals. Gretzky had been foiled on six shots through two periods and during more than half of the third he missed on two more.

Then, *pow!* in a space of six minutes he put three shots into the Sabre cage. The first one, the one that broke Esposito's record, was achieved unaided. He swiped the puck from one Buffalo defenceman, whirled past the other, and as he sped diagonally across the front of the net in those quick darting little strides of his he blistered a high shot past Edwards.

For five minutes the mob would not sit down or stop hollering. Espo went onto the ice and embraced the new champ. Later, he and Wayne sat in a steamy makeshift press room upstairs where a long congratulatory telegram from President Ronald Reagan of the United States was awaiting Wayne's arrival. There was no word from Pierre Trudeau, the Prime Minister of Canada. In this sardine can of a room the old star and the new one sat under bright television lights and guys with tape recorders and notebooks leaned forward expectantly, crowding close and sweaty. Phil said he'd known about Gretzky since Wayne was 14.

"My dad phoned me one day from Sault Ste. Marie. 'Hey, Phil,' he said, 'there's a kid here's gonna break your record some day.'

"'Yeah,' I said. 'Who?'

"'He's called Gretzky,' my dad said. 'Geez, Phil, what a kid.' So I've been waiting."

A scribe wanted to know what it was that set apart this paragon just turned 21.

"Intensity," Phil said instantly. "Intensity and concentration and desire. He can put these three things together better than anybody I ever saw."

Wayne sat silent through all of this. I can see him now, sitting back of a bank of microphones, his fair complexion flushed, a green towel around his neck that he kept rubbing through his sweat-matted hair. When time came for him to speak he made an observation that was to become typical of him as the years moved along.

"I just feel very fortunate to be playing in the era that suits my style. Players like Phil, Bobby Hull, Bobby Orr, and Gordie Howe were great players and would have been great in any era. I'm glad that the way the game's played now I've been able to join them, sort of."

That season he wound up with 92 goals, miles ahead of everybody in history, and an unprecedented 120 assists. Four seasons later he got 163 assists. Before Gretzky the record was Bobby Orr's 102. "Mathematically," a guy wrote, "if he had been hitting home runs, Gretzky would have thumped number 97."

The thing about Wayne, he loves the game. I got a letter from him one time thanking me for columns about him – imagine, a guy *thanking* a scribe – and it emphasized how he really loved to play this game, the pure pleasure he got from it. It's hard to know if Mario feels this strongly about his work. You get the feeling watching him that he does it because he's good at it and can gain a lifetime of security by playing it. Mario doesn't make speeches about it, he just goes about his business. All through the 1980s Wayne did both. When the international spotlight lands on him, as it did when he surpassed Espo's record and later, in December of 1989, when he overcame Gordie Howe's once seemingly insurmountable points total, he always preached the gospel of the game.

He did this especially on behalf of the Oilers, another sorry reflection on Pocklington's callousness in selling him – oh, yes, in the sense that other players were involved it was a trade, but there was also the $18 million price tag that eased the owner's business difficulties. It didn't matter to him apparently that whenever the spotlight had hit Gretzky in his Edmonton days he always spoke of the Oilers, saying things like:

"Winning games and having people follow the team is very satisfying to me. One guy can't sell hockey but our team can because we play fast and we play clean. Almost every rink is sold out where we play. That's good for our team and good for hockey."

And he said things like:

"Hockey's really a terrific game. I don't think the bench-clearing stuff is typical, at all. People in the United States have a misconception about the game. They should know that it can be played the way our team plays – you know, fast and hard but clean, too."

Which was the way Gretzky and Lemieux played their game. It wasn't until his fifth season that brawny Lemieux hit 100 minutes in penalties, an average of less than one minor penalty a game, and of course Gretzky's company was unknown to half the league's penalty timekeepers. When Pittsburgh played Edmonton – or the Kings, after Wayne was shipped to Los Angeles – the meeting of the giants was practically a love-in. One time the *New York Times* dispatched a beat writer, Robin Finn, to do a feature on the pair and she was dismayed by their attitude toward one another. "The two men are infuriatingly humble," she wrote. Then she quoted Gretzky. "You never lie awake nights worrying about who's better because where does that get you?" Wayne told her. When she caught up to Lemieux it was more of the same. "The comparison has gotten kind of tiring," Mario told her. "I'm sure Wayne feels the same way about it as I do. We have fun pushing each other to be better but we each want to be known for just ourselves."

It was hardly like this 40 years ago with the brooding, explosive Maurice Richard, the hero of French Canada, or with the seldom perturbable strongman of Floral, Saskatchewan, Gordie Howe. Their rivalry in the 1950s was an endless source of comparison among fans and newshounds and they rarely had a kind word for one another. Richard was seven years older so his eminence arrived earlier. When the 18-year-old rookie Howe landed in the NHL in the autumn of 1946 Richard was firmly established as the league's premier right-winger.

There is no question in my mind that Rocket Richard was the most spectacular goal-scorer who ever played hockey. I never saw the old, *old* stars Cyclone Taylor, Joe Malone, or even Howie Morenz, but from what I'd hear from people who had, newspapermen such as Montreal's Elmer Ferguson and Baz O'Meara and Toronto's Bobby Hewitson and Andy Lytle, none of them electrified onlookers the way the Rocket did, dashing from the blueline in. And nobody I've seen since had his hypnotic flair, either. When he was battling for the puck near the net, driving for it with guys clutching at him, you could actually see a glitter in his coal-black eyes, the look wild horses get.

The Rocket was not a classic player in any sense. He skated in a disjointed way. Sometimes his shoulders rocked as he hopped into stride and you'd think of Ray Charles teetering at the piano. Looking back, I can see him whirling in front of the rival goal to free himself of a draped defender, and I can see him rearing back on one leg from a fierce check, but I can't visualize him at all in his own end. Was he ever there? I don't know. Yet it wasn't that he loafed; not at all. It was that he put so much effort into his quest for goals that who'd expect to remember him backchecking? He wasn't particularly big, around 175 and a little under six feet, but he was lean and trim as a welterweight fighter, a stick of dynamite. He had smooth black hair parted on the side and combed almost straight back, thin lips, hollow cheeks, and, when he was straining to control the puck with the net in sight, a really terrifying intensity.

Terrifying? Well, it was for referee Hugh McLean for one and for a lanky Boston defenceman, Hal Laycoe, for another. McLean attracted the Rocket's animosity one Saturday night in Montreal when the Canadiens were playing the Red Wings. It began when Richard drew a penalty and Red Wing defenceman Leo Reise jeered him as he moved sourly to the penalty box.

Later on he was grabbed in back of the net in a headlock by Sid Abel and flung to the ice.

"You must have seen that!" cried the Rocket, chasing after McLean, but the referee merely skated away. Reise needled him again for crybabying, whereupon the Rocket swung his stick at Reise. McLean caught that one and gave Richard a misconduct penalty, frustrating him further.

In his Pullman berth that night he continued to seethe en route to New York for a Sunday game. Shortly past noon he happened to encounter McLean and linesman Jim Primeau in the lobby of the team's hotel. He rushed McLean, grabbed him by the collar, and was punching at him when Primeau flung his arms around him and pulled him away. He was fined $500 by the league president, Clarence Campbell. The Rocket was a brooder, all right.

But the McLean outburst was a mere warmup for the incident involving Laycoe, in which Richard went after the Boston defenceman with his stick, wielding it across Laycoe's shoulders and neck as though taking an axe to a tree. A linesman, Cliff Thompson, rushed to Laycoe's defence, wrenching away Richard's stick, but the Rocket found a loose one lying on the ice and attacked Laycoe again, breaking this stick across his back. Again Thompson grabbed Richard, again the Rocket broke free, picked up yet another stick, and again attacked Laycoe. The indefatigable Thompson leaped after him a third time, strong-arming him to the ice and hanging on. But then a Canadien player pushed Thompson away and Richard leaped to his skates and this time punched Thompson twice in his persistent kisser.

And that, scholars, was when the shit really hit the fan. President Campbell suspended Richard for the balance of the season (there were only a few games left on the schedule) *and the playoffs*. The fans in Montreal went into deep shock.

A few nights later the Red Wings arrived at the Montreal Forum tied with the Canadiens for first place. Campbell and his then secretary, Phyllis King, who later married him, sat in

The *Winnipeg Tribune*'s sports department in 1940 had a four-man staff plus one golf writer from the news side, Allan Anderson, lower right wearing the pipe. Vince Leah, far left, did most of the work; Herb Manning, next to him, wrote the column; and the boss was Johnny Buss, editing copy. Intrepid reporter answered the phone.

Hatted scribe stares off into the sunset thinking up tough questions for Joe DiMaggio at 1941 World Series.

Speaking of hats, this guy had a million of 'em. Under the grey one he poses penetrating queries for Olympic skating champion and film actress Sonja Henie, another exclusive interview for the *Tribune*.

In the early 1940s the former star left-hander of the New York Yankees, Lefty Gomez, was lured to Brandon, Manitoba, as an after-dinner speaker. After the after-dinner speaker spoke, he and the *Tribune's* toothy scribe posed at a hockey game in the Brandon arena, letting on they weren't posing.

In the mid-1940s the high-collared owner of the Philadelphia Athletics, Connie Mack, was visited by a couple of Toronto scribes (that's Gord Walker of the *Star* at left) at the A's rustic park in West Palm Beach.

What's this, a Pepsodent commercial? Nope, wedding day for a couple of *Globe and Mail* reporters on May 13, 1944. The gorgeous creature is June Callwood.

Toronto sportswriters, Trent Frayne, left, and Gord Walker, visit ex-Leaf pitchers at Philadelphia's West Palm Beach training grounds. From left: Toronto's Dick Fowler, only Canadian to hurl no-hitter in majors, Frayne, Joe Coleman, Walker, and Phil (Babe) Marchildon of Penetanguishene.

Old Maple Leaf Stadium (what's this, real grass?) was the setting in the early 1950s for a benefit ball game between the Toronto Maple Leafs and an assortment of newshounds. Posing to promote the game, decked out in Leaf uniforms, are Joe Crysdale, the play-by-play announcer from CKEY, and Ed Fitkin, baseball writer for the *Star*, flanking the *Telegram*'s chubby righthander.

The revered (and now defunct) American magazine, the *Saturday Evening Post*, bought an article on Elmer Lach, Montreal Canadiens centre, titled "You Can't Kill a Hockey Player," and sent the author to the Montreal Forum to promote it by presenting a leather-bound copy to Lach. With him are Glen Harmon, left, Lach, Billy Reay, coach Dick Irvin, and Ken Reardon.

The *Toronto Star* dispatched its man to the 1972 Olympics in Munich, Germany. Here he is, beaming on a hillside, a few days before the tranquility was shattered by Palestinian terrorists invading the Israeli sleeping quarters in Olympic Village.

Peace reigned 24 hours before the terrorists struck when the author and *Star* photographer Graham Bezant travelled south from Munich to the Winter Olympic site of Innsbruck, Austria, and went sightseeing.

One of the great thrills in 1964 was watching Northern Dancer win the Kentucky Derby, the first Canadian-bred colt ever to win the American classic. In the stable area here's the horse who became the world's most productive sire, with his dapper trainer Horatio Luro.

Visiting celebrities are always welcome at racetracks and, indeed, they add colour and excitement to the spectacle of thoroughbred racing. One of the biggest stars to visit Woodbine in 1966 (at least anatomically speaking) was Sabrina. The cantilevered actress was in Toronto for an engagement at the Royal Alexandra Theatre and her appearance at Woodbine brought a smile to Jockey Club publicist Trent Frayne.

In 1989 the latter-day, right-handed Rod Laver tippy-toes across the court in a tournament devised by CBC-TV producer Don Goodwin – likely for 4 a.m. insomaniacs.

their box through the first period while fans booed, hissed, and threw eggs, rubbers, and other debris at the pale, impassive president. Then a smoke bomb exploded near him. As the period ended a hoodlum leaped at Campbell and punched him. The police chief escorted the president and his fiancée to safety. The city fire director ordered the Forum evacuated. The p.a. announcer, voice crackling above the din, shouted that the game had been forfeited to Detroit! Wild men surged into Ste. Catherine Street and began smashing store windows and looting the stores, upsetting cars and shouldering pedestrians from the sidewalks.

The city simmered for two days and what finally quelled a dangerous situation was the Rocket himself. He suggested that he go on the air and tell the fans to end their rampage. A studio was set up in the Canadien dressing room, bright lights flooded the Rocket, and he spoke into banks of microphones and cameras. This is what he said, first in French and then in English:

"I will take my punishment and come back next year to help the club and the younger players win the Cup. Because I always try so hard to win and had my trouble in Boston I was suspended. At playoff time it hurts me not to be in the game with my team. However, I want to do what is good for the people of Montreal and my team. So that no further harm will be done I would like to ask everyone to get behind the team and help the boys to win the Cup."

The fans did but the boys didn't. Without the Rocket, the Canadiens lost to Detroit in the Stanley Cup final. But he was right in his prophecy: he did indeed come back the following year and help the team to the Stanley Cup – and not just in 1956 but in '57, '58, '59, and '60, as well. Twice in that span he scored overtime goals to deliver the victory, a playoff achievement he performed six times in his career. Once, in the spring of 1951 on the road against Detroit, he drilled twin backbreakers. The first came after 61 minutes and nine seconds of overtime and the second arrived a mere two nights later after 42 minutes and 20 seconds of extra time. The Wings couldn't recover from those blows.

In the autumn of 1960 the Rocket reported to Montreal's training camp in the Forum to prepare for his 19th season. Unexpectedly, one afternoon following a routine workout he walked into the office of his old linemate, Coach Toe Blake, and said he'd had enough, he was through. In so ordinary a fashion this extraordinary man retired.

But the fire never really died. Even in 1989, approaching 70 years of age, the Rocket flared into life one December day when he got an impression that his old rival, Howe, had mocked him. At the time, his name and photograph were appearing each Sunday over a sports column in the Montreal newspaper *La Presse*. The writing was done by a staff person but the opinions came straight from the Rocket. The column said that Howe had been a big scorer who couldn't deliver in the clutch.

"Howe scored goals at a constant pace," the piece said, "but he really didn't distinguish himself with important goals."

What the Rocket didn't say but what French-reading fans knew was that Howe had been quoted earlier in *La Presse* describing Richard as "a bastard."

When I read the report of the Rocket's column I phoned Howe at his home in Hartford and asked him about it.

"It didn't hurt my feelings at all," Gordie said cheerfully. "The truth is, I did hate the old bastard."

"You *hated* him?"

"Sure, sort of. See, when we played you couldn't fraternize. In those days it was a hatred situation. The coaches preached it and built it around us. Hey, I wouldn't *talk* to a guy on another team even in the off-season."

"Did you and the Rocket tangle?"

"Not a lot. We were both right-wingers so if we were on the ice together we were on opposite sides of the rink. But there was one time, in Montreal, when we had a go."

"How did it turn out?"

Howe chuckled on the telephone. "I remember his head came out from under my left leg. Sid (Abel) skated by and yelled

at him, 'You damn Frog, you got what you deserved that time.'
Oh, I tell you, we used to have fun all right."

"And did you call him a bastard lately?"

"Oh, heck, there was nothing serious about it. When I was
promoting the book somebody asked me about him and I said
something like, 'That old bastard used to cause us a lot of
trouble.' I meant it in a harmless way."

This book he was talking about, *After the Applause*, was a big
seller in the autumn and winter of 1989 and well into 1990.
Written by Charles Wilkins, it was the idea of Gordie and his
wife, Colleen, and in it 10 hockey legends discussed life after
the game. Rocket's story was one of those in the book, and he
and Howe travelled together for interviews in Montreal and
Ottawa as part of the book's promotion, a round of visits to
television and radio studios and newspaper offices that book
publishers organize to familiarize buyers with new releases.
The old right-wingers got along fine and each was a hit with the
interviewers.

These days Howe has grown from the shy and solemn loner
from a northern Saskatchewan farm into a chatty, light-hearted
fellow entirely at ease in speeches and interviews. Indeed,
during his book tour he sat down with Peter Gzowski, the host
of the popular CBC network radio program *Morningside*, for a
conversation of such interest that Gzowski's producers sepa-
rated it into three segments aired over three mornings.

This was a long way from the Howe I got to know back in the
early 1950s when he was beginning to push Richard onto the
second team in the NHL all-star selections. One afternoon at the
Mississauga Golf Club on Toronto's western outskirts he was
booked to play a golf exhibition for charity with a pair of this
country's best professionals, Stan Leonard and Al Balding, and
the host pro, whose name escapes me. Howe was pale and
withdrawn in the locker room before the round. I asked him if
he felt ill. He said no, he was simply nervous. He said he felt
shakier knowing a large handful of people would be following
the golf foursome than he'd feel in front of 16,000 or so in a
Stanley Cup final.

"Holy cow, why?" I cried, no amateur psychologist me.

He hesitated, then offered tentatively, "Pride in not making a fool of yourself?"

He had this laconic way back then. One time a guy noted that he seemed to score a lot of goals by setting up in front of the net looking for rebounds and passouts. "You don't score much from behind," Gordie replied, blinking rapidly.

The blinking, which I haven't noticed for years, was so pronounced in his playing days that he picked up the nickname Blinky. Once, asked if he knew the source of his palpable determination, he blinked his blink and answered in that laconic way, "Shyness, maybe, eh?"

But he was a hard man in a hockey game, earning another nickname, Elbows. In that Gzowski interview he voiced philosophies he had taken to the arenas: "Don't drop your stick first" and "Each time you go out, take two seconds to see who's on the ice so you'll know where trouble might come from and where help will be coming from."

Once when I was working for the *Toronto Telegram* the boss, Bobby Hewitson, assigned me to accompany the Leafs on a Detroit trip. The teams travelled by train in the old six-team league, usually overnight in a Pullman. The railway car would be put on a siding and the team would return to it after a game for the overnight trip home. Nowadays, of course, the teams zip in and out of towns by air.

This night, following the game in Detroit, I was sitting in the smoking compartment with the regular beat men, Red Burnett of the *Star* and Al Nickelson of the *Globe and Mail*, listening to the coach, Joe Primeau, review the game. A Leaf defenceman, Leo Boivin, was standing at the wash basin, bare to the waist, pressing a wet, steaming, white towel to his face. Boivin was a stocky man, shorter than most defencemen, with black curly hair and pale skin. His face was bruised, bore a few red welts and a couple of scratches, and it was obvious he was tired as he slowly soaked the towel into fresh hot water for another soothing massage.

At length he was finished. He gathered his things and left the compartment to climb into his berth. Watching, Primeau permitted himself a soft smile.

"Poor Leo," Joe said. "When he goes into the corners for the puck he's just the right height for Blinky's elbows."

Howe rarely picked a fight but he certainly never avoided one. There is the famous story of how, late one season, he absolutely pulverized Louie Fontinato's nose in a brief fight behind the New York Ranger net. The Rangers had practically cinched a playoff berth but their coach, Phil Watson, said the beating Howe administered so demoralized his players that the oncoming Maple Leafs were able to overtake them and win that last playoff spot.

Detroit's coach and general manager, Jack Adams, used to stand in the Wing dressing room beaming fondly at his right-winger. "He could have been a star at any sport," Adams remarked to me one night, peering across the room at Howe. "Look at those shoulders, see how they slope from his neck. He used to hang from a door-frame when he was a kid developing those shoulder muscles. He could have been a prizefighter, he could have been a ballplayer. He's a friend of Al Kaline's of the Tigers, you know, and works out with them sometimes."

Adams wasn't always in so expansive a frame of mind. He could be harsh and intractable, too. He and Toronto's Connie Smythe broke up the first attempt that hockey players made to form a union before they hired Alan Eagleson to do the job for them. Also, Adams and Smythe forbade their players to have any dealings with Lloyd Percival, a Toronto sports analyst and theorist, who was roughly 20 years ahead of his time in the development of training techniques. He was far too smart for the old guard of hockey, which was one reason they ostracized him.

Percival got into the middle of the Richard-Howe controversy when he released a detailed analysis of the two players after he and a couple of his researchers watched them over a 17-game period and recorded various statistics arrived at by stopwatches, graphs, and charts. In noting 17 points about their play Percival's people concluded that Howe was superior in 16 of them, including such items as "carries puck out of defensive zone more often," "completes more passes," "hands out more body checks," "backchecks more often and travels faster when so doing." The research showed Richard superior only in "acceleration from a complete stop." No plaques were erected in Montreal to perpetuate Percival's name. Dick Irvin, the Habitant coach, said in real anger, "It is obvious to me that this is an attempt to rob Richard of the right he deserves as the greatest right-winger in hockey today."

About that time and for the next 20 years Percival tried to get NHL bosses to inject imagination into their game. The things he wanted them to embrace were the very things that Soviet teams introduced into hockey on this side of the Atlantic in the classic September Summit series of 1972, the style that came to be known in the 1980s as "European hockey." What irony.

One night in Percival's recreation room in Toronto I listened to him discuss a script for a weekly CBC network radio show of his called *Sports College*. In the midst of it Howe and the Detroit goaltender Terry Sawchuk arrived at Percival's home, escaping the vigilance of Adams so they could discuss training and tactics with Lloyd. This was the sort of thing Lloyd especially enjoyed, for he was hooked on sports theory and, later, its practical application. Once he'd worked something out, he'd try it on a testing group. Of course, first-hand discussions with players of the stature and experience of Howe and Sawchuk provided invaluable research. Still, the lords of hockey wouldn't listen. Lloyd died of a heart attack one summer afternoon in 1974 at age 61. Suffering his detractors, he'd endured a great deal of stress.

Percival was a pudgy guy with a muffin face, a vibrant and sometimes long-winded talker with a nice wry turn of humour. He was an expert in many fields. George Knudson and Al Balding benefited from his counsel in golf and his training programs produced personal bests for numerous track and field stars long before steroids became universally ingested. But hockey, being Canada's national game, got most of his attention. He wrote a book in 1951 called *The Hockey Handbook*, the foundation for that European style people were raving about 25 years later. Percival advocated keeping the other team off-balance with tough forechecking, positional play, and swift sustained skating. "The whole idea when you have the puck is to pass, pass, pass," he wrote. He thought deliberately turning over the puck, the mindless shooting from the centre red line, was dumb. Of course it still persists and of course it is still dumb.

No one on this side of the Atlantic, least of all the NHL geniuses, would listen. Percival's ideas were sufficiently advanced to make people in high places resent him. Partly, too, Lloyd was an impatient guy and an undiplomatic one. He grew weary of the stubbornness of the people in control and ridiculed their archaic ways. Hence, the players were told to avoid him.

But wily Anatoli Tarasov, the first Russian coach of international prominence, didn't mind learning from a master. He made the Percival book his very own. In his own book, *The Road to Olympus*, the father of Soviet hockey duplicates diagrams of Percival plays, freely employs Percival philosophy and technique. He sent a copy to Lloyd and wrote in it: "I have read, like a schoolboy, your wonderful book which introduced us to the mysteries of Canadian hockey. Thank you for a science which is significant to world hockey."

And here was the true irony. A generation later Wayne Gretzky was expressing thanks that he happened to arrive on the scene with a style that perfectly suited the times. That style was the product of the NHL's learning experience in 15 years of competition with the Soviets. And where did the Soviets learn to play the game? Why, from the outcast Lloyd Percival, a man unhonoured and unsung in his own land.

Chapter 8

When it's springtime
on the diamond

Baseball's spring training was invented in 1885 by a spoilsport manager named Adrian Constantine (Cap) Anson, who ran the Chicago White Stockings for 19 seasons. Cap was a great first-baseman for 22 years with the Chicago nine, compiling a lifetime .334 batting average. In all but the first three of those years he was also their manager, winning the pennant in 1880, '81, and '82 and finishing second in '83. When the team slipped to fourth in 1884 Cap realized something had to be done.

In the 1880s, ballplayers spent the long cold winters catching up on their beer-drinking, and as John Lardner once wrote, "their appetites were as wide as their mustaches." With each new season they needed two months to fit into their woollens. Accordingly, when the overstuffed players assembled in Chicago a short time before the 1885 season their manager was struck suddenly by an exceptional array of paunches. He decided to lead them to the famous health spas of Hot Springs, Arkansas, and let the healing waters steam the brew from their pots. Worse, he banned beer from the menu.

But that year the White Stockings won back their pennant (you could look it up) so the following spring rival teams sent *their* soggy, beer-logged players to warmer pre-season climes, and they have been doing so ever since. Connie Mack, who later became the owner and manager of the A's (he'd sit on the bench in a three-piece suit, a high starched collar, and a straw boater, positioning his players with a scorecard), once told of those early training days when he was a catcher for the Washington Nationals. To accommodate the players in Jacksonville, the management rented two wooden shacks at a dollar per man per day, including breakfast. These days some of the millionaire ballplayers will sometimes leave that much in a restaurant as a tip (two people, of course).

The value of spring training for the players is open to scrutiny and certainly six weeks of it are more than enough, as a lockout of players by the big-hearted owners demonstrated in the spring of 1990. Ordinarily for the owners six weeks are fine; tickets can scarcely be printed fast enough to gratify the pale-faced tourists who flock to the exhibitions. But in the late years of World War Two travel restrictions kept teams in the chilblain sectors of the north. They spent a few weeks at such outposts as Bear Mountain, New York, Asbury Park, New Jersey, and French Lick Springs, Indiana. There, most days were passed in large fieldhouses in which the players played catch, did push-ups, and swung their bats in a net-enclosed area with a pitching machine. Yet pennant races were close, nobody damaged a rotator cuff, required arthroscopic surgery, demanded a renegotiated contract, or filed for arbitration, and the World Series miraculously went off as scheduled.

Spring training has always been an excellent time for scribes to grow a little closer to their subjects, listening to their complaints and occasionally encountering at close range characters as unforgettable as, say, the all-time champion of the malapropism, Casey Stengel.

Charles Dillon Stengel traversed National League outfields for 14 seasons until 1925 and then he was the manager of the Dodgers and the Braves before landing with the Yankees in 1949. He led them for 12 years during which they won the American League pennant 10 times and the World Series seven.

Sports, even as politics, has seldom been devoid of persons born to manipulate the mother tongue; sports more so, perhaps, since the practitioners are concerned not so much with worldly affairs as with children's games and can afford to take more liberties with the truth. People such as Jack Kent Cooke and Bill Veeck and an engaging old friend of mine, Nat Turofsky, are merely three of many who mesmerized me one way and another during the springtime exercises, among other times. However, nobody, positively no one, could manoeuvre his way around a split infinitive as spectacularly as the man everybody knew as Ol' Case.

Partly because the Yankees kept him endlessly in the spotlight, Stengel was the most quoted man in baseball and one of the most quoted men in the explored galaxy during the 1950s. Another reason was his unsurpassed skill in mangling a perfectly sensible thought and still getting his point across. Examples of this abound but none caught the eye of the public at large as strikingly as reports of his 1958 appearance in Washington before Senator Estes Kefauver's U.S. Senate subcommittee hearings on antitrust and monopoly. At one point he was asked how many minor leagues existed in baseball when he started out, and here, from a transcript of his testimony, is part of his reply:

"Well, there were not so many at that time because of this fact: anybody to go into baseball at that time with the educational schools that we had were small, while you were probably thoroughly educated at school, you had to be – we only had small cities that you could put a team in and they would go defunct.

"Why, I remember the first year I was at Kankakee, Illinois, and a bank offered me $550 if I would let them have a little notice. I left there and took a uniform because they owed me two weeks' pay. But I either had to quit but I did not have enough money to go to dental college so I had to go with the manager down to Kentucky.

"What happened there was if you got by July, that was the big date. You did not play night ball and you did not play Sundays in half of the cities on account of a Sunday observance, so in those days when things were tough, and all of it was, I mean to say, why they just closed up July 4 and there you were sitting there in the depot. You could go to work someplace else, but that was it. So I got out of Kankakee, Illinois, and I just go there for the visit now."

When Ol' Case was through, the bewildered Senator Kefauver thanked him and called the Yankee centre-fielder Mickey Mantle and asked, "Mr. Mantle, have you any observations with reference to the applicability of the antitrust laws to baseball?"

And Mr. Mantle, bless his heart, replied: "Well, I'd say my views are just about the same as Casey's."

One time I caught up to Stengel in the spring of 1960 at the beginning of his final year as manager of the Yankees. He was holding court in room 235 of the comfortable old Soreno Hotel in St. Petersburg. These days, the Yankees do their Florida training in Fort Lauderdale but in Stengel's time they shared Al Lang Field with the Cardinals in St. Petersburg. Each late afternoon when the day's work was done Casey met with the newsmen who followed the Yankees – he always referred to them as "my writers" – over cold cuts and liquid refreshments until seven o'clock, at which time he and they went their various ways, no doubt to eat and talk and enjoy liquid refreshments.

Stengel was the dominant figure in a room that often housed perhaps 30 people, partly because he was the manager and partly because his resonant voice precluded most other conversation. He was closing on 70 then. He was a prowling, gesticulating, loud, stooped, profane, and fascinating figure rasping out his renowned double talk and frequently pausing to lubricate it. I see him now, a thick, squat man with deep furrows lining his cheeks and neck, thick iron-grey hair curling in a half-moon across his forehead, a big hook of a nose, and enormous ears.

I dropped into that room to hear him a couple of times after Yankee games. Once, he got talking of his youth, slightly more centred on the point than he'd been at the Kefauver hearings. "Fifty years ago on the outfield fence there is this big Bull Durham sign, which is why they call the warmup spot the bullpen, and they had cash money for batters who hit the wall out there. They didn't give away much money for the sign was a mile and a half away, and one day I got lucky in Fond du Lac and won myself 50 bucks which was a big windfall and I went home quite dapper. I bought me a stiff straw hat like that French singer which I wore until December."

Though as a manager he obviously had great talent at his disposal, Ol' Case was noted during his Yankee reign as a clever manipulator of manpower, platooning outfielders with catchers and often, on hunches, bringing in a left-handed pitcher to face a right-handed hitter or, conversely, sending up a right-handed pinch-hitter to replace a left-hander against a right-handed pitcher – all these moves unorthodox even in the enlightened age of the 1990s. One afternoon in room 235 he said that a manager had to use common sense in manoeuvring his ballplayers.

"It's like everything else; common sense is the best thing you can have except steal a little." And he tilted back his head and drained his glass. In describing how the economy had changed since he was a boy, he growled, "I went into dentistry to keep out of pool halls. Now you look at pool halls; they are built better than buildings."

The first time I went to this Yankee room I could hear his voice before I knocked. The man himself, in the middle of an oration, opened the door. He glanced at me cursorily, offered a welcoming handshake, and as I moved on into the room he closed the door behind me, the flow of words uninterrupted.

At that time Branch Rickey, the man who had built the powerful Brooklyn Dodger organization, was heading a group that included Toronto's Jack Kent Cooke in organizing a proposed major league, the Continental League. So at one point this day in the Soreno Hotel I asked Stengel what he thought of the idea.

"Now I am the manager of this ball club and I am not the

owner and, look here, the Continental League is not under my province of jurisdiction," he replied, frowning and gesticulating. "I have nothing against the Continental League. I wish it good luck and I have my own problems as manager of the New York ball club." That was it; for the rest of the evening, as far as I could tell, he never looked at me again.

But a couple of days later I was in for a shock. I thought it would be a good idea to get down the flavour of Stengelese, so when he was answering somebody who'd asked why he felt the Yankees would prosper in the coming season I began taking down his words as fast as I could write (I didn't own a tape recorder and, upon reflection, can't recall other scribes using them that long ago). Anyway, here is approximately what he said:

"Pitchers in the second line I have four of 'em which is this fella Coates who could start, Terry we don't know about because he's in the service and did they get any work, and there is Ford and what about this rule that there is nobody taking notes in this room only talking among ourselves and I am referring to you young man over there who I let into this room the other afternoon and you wondered about the Continental League, is that right?"

I was stunned, scribbling away, realizing suddenly that he meant me. I felt embarrassed in this large roomful of people and mumbled that I didn't know there was such a rule.

"That's all right, my boy," Ol' Case said in a kindly way. "Now you do."

Some years later, in one of Red Smith's visits to Toronto I told him of this incident. He chuckled and said that anyone who thought Stengel a buffoon because of the way he sparred with the language was making a very large mistake.

"When he first joined the Yankees he had never before been exposed to the numbers of newspapermen who follow the club," Red said. "He had managed the Braves and the old Dodgers in comparative solitude, and I think his constant flow of words was protective while he found his bearings. He told me once that Ring Lardner had advised him years ago, 'Casey, you have a wonderful gift of gab. You would be a fool if you ever quit talking and tried to act dignified.' I think Case did that at first, and afterwards his language was so publicized he chose not to change."

By 1960 I had been going to ball camps off and on for 15 years as a freelancer. In the mid-1940s none of the Toronto or Montreal newspapers was sending staff people to Florida to write about baseball, not even about the home-town Maple Leafs and Royals of the Triple A International League. The Montreal Royals, as best I can recall, had no camp of their own; their prospects, of which Jackie Robinson was one who made it in spectacular fashion in 1946 with the Royals, congregated with the rest of the players in the vast Brooklyn organization at Dodgertown, the Brooklyn training base at Vero Beach. The Maple Leafs went through their spring exercises at Fort Lauderdale, now a tourist mecca but then a quiet little ocean-side town not much more than a Miami adjunct. A few miles south of Lauderdale was Hollywood, where the Baltimore Orioles, another International League team then, trained and played frequent exhibitions with the Leafs.

Since Toronto staff scribes rarely appeared, Lauderdale was an agreeable place for a freelancer, and on a couple of occasions I made a deal with Andy Lytle, the *Star* sports editor, to write feature stuff for him. The first trip south was in 1945 by car with Nat Turofsky who, partnered by his brother Lou, owned the Alexandra Studios photography shop in Toronto. The town's three newspapers were serviced by the Turofsky brothers. Lou was hired by the Ontario Jockey Club to provide the papers with pictures from the thoroughbred racetracks and Nat was paid by the ball club to send pictures of the Maple Leafs. Alexandra Studios did the work for the hockey club, too. When Nat was away in Florida a youngster from their dark room, Michael Burns, covered hockey. Eventually, he bought the business.

A guy could go around the world these days faster than Nat drove the 1,600 miles from Toronto to Fort Lauderdale. In this first trip we were accompanied (in the back seat, naturally; the men sat up front) by Thurza Hesk, the Turofskys' office manager, a quiet-spoken woman without whose business acumen the leisurely brothers would have had to find another line of work.

The trip took forever. Now and then Thurza would say quietly from the back seat, "Nat, a boy on a pogo stick just passed us," but her words had no effect.

"So what's the rush?" he'd reply equably. "A hundred years from now what'll it matter?" Nat had that easy philosophy for a lot of things other people might have found irritating.

Anyway, the first night out we reached Mansfield, Pennsylvania, and in the morning we found there was snow on the window sills.

"We'll wait till she clears," Nat said.

Luckily, she cleared by noon and we made it all the way to Leesburg, Virginia, just outside Washington, easily 200 miles, the second night. Raeford, North Carolina, was the next overnight, then Savannah, then Daytona Beach, and finally on the sixth night Fort Lauderdale. It was late at night and raining when we pulled up beside the old three-storey Broward Hotel in the heart of town, our destination.

Nat had reminisced through most of the drive. "There used to be this real good right-hander back a couple of years, um, what was his name, Thurz?"

"Tom Drake," from the back seat.

"Tom Drake," Nat said. "I'll never forget it."

At the ballpark Nat unloaded his Speed Graphic and began shooting his pictures of Maple Leaf players. He'd get the pitchers in their follow-through poses and the hitters slugging imaginary home runs beyond the neighbouring palms. One morning while he worked, along came the team's owner, a snappish, fiftyish, bald-headed guy named Peter G. Campbell. This was an era when owners were sometimes a trifle less affluent than owners are today. Peter G. Campbell, for example, worked in the advertising-sales department at the *Globe and Mail* when he wasn't telling the ballplayers they were overpaid.

"Whattayuh shooting, are yuh shooting 'em full length?" he growled at Nat.

"Yeah, that's it, full length, Mr. Campbell."

"Well, look, if you just shot head-and-shoulders, would I get 'em half-price?"

Hockey was by far the biggest game in Toronto in this era before the Blue Jays. Interest always peaked during the playoff weeks of March and early April. In Florida, Nat and I would drive beyond the Fort Lauderdale city limit, park on the side of the two-lane dirt road that led to West Palm Beach, and sit there under the stars trying to pick up on the car radio the voice of Foster Hewitt from Maple Leaf Gardens.

The Philadelphia Athletics trained at West Palm back then, a time when Canadian ballplayers were as scarce in the big leagues as they are in the 1990s. Phil Marchildon and Dick Fowler were two standout pitchers for the A's, the parent club of the minor-league Leafs for a few years. Fowler, the Toronto-born giant who faced Ted Williams the day Ted took his average to .406, had two 15-win seasons in surviving 10 years with the A's. Marchildon came from Penetanguishene, Ontario, a highly strung right-hander with a herky-jerky motion who won 19 games in his best year, 1947. Both pitched for the Maple Leafs, where they made $400 a month, before going up to the lacklustre A's. Reflecting on those times not long ago in his Toronto home, Marchildon remembered that after his 19-win year he was in an excellent position to bargain with the parsimonious Connie Mack and collected his best big-league salary, $17,000.

Ralph Kiner, the Pittsburgh slugger of the late 1940s and early 1950s (54 homers in 1949), spent part of a season with the Leafs, driving baseballs in great climbing arcs far beyond the double-deck advertising billboards that circled the outfield of old Maple Leaf Stadium. Back then, a couple of incorrigibly argumentative Toronto fans, Sammy Gold and Sam Shefsky, usually turned up at the Leaf camps, and one day their names burst into a troubled observation by Nat.

This time, he and Gord Walker and I were driving north, accompanying the team. Walker was the baseball writer for the *Globe* and I was with the *Telegram* by then. We stopped for a night game in Savannah where we found a pleasant-looking restaurant and sat down for dinner a couple of hours before the game. Walker and I got into a dispute about Ralph Kiner's value to the Leafs in his brief stay in Toronto and as our voices rose Nat grew increasingly uneasy. He disliked scenes and was concerned that Gord and I were drawing the attention of other diners. From time to time he glanced quickly over each shoulder. Then his patience ran out.

"Walker," he snapped in a stage whisper, "you and Gold and Shefsky are a pair."

It was also in the springtime that I first encountered Bill Veeck, an owner whose every move in baseball was directed toward the enjoyment of the fans. It's a pretty scandalous thing to say in the 1990s but I don't think profit entered his mind. Not directly, anyway.

Like the unforgettable time he sent the midget up to the plate to bat, little Eddie Gaedel emerging from the dugout waving three sawed-off bats. "For the Browns," said the guy on the p.a., "number one-eighth, Eddie Gaedel, batting for Saucier." The fans in the old St. Louis stadium, Sportsman's Park, couldn't believe it. The plate umpire couldn't believe it. The Detroit catcher couldn't believe it, and the Tiger pitcher, a left-hander named Bob Cain, was aghast. He had to pitch to a 3-foot-7-inch batter who weighed 65 pounds. Of *course* the fans went nuts; that was Veeck's whole idea.

Listening to Bill Veeck was always one of the highlights of the spring for me. The day I introduced myself to him, saying I worked for a Toronto newspaper, he said he'd bet I didn't know that if it weren't for him there'd be no Toronto Blue Jays.

He was always good for a column. A couple of hours before a spring game he'd be sitting alone, sprawled across two or three seats in the wooden bleachers at Payne Field in Sarasota watching his Chicago White Sox in batting practice (at various times he owned the White Sox, the Browns, and the Cleveland Indians). The stands would be empty this early and Bill would be bare to the waist absorbing the sun, puffing endlessly on mentholated cigarettes, his peg leg stuck straight out. Or you could catch him after a game in a little office at the team's motel across the street from the ballpark, uncapping beer after beer from a big glassed-in cooler, talking and chuckling in a deep-down voice. He was a man born to baseball. His dad had been the president of the Chicago Cubs and Bill grew up surrounded by the game. He was a maverick and an innovator, a fan's man.

Bill Veeck died early in January of 1986. He'd been dying in bits and pieces since he'd lost a leg at Guadalcanal in the war in the Pacific. The area above the knee never did heal properly and he had to undergo surgery every few years. Before he died of a heart attack following respiratory problems, the most recent time he'd been in the hospital was to have part of a lung snipped out. He had a hearing impairment, too, and he used to laugh and cup an ear and cackle, "Aye-e-e? Howzzat?" if he didn't hear something clearly. After the final surgery on his leg, he said, "I've got a lung and a third, a leg and a quarter, one working ear, and lousy eyesight. I've given the world all the edge I'm going to."

Veeck was a man of scruples and integrity, not the most common characteristics of owners. He was enormously upset the summer before he died by baseball's drug hearings in Pittsburgh. At these, such prominent players as Keith Hernandez and Dave Parker were given immunity from legal action if they testified that they had used cocaine or if they squealed on their peers. What a splendid group they were, too, sitting there in court, immune from prosecution, blowing the whistle on one another and on their former friend and companion, their provider Curtis Strong, who was on trial, did not have immunity, and got 12 years for supplying the ballplayers. Of these players Veeck wrote in *The Sporting News* that autumn:

"They strolled into the courthouse in $500 three-piece suits, $150 custom-made shirts, $200 shoes by Gucci and a quarter's worth of character. What they had in common were a good but not too good memory, a lack of moral courage and principle, a highly developed sense of self-preservation. They had to be malleable, amoral, arrogant and, above all, completely selfish."

He was often as outspoken about the owners. One of them, George Steinbrenner, the H. Ballard of the batted ball, announced once that the Yankee manager of the moment, Yogi Berra, would keep his job all year "no matter what," then fired him two weeks into the season. Steinbrenner grew quite touchy when he was accused in the papers of saying things he didn't mean. "Why would Steinbrenner get mad about that?" Veeck innocently asked a nest of newspaper people. "I'd always assumed he thought being accused of not telling the truth was a compliment."

But the best of Veeck for me was his revelation that the lords of baseball hadn't bestowed a franchise on Toronto simply because the city was too irresistible for any other consideration. Bill didn't see it quite that way.

The Blue Jays were born in November of 1976, but sitting in the sun this morning at Sarasota, peg leg stuck out in front of him, occasionally running his hand back to front across the few short stray hairs on his freckled head, Veeck said the saga had begun in 1970. That was when the Seattle Pilots of the American League fled to Milwaukee and became the Brewers. The reason they jumped to Milwaukee was that the Braves of Milwaukee had jumped to Atlanta and the Pilot owners felt Milwaukee was a better market for them than Seattle.

But when their fellow owners endorsed the shift to Milwaukee they hadn't reckoned with the outrage of the civic leaders in Seattle who threatened a lawsuit over the loss of *their* franchise. By 1975, as the courtroom beckoned, the league owners believed they'd found a solution. In Chicago, the White Sox were the Sad Sox. Attendance for the team that once had been owned by Veeck was falling off and costs were going up. When attendance dipped to 770,800 that season the current owner, John Allyn, was anxious to sell. But the owners didn't like that idea. The solution they favoured was to ship the Sox to Seattle, solving Allyn's financial difficulty and, better than that, extirpating the lawsuit in Seattle where the roofed Kingdome was nearing completion.

But that wasn't Bill Veeck's idea of an ideal solution. He was concerned by the prospect of the loss to the fans in Comiskey Park on the city's south side. He rounded up enough backers to buy the Sox from the beleaguered John Allyn and keep the team where he felt it belonged. But when the AL owners met to ratify the sale they boosted the financial requirements needed to satisfy them. Veeck was confronted by a case of the shorts.

So he launched a Save-the-Sox campaign and enlisted the aid of tough old Democratic mayor Richard Daley for civic backing. The campaign caught on; a public that had ignored the Sox suddenly couldn't countenance the prospect of seeing them depart. Enough heat was generated and money raised that the league owners had to ratify Veeck's bid or expose their prejudice.

Telling this tale, running his hand across his head again, chuckling from time to time, chain-smoking his menthols, Veeck gave voice to its conclusion. "With the Sox set in Chicago, the lords of baseball had to find a way to get out of the fix they were in in Seattle," he said. "They did it by granting an expansion franchise. But they couldn't go with 13 teams, could they? That'd drive the schedule-maker daffy. So they brought in Toronto, who only a short time before had narrowly missed getting the San Francisco Giants. See, without me, you'd still be outside looking in."

Not everybody agreed with Veeck's version, however. Bowie Kuhn, for one, scoffed at it one winter morning in 1987 when he arrived in Toronto to promote a book he'd written reflecting on his days as baseball commissioner. It was Kuhn's notion that the success of the Expos in Montreal in the early 1970s had ignited the interest of owners in both major leagues in settling in Toronto. He recalled how Montreal mayor Jean Drapeau had romanced National League visitors in 1968, telling them in that characteristic offhand manner of his, "There are no problems, only solutions."

Kuhn smiled, reflecting on the mayor's insousiance. "He took us to Jarry Park at nine o'clock at night, got some lights turned on, and at first blush I thought I was going to cry," Kuhn said. "It was a lovely little place but it was no major-league ballpark. Still, the more the mayor talked, the more it seemed possible, and finally Warren Giles, the league president, said okay, he thought it would work. And of course it did."

I thought it only fitting to tell the former commissioner the way Bill Veeck had seen the Toronto acceptance. "Oh," he said, virtually dismissing the intrusion, "Veeck was never bothered by the niceties of accuracy." In his book Kuhn had written, "In an earlier age Veeck would have been the Music Man, shamelessly selling elixirs to the unwary. His fumbling, self-effacing charm and his iconoclasm toward the baseball establishment endeared him to millions of fans. In his heart he was a beer-drinking, fun-loving populist, ill at ease with his baronial peers. He reminds me of what Bugs Baer wrote about Ping Bodie as a base-stealer, 'He had larceny in his heart but his feet were honest.'"

Maybe Kuhn was right, but with Veeck lying in his grave there was no way to hear a rebuttal, if any. There's no question, though, that the lords of baseball had to find a solution to the impending litigation being brought by the city of Seattle, and it's assuredly a fact that the American League could not have avoided a scheduling nightmare with 13 teams. Locating a team in Toronto settled numerous looming problems. And all Veeck ever contended was that, by keeping the Sox in Chicago, he compelled the lords of baseball to find other means of staying out of a Seattle courtroom. Without that, there'd have been no Blue Jays. Not then, anyway.

These days, with its Taj Mahal ball park and a contending team, Toronto has prospered as an American League town, but there's no doubt that things would have been different – not necessarily better, just different – had the bid for the San Francisco Giants succeeded. Rivalry with the Expos would have engendered sparks, of course. The NL's Cubs are a better draw than the White Sox, the Dodgers than the Seattle Mariners, the Cardinals than Cleveland. Conversely, the Yankees and Detroit would be missed, and Oakland, too, these past couple of years.

What would be sharply altered would be the patterns of spring that now take many hundreds of Canadian tourists to the dopey little town of Dunedin on the gulf side of Florida where the Blue Jays train. One of Dunedin's liveliest attractions is that it's close to St. Petersburg, the afternoon-nap capital of the universe.

Instead, the Toronto Giants would have inherited the San Francisco winter property in fashionable Scottsdale on the eastern outskirts of Phoenix. For fans, the scenery is more restful than Florida's endless flatlands and billboards and fast-food franchises. The clear air illuminates the desert's spectacular camelback eruptions, sharply defined as some of them climb almost as tall as mountains. Florida's perpetual freeway construction is absent; traffic moves in a leisurely way and is unconstrained. A city ordinance limits buildings to 24 feet in Scottsdale's broad-based civic centre.

The air is dry-on-dry. With the Pacific Ocean 360 miles west across cactus and mountains to San Diego, there's no humidity. I was out there for the *Globe* for three springs in the late 1980s, peering at the eight clubs that train in Arizona, and one morning sat down beside Jim Gott, a most amiable man, who had gone from the Blue Jays to the Giants.

"The first thing I noticed out here is that you don't sweat much," he said. He was squeezing a baseball between his right paw's index and middle fingers as we talked, getting accustomed to the grip of a split-finger fastball that the Giant manager, Roger Craig, teaches every pitcher who works for him and some who don't – such as the Houston ace, Mike Scott. "The dry air lets us work longer – all of us, the position players, too. That Florida humidity drains you."

The Giants were prevented from moving to Toronto by George Moscone's election as mayor of San Francisco in early January of 1976. It was in that time and place that Horace Stoneham, whose family had owned the Giants even in their New York days, said yes to a $13 million bid by the dashing young president of Labatt's brewery, Don McDougall. All that was needed to seal the deal was the approval of NL owners meeting in Phoenix.

At that time nobody really wanted the Giants, no American

money, anyway. Age had taken the stars who had made them an attraction – Willie Mays, Juan Marichal, Willie McCovey – and the team had sunk to the league's darker regions. In 1974 and 1975 they'd barely drawn half a million fans each season.

But with the Toronto deal all but consummated late in January, down the wide spiral staircase from the main floor of the Adams Hotel swept the trim, brisk, alert figure of San Francisco's newly elected mayor George Moscone. He dashed into the meeting room while we scribes stood there waiting for the word of the transfer, and soon emerged to advise us that the last thing a new mayor desired was to lose an attraction as deeply steeped in tradition as the Giants. "I have 10 days," he announced. "I'll find us an owner. The Giants *belong* in San Francisco."

And they stayed. At the last moment Moscone did indeed come up with an owner – two, in fact – a Phoenix cattleman named Bud Herseth and Bob Lurie, the son of a wealthy San Francisco financier. In 1978 Lurie bought out Herseth and became the sole owner, a quiet-spoken guy of 49 at the time.

As far as I know, Moscone never got to the Scottsdale training headquarters. Actually, he wasn't much of a baseball fan. And two years after his spectacular entrance at the meeting room in the Adams Hotel, a guy walked into his office in the San Francisco city hall and shot him dead.

The Toronto Giants surely would have prospered had they acquired the lush green training base in Scottsdale. George Moscone did them no favour when he became the San Francisco mayor. Of course, he didn't do himself a lot of good, either, did he?

Twenty-five years before Toronto missed out so narrowly on the Giants, the International League's Maple Leafs had suddenly begun attracting large and lively baseball crowds. For it was in 1951 that 38-year-old Jack Kent Cooke lay down $200,000 for the team and undertook a marketing campaign that turned the Leafs into the biggest drawing card in all the minor leagues. In his first training camp at Fort Lauderdale, Jack got into an argument with a Toronto scribe and banned the lout from his ballpark. I was the lout.

This is the Cooke, of course, who became a big-league tycoon in a lot of areas – he owns, or owned, the Chrysler Building in Manhattan, the Washington Redskins football team, the L.A. Lakers basketball giants, the pre-Gretzky L.A. Kings, and he is the man who built the Forum, the beautiful Los Angeles home of the Lakers and the Kings.

Forty years ago or so, on his way to tycoondom, Jack merely owned the No. 1 radio station in Toronto, CKEY, a couple of magazines, *Saturday Night* and *Liberty*, and the ball club. He promoted the Leafs on his radio station, induced scores of top-flight entertainers such as Kay Starr, Gloria DeHaven, Victor Borge, and Danny Kaye to throw out the first pitch at ball games in return for free plugs on Cooke's station for their stage shows, turned loose his disc jockeys between innings on the ballpark's p.a. system, and worked contra arrangements with advertisers – free commercials in exchange for gifts for door prizes for ball fans. Jack had scarcely arrived as a club owner than he was named by the *Sporting News* as the top minor-league baseball executive of 1952. That year the Leafs set a minor-league attendance record of 446,800 fans. That year, too, was my third in the *Telegram*'s sports department, covering the Leafs in the spring and summer and the Argonaut footballers in the fall.

Anyway, one evening in the courtyard of the Broward Hotel after a game with the Orioles, a tourist from Toronto, Sam Shopsowitz, invited a group of us who were having a post-game drink to join him for dinner at the Sea Horse Restaurant, a popular spot along Las Olas Boulevard, the town's main drag. Back home, Sam ran Shopsy Foods, a well-patronized delicatessen, and Sam himself was a beaming, moon-shaped baseball fan known, of course, as Shopsy.

So off we went. Just as we were leaving the hotel Cooke turned up and, perhaps having nothing better to do, decided to join us. By coincidence, in the seating at the Sea Horse I was at one end of the table and Shopsy, our host, at the other. My wife June was on my left and Cooke sat down opposite her on my right. He had recently become a magazine publisher so, since June and I both freelanced in magazines, the conversation turned to them.

Jack said he had great plans for *Saturday Night*, a magazine of literary quality that he said he planned turning into a Canadian version of *The New Yorker*. Also, he said he was thinking of making *Liberty* a newsweekly like *Time*.

"Jesus, Jack," I said, startled by such grandiose plans. "If you do that you're going to have to start paying decent dough for articles."

Cooke's bright blue eyes turned icy. "And just what is that supposed to mean?" he asked.

"Well, you just can't get quality stuff for the rates you're paying now," I blundered on.

And he said, "That's insulting. If I weren't your guest I'd leave right now."

And I said, "Geez, you're not *my* guest."

And he said, "That's enough. I'm advising you now to stay the hell away from my ballpark tomorrow."

Whereupon I rose haughtily to my feet and walked June back to the Broward. There, the first person we encountered was Dave Price, a CBC sports broadcaster, who was sending occasional reports back to Jim Vipond, the *Globe*'s sports editor. Dave wanted to know what was up and I told him about the restaurant scene with Cooke.

The next morning, nervous and apprehensive, I turned up early at the ballpark. The entrance was at the left-field foul pole and as I walked in along the third-base line I could see that Cooke was already there, near the first-base dugout talking to Allan Lamport, the Toronto politician who had been instrumental in changing legislation to permit Sunday games in the pious old burg. I can remember thinking, "If I'm gonna be tossed out I may as well find out right away."

So I walked around behind the plate and past the two men and Lampy called out, "Hello Trent," and I said, "Hi Lampy," and Jack didn't say anything and I didn't say anything and just kept walking and that was the end of that.

Except that when I returned to the hotel there was a message to call Bobby Hewitson, the *Tely* sports editor, who wanted to know about the Cooke fiasco. It turned out that Dave Price had phoned Vipond and Jim had written in the *Globe* that I'd been banned by the owner. I told Hewitson there was nothing more to it, that I'd gone to the park and there was no problem.

But when Cooke heard about it he adopted an air of outrage. "Goddammit," he cried next day at the park, "if I'd known they were going to write about it in the papers I'd have chased your ass out of here for as long as we took the space from hockey."

Cooke never was much of a drinker, but on the rare occasion when he had one too many he became red-faced and excessive and sometimes outlandish. One time he accompanied the team on a road trip, and I remember sitting with him in a bar in Baltimore after a game.

"Bill, tell me this," he said. "Have you ever screwed a nymphomaniac?"

I placed what I hoped to be a thoughtful expression on my face and replied, "As far as I can remember, I guess not, Jack."

"Well, goddammit, if you had, I'll tell you this: you'd remember."

I suppose the reason I recall this brilliant exchange is that it was the first time I'd encountered the word nymphomaniac. Back then, I hadn't the slightest idea what Cooke was asking me.

Some 30 years later, by then working for the *Toronto Sun*, I was dispatched to Pasadena for the Super Bowl game between Jack's Washington Redskins and the Miami Dolphins. This was Super Bowl XVII, in which the former Argonaut quarterback, Joe Theismann, led the Redskins to a win over the Dolphins by XXVII to XVII. Jack was ensconced in a penthouse suite in the team's hotel at Costa Mesa, down the road from Los Angeles, and I went there to see how the years had treated him. I found him at 70 the same flamboyant fellow he'd been at 40, the eyebrows greyer, the beam broader, but the whole still full of fire.

Since he was now the owner of a Super Bowl team, about as close to knighthood as an American celebrity ever gets, I asked if he was apt to become the NFL's George Steinbrenner.

The eyes became the icy blue slits of yore.

"*What!*" Jack cried. "That's an absolutely asinine question. It doesn't deserve an answer, it's utterly stupid and ill-conceived. I have been the majority shareholder of the Redskins since 1974 and if I haven't revealed the character and nature of my ownership by now, I don't know when I'm going to. That is simply a *grotesque* question." (I was getting the notion that Jack didn't think much of my line of questioning.)

So I asked him how he'd become a football person. He'd owned a baseball team, a basketball team, and a hockey team but I said if he'd had a football interest I'd forgotten it. Jack was appalled.

"What a question!" he exclaimed. (I guess I wasn't having a nice day.) "Everybody knows the answer to that. It's been written a thousand times."

He sighed. "Well, back in 1960 when I was still in Toronto, George Preston Marshall, the principal owner of the Redskins, wanted to oust one of his directors, Harry Wismer, and announced the shares were for sale, a 25 per cent interest. I felt intrigued so I took them. You surely know that I'd been interested in buying the Argonauts, but was unsuccessful. You'd forgotten? Good God! Anyway, since then I've been adding to my Redskin stock."

As he talked Jack watched me scratching away in my notebook. "You should get a tape recorder, you know," Jack said. "Good reporters carry tape recorders."

I haven't seen Jack since but I get a Christmas card from him each year. The card is signed Jack in a familiar handwritten sweep and the envelope is handwritten, too, but I don't think it's Jack's hand. The envelope calls me Trint.

Chapter 9

Eyeball to eyeball with the mighty

The Jack Cooke contretemps had no lasting residue; we got along fine through the rest of his reign in Toronto, which terminated in 1960 when he abruptly took off for California. It's entirely possible he'd be in Canada yet if a couple of his sports projects hadn't received bizarre rejection.

First off, in 1956 the Argonaut Rowing Club, which had run the football team for generations, decided to ask for bids for the team's purchase. It was done in a quiet manner, just a few wealthy sports people such as Cooke, John Bassett, the publisher of the *Telegram*, and a stockbroker named Eric Cradock, a former owner of the Montreal Alouettes, among others, being made aware of it.

Cooke submitted the highest bid but Bob Moran, the chairman of the Rowing Club's football committee, whispered to me years later that "somebody blabbered to Bassett and Cradock." This pair joined forces, undercutting Cooke, and Bassett became the new chairman of the Argos.

Cooke sizzled when he discovered he'd been hoodwinked but Bassett wasn't finished with him yet. In 1959 both Cooke and Bassett began urging city hall to turn CNE Stadium into a multi-purpose facility so that the Argonauts could move there from Varsity Stadium and Cooke could press for the big-league baseball franchise he'd been pining for.

But one day, according to Cooke, he was called out of town and Bassett took advantage of his absence to urge the city fathers to opt for a football-only renovation. Bassett felt a playing field designed to cater to both sports would not properly serve either, and he wasn't about to flip a coin with Cooke over which game to opt for. Bassett's lobby was successful. He moved the Argonauts to a new home on the waterfront and Cooke, shut out again and furious, used influence he had in Washington to expedite an application for American citizenship and quickly set sail for a new life in Los Angeles.

Cooke was not the first sports figure whose ire I had attracted, nor was he to be the last. Team owners and players often have the notion that newspapers are in business to promote them the way television does, but this is hardly so. That's not because newspapers are run by steely-eyed, high-minded publishers, it's simply that newspapers have no financial stake in a sports operation; their coverage doesn't attract millions of advertising dollars as television's does. So they can afford to be virtuous and independent.

This enables scribes to adopt an adversarial position with impunity, and over the years I had my moments with various field-of-play bosses, though rarely with players. That was because until the lowly serfs began turning into overnight millionaires they were at the mercy of the whims of greedy owners. So I rarely encountered difficulty with players, either before Cooke or for a long time afterwards, with one notable exception. All through the 1980s the No. 1 pitcher of the Blue Jays, Dave Stieb, was a hard guy to love.

Dave arrived, cocky and brash and not quite 22, halfway through the 1979 season, a square-set six-footer with a live arm, a crackling slider, and a facial resemblance to actor Tom Sellick. He won eight games and lost eight for a terrible team in only its third year of existence, a team that won 53 games and lost 109.

So far so good.

In his second year Dave won 12 and lost 15 for an improving team that won 67 games and lost 95, and it was about then that he began to behave as though he had mistaken himself for Cy Young. When teammates erred behind him Dave fumed. He'd stare at the heavens or, hands on hips, glare at the culprit or, variously, pick up the resin bag and slam it into the mound at his feet.

After his third season, when he won 11 and lost 10, Dave went to arbitration, seeking a $325,000 salary instead of the $250,000 the Blue Jays offered him. "I want to be traded," Dave told the scribes. "I want to move on. As long as I stay here I'm gyping myself. I'm not going to see my true potential here."

When the Yankees came to town Dave unburdened himself to Murray Chass, a *New York Times* scribe. "I could pitch anywhere," Dave said. "Here, what can I hope for? Maybe 15 wins a year? But win 15 games a year for 10 years and where are you? You're not close to anything. I feel as long as I'm here I'm stagnant."

As time marched on Dave began to bellyache about the fans. They didn't understand the sensitivities of the players, Dave said, and cheered at the wrong times because they just didn't know the game. Often they'd holler louder for Detroit or the Yankees than for the Blue Jays. That made it hard on the home team's players, Dave said.

After 10 seasons with the Blue Jays Dave had won 131 games. On only four occasions had he reached or topped the 15 wins he'd so disparaged. He'd started out with an expansion team in 1979 but from 1983 on the Blue Jays were a power in the AL East and Dave was nowhere near a 20-game winner. It's difficult to know what salary Dave might have regarded as adequate for his Herculean efforts but players' association figures showed him receiving $1.6 million for 1990. That seemed pretty good for a guy figuring he'd stagnate.

So, writing about Dave back in 1981 when he'd expressed displeasure with the $250,000 offer, I mentioned that there were some people paying to watch him pitch who weren't

making a quarter of a million dollars for seven months' attendance after three years on the job. And then I wrote that a lot of
people were lifelong Yankee fans who drove to Toronto from
Buffalo and Syracuse to see their favourites, and a lot of fans
were lifelong Tiger fans who drove from London and Sarnia to
see their favourites. That could account for a lot of the cheering.

And so Dave and I didn't often see eye to eye. Literally. I
mean, I didn't attend the post-game scrums in front of his
locker after he'd pitched, and in the pre-game hours when the
scribes stood around the batting cage or the dugout gabbing
with players, Dave would be in the outfield with the pitchers
shagging fungoes or running. I've no idea whether he read any
of the stuff I wrote.

One Sunday during the 1986 season, though, I had a notion
for a column on pitching and sat on the bench talking about it
with Al Widmar, the pitching coach. Then I wanted to get a
pitcher's viewpoint but they all seemed to be in the outfield. I
walked from the dugout to the clubhouse and there in the
otherwise empty room was a pitcher – Dave Stieb. He was down
on one knee over a tote bag putting equipment from his locker
into it.

"Um, Dave," I said tentatively. "Have you got a minute?"

He glanced up, saw who it was, then went back to his
equipment bag.

"I'm not interested, really," he said pleasantly. I remember
that word really – "rilly" is how he said it, "rilly."

"Oh," I said, off balance. "Well, when do you think you
might be interested?"

He didn't look up this time.

"I'm just not interested," he replied, still pleasant. "Rilly."

I stared at him for a couple of seconds and then departed.
After a while, when the other pitchers came in from the
outfield, I grabbed one of them to ask whatever it was I had
planned asking Stieb.

Dave and I didn't exchange birthday gifts or Christmas cards
or even nods of recognition for the next couple of years. It

wasn't that I was mad at Dave or whether he even knew I was above ground; it was just that I didn't need him for anything I couldn't get from somebody else and he sure as hell didn't need me for anything. So our paths didn't cross.

That isn't unusual. It's my experience that a tall indifference exists between the ballplayers and the scribes who flock to find something to write about besides who won. The players go about their business and the scribes go about theirs, and eyes often meet with no flicker of recognition or greeting. Newshounds spend a lot of time interviewing one another and ballplayers flock in tight little groups of their own or hide in the trainer's room, which is off limits to the lowly scribes.

But one early evening after a Sunday game midway through the 1989 season that ended a Blue Jay homestand, my wife and I were having dinner at a restaurant near the Toronto airport. Two or three young men brushed past our booth on their way to the exit and I heard a voice say in a friendly way, "Hi Trent."

I looked up at the receding figure and called in real surprise, "Hey, *hi Dave*."

"Holy shit!" I said to my wife. "Do you know who that was, Dave Stieb."

"Holy shit indeed," echoed my dear wife, who hardly knows Dave Stieb from Grapes Cherry. "I think I'll have the fettucini alfredo."

And so, with Dave and I back being buddies, I thought of him at the ball yard a couple of weeks later as an idea assailed me. On a given day a major-league pitcher can throw a three-hit shutout and later the same week he can be knocked out early. So I decided to ask my pal Dave, a guy who has pitched back-to-back one-hitters and has also exited early, what accounts for this broad discrepancy.

As Dave strolled toward the dugout from the outfield, crossing the third-base line on his way in, the conversation went as follows:

Me: "Ah, Dave, can I see you a minute?"

Dave: "Got a team meeting."

Me: "Well, after it?"

Dave (nearing the dugout): "What about?"

Me: "Pitching."

Dave (disappearing down the dugout steps): "Nah."

The irony was that across the way in his grey Texas uniform was Nolan Ryan, whose record showed five *no-hitters* and *nine* one-hitters. This day he'd been doing pushups and situps out along the right-field line, and when he came in the conversation went like this:

Me: "Ah, Nolan, got a minute?"

Nolan: "Oh, now? Well, I haven't quite finished my workout. How long will this take?"

Me: "Just a couple of minutes. I just have a couple questions."

Nolan: "Oh, okay. But let's do it right now."

And we did.

Nevertheless, in defence of my former buddy Dave, I must say that he occasionally gets a bum rap. For instance, in the 1989 American League playoff the Blue Jays were kayoed in five games by the Oakland A's. The first two games were played in Oakland and the next three in Toronto, where the series ended.

A week or so later I got a letter from a reader in Calgary who wanted to know why the Toronto scribes were homers, refusing to be critical of the home-town boys. He said that a columnist in the *Calgary Herald*, name of Allan Maki, had advised his readers that Dave Stieb had given up early on the Blue Jays' chances of prolonging the Oakland series. Stieb had brought his packed bag and his golf clubs to the clubhouse *before* the fifth game, itching to get home. None of this had been in the Toronto papers, this Calgary fellow wrote me. How come? So I wrote back that there was nothing surprising about Stieb taking his stuff to the ballpark. So had everybody else, give or take a pile of golf bags. If the Blue Jays had won that fifth game the series would have gone back to Oakland. The Blue Jays had a chartered airplane waiting at the Hamilton airport. The team would have been Oakland-bound that evening.

A couple of weeks later I was surprised to read a piece by

Marty York in the *Globe* with the same charge against Stieb. I sent a little note to Marty about it. But I didn't hear from him until I ran into him at the Grey Cup game five or six weeks later.

"Hey, you haven't answered my note," I said.

"Oh, I wanted to wait until I saw you. It was after the *fourth* game that Stieb had his bag packed, not the fifth."

I thought about that for a minute and then I said, "Nope, going into the fourth game the series was two to one for Oakland. No way it could end in four games, so why would Stieb be packed to go home?"

"Oh yeah," said Marty, blinking.

"A guy named Al Maki in Calgary wrote the same thing a few weeks ago," I said.

"I know," Marty said. "It was Maki who tipped me."

But Marty never bothered slipping a correction into his stuff.

My first confrontation with the mighty was in the early 1940s when the New York Rangers trained in the old Amphitheatre rink in Winnipeg and I worked on the *Tribune*. Lester Patrick was running the Rangers then, an imperious figure of about 6-foot-2 with a lean, handsome face, arresting blue eyes, and a crown of wavy grey hair that eventually brought him the name Silver Fox.

It was a source of real annoyance to us local scribes that Lester was often an elusive figure for us but that he'd sit all through a practice high in the seats in the Amphitheatre talking to Andy Lytle. Lytle, the sports editor of the *Toronto Star*, wrote training-camp pieces about NHL teams, and we'd read stuff from Lester in the *Star* that he never bothered to tell us.

But one day Lester got real chummy with me and with Cam McKenzie from the *Free Press*, telling us that although the Rangers were a set team defending the Stanley Cup they'd won in the final the previous spring against Toronto, there was one position open. He told us the names of three players who were in the running for it and said he'd determine the winning candidate during three exhibition games coming up against the rival New York team, the Americans. I don't have the faintest recollection who the three players were but I do remember a coincidence that dawned on me while I was writing about Lester's dilemma in the *Trib* office that night.

The exhibition games were booked for Port Arthur, Winnipeg, and Saskatoon, and I noticed that a candidate whose home town was Port Arthur had been pencilled in by Lester to play in Port Arthur, a Winnipeg prospect would play in Winnipeg, and a Saskatoon lad would get his chance in, yep, Saskatoon. So that's what I wrote about, that home-town boys were getting their chance. I also noted that such an arrangement wouldn't hurt the box office for the exhibitions, either, and that Patrick likely had his mind made up anyway and was hoping to sell a few extra tickets.

The next morning at the Rangers' practice I was sitting in the dressing room in a conversation with the goaltender, Davey Kerr, when Lester loomed over me, surely 6-foot-9 if not 9-foot-6, his gaze unwavering and cold. He ordered me from the room and told me not to come back. He said that big-league hockey teams had no time for small-town smart asses.

That, I guess, was the last time I saw Lester. The Rangers soon left Winnipeg and so did I. I went to Toronto, where I spent the next three years on the *Globe and Mail* on the military beat.

But not before I'd had one more run-in with the mighty. This time it was Mervyn (Red) Dutton, a former great defenceman for the Montreal Maroons and the Americans, who just before the demise of the Amerks had become their coach and principal benefactor, lending money to their beleaguered owner, a famous Manhattan bootlegger named Big Bill Dwyer.

Dutton was a marvelous hot-head. At one time he held the NHL record for penalties. Jim Coleman used to tell a story of how Dutton took so many penalties that his coach, Eddie Gerard, once benched him for three games. Dutton was deeply hurt by this and marched into Gerard's office to insist he be reinstated or traded forthwith.

"If I put you back in the lineup, can you control your temper?" Coleman quoted Gerard.

"*Temper*," cried Dutton. "It's not my temper. It's my *enthusiasm* I can't control."

In one of my favourite Dutton stories a game is about to begin and Red is tense and ready at the blueline, but no one has handed the referee a puck for the face-off. He stands at centre looking toward the timekeeper's bench, and Dutton's patience snaps.

"Never mind the damned puck," he growls at the referee. "Start the *game*!"

On the day that the Americans arrived in Winnipeg for their exhibition with the Rangers I ran into Dutton in a wide corridor in the legislative building just along Broadway Avenue from the Amphitheatre rink on Whitehall. Wartime regulations from Ottawa had decreed that civilians of military age required special border-crossing cards to enter the United States. I had just learned that the applications of a couple of Winnipeg players Dutton was counting on for the Amerks had been rejected and was on my way to the *Tribune* with this piece of news for the afternoon edition.

"Bad luck for you," I told Dutton. "Those two players of yours have been turned down."

I guess he thought I was the guy who'd rejected them.

"What!" he cried, grabbing me in one hand by the coat lapels. "*What did you say?*"

"Hey, whoa!" I yelped, my back now against the marble wall. "What'd *I* do? I'm just telling you what they told me."

"I'll be a son of a bitch," Dutton muttered. "The bastards!" Finally the fire went out of his eyes and he turned me loose.

Thirty-odd years later I went to Calgary to talk to Dutton, by then retired and living on his money. Following his stint with the Americans, he became the NHL's president for a couple of years, then gave it up to run his construction business. In 1973 I was researching a hockey book and wanted to talk to him about the defunct Amerks, my all-time favourite hockey team, an assortment of high-living guys in New York during the speakeasy era of Prohibition. I have told this story before but it bears repeating to illustrate the kind of open and impulsive and vigorous fellow he was even late in his life.

He came to my room in the Pallisar Hotel, a millionaire of 75, a six-footer expensively dressed, the red hair now snow white. We made no mention of the meeting long ago in the legislative building in Winnipeg; I doubt it ever crossed his mind again. He stood at the window looking across the rolling Alberta hills and then he turned, talking of his youth in the infantry in France during World War One, and suddenly he dropped his pants.

"It was high explosive," he said. "It took 10 pounds of meat out of my ass. Right here, look. Shrapnel hit me right here in the ass, in my thigh, and all down the calf, see?"

His fingers traced tiny pock marks on his leg as he talked, his pants at half-mast at his knees. Then he hiked them up, still talking, zipping up the fly, tightening the belt.

"I'd been 20 months in the front line. I was 18 years old and a buck private. A couple of years before, I'd lied about my age when I enlisted. We were carrying ammunition to the front at Farbus Wood. I had this ammo over my shoulder and I remember the quiet. So still. And then suddenly the German guns opened up, and a shell exploded and the shrapnel hit seven men in a row, killed 'em right there, and then hit me. I crawled into a gun emplacement and lay there for many hours before they found me.

"I was in hospitals for 18 months. The doctors wanted to take the damn leg off but I said no way. When I got back to Canada in the spring of 1919 I was determined to play hockey. I took a job on one of my dad's railway construction projects. I wore the heaviest work boots I could find and I ran from construction gang to construction gang to strengthen my leg. At freeze-up I went back to my folks' place in Winnipeg and skated every day from early morning until late at night. By God, I played hockey in *seven* different leagues, sometimes two leagues on the same night, playing well past midnight."

The last time I saw Dutton was on television in the spring of

1986. The Calgary Flames were honouring one of their city's famous sons, inviting him to drop the puck at the opening game of the Stanley Cup final. He was 88 then and had been ill most of the winter. But the Flames sent a limousine for him, had a golf cart at the back door of the Saddledome to run him to rinkside, and the television cameras showed him there holding tight to the bar of one of those walking cages and then creeping slowly along a red carpet toward centre ice, followed by a nurse and a couple of dignitaries. He was pale and gaunt, inching along toward the face-off circle. It crossed my mind that he had lost three sons in World War Two, two fliers in the RCAF and a sailor in the RCN. My thoughts went to the fiery young player who had growled, "Never mind the damn puck. Start the game!" It was all very sad.

In his way Jack Adams was as competitive as Dutton, and one thing they had in common when they were running their hockey teams was a sudden explosive temper. I ought to know.

Though he was called Jolly Jawn in his latter years, Adams had been a rugged player, a forward and a smaller man than the raw-boned Red. He grew fat as he grew older and he liked to talk about how tough hockey was when he played for the old Toronto Arenas, who preceded the St. Pats, who preceded the Maple Leafs. He told me once that the team's trainer used to stand at the bench with a pail of water, a sponge, and some strips of adhesive tape. He said that when players were cut they'd skate to the bench and stand at the boards while the trainer sloshed away the blood with the sponge and covered the cuts with the tape.

One night, Adams said, he'd been so badly cut in a game in the Montreal Forum that a couple of his Toronto teammates took him to the Royal Victoria Hospital after the game to be patched up properly. The blood had dried here and there on his face and a nurse gently patted away at it. He didn't pay any attention to her until her startled cry, "My God, it's you, Jack!"

It was his sister Margaret. She hadn't recognized the bloodied mug.

Jolly Jawn's sobriquet overlooked the tough side of him. After his playing days he became the boss of the Detroit Red Wings for 35 years, given virtually a free hand by the owner, burly old James Norris, a Chicago grain millionaire. Adams spent 50 years of his life in the game, first as a player in 1918 when hockey was a cruel and vicious pastime, and finally as the president of the Central Hockey League, the job he was holding in 1968 when a heart attack killed him at his desk. In the middle, when Gordie Howe and Terry Sawchuk and Terrible Ted Lindsay were at their best in Detroit, the Red Wings had an exceptional seven-year run from 1949 through 1955: seven first-place finishes, five Stanley Cup finals, four Stanley Cups.

In those years Adams was a round, beaming, voluble man who laughed a lot but didn't have much humour. His laughter was more mechanical than reflective of a warm personality. He bore grudges. He stopped speaking to Lindsay for two years after Ted joined an unsuccessful effort to form a players' union. After a heated exchange with his all-star goaltender Glenn Hall he stopped speaking to him, too, then shipped him off to Chicago, the league doormat.

In 1959 the *Maclean's* editor Ralph Allen dispatched me to Detroit to write a two-part piece under Adams's byline, a sort of abbreviated autobiography. We got along fine. Adams escorted me here and there, to sportsmen's luncheons where I was introduced as the person who was writing his life story, to the ballpark, then called Briggs Stadium, where we watched the Tigers play the Yankees, and Jolly Jawn, at his expansive best, led the way to the Tiger clubhouse to meet the manager, a former Toronto outfielder named Bill Norman.

"He's doing my life story," Jolly Jawn said in an offhand way, adding that mechanical laugh of his.

After this social whirl I went home to organize my notes and think about a lead, and in the middle of that the Red Wings came to town and I went down to the Royal York Hotel to see

Red Kelly, their rock-steady defenceman, who was having a below-par year. I thought there might be a fast piece in that, if Kelly, a pleasant, shy man, had anything startling to say.

He did. He said he'd been playing pretty well lately but that his recovery had been slower than he'd expected.

"What recovery?" I asked. "Were you sick?"

"Well, no, not sick," Red said. "But I broke my ankle and, see, there was nothing in the papers because the club wanted to keep it quiet. I broke it a year ago and right afterwards a couple of other guys were hurt and Mr. Adams asked me to play. I wore a plaster cast and played. It's just beginning to feel right again now."

Red said he assumed the Red Wings had kept his injury quiet because they didn't want rival players beating on it. He said he was a little surprised, though, when he was fined $100 by the coach, his old teammate Sid Abel. Sid told the papers the team was slumping because veteran players weren't producing. He'd fined them $100 each for lack of effort, including Red.

I sold the Kelly piece to the *Star Weekly*, finished my second *Maclean's* part on Adams, and then the magazine received this telegram from the man himself: UNDER NO CIRCUMSTANCES WILL MY NAME APPEAR OVER YOUR STORY STOP PERMISSION TO USE MY NAME HEREBY WITHDRAWN STOP DETROIT HOCKEY CLUB IS AN HONORABLE ORGANIZATION STOP AM CONFERRING WITH MY LAWYERS STOP SUIT MAY FOLLOW.

Taking off in all directions, Adams turned on Kelly, too. In eight of the previous 10 seasons Red had been on the NHL's first or second all-star team but that didn't deter Jolly Jawn; he traded him and a young forward named Billy McNeill to the New York Rangers for Bill Gadsby and Eddie Shack. But Red decided he didn't want to move to New York. He said he'd retire if the deal was not voided. When McNeill, whose wife had died that summer, said he'd prefer to retire, the trade was abandoned.

But this didn't derail Adams for long. Still mad at Red, he readily agreed to a swap suggested by Toronto's Punch Imlach: Kelly for a rookie Leaf defenceman, Marc Reaume. Red concurred so the deal was made. It was one of Imlach's best; he turned the all-star defenceman Kelly into a centre and Red helped the team win the Stanley Cup four times in the 1960s.

The lawsuit didn't materialize. Ralph Allen was successful in several phone calls persuading Adams to let the magazine run his story. I was relieved; I had a month's work and a $1,500 fee invested in Jolly Jawn. That was a lot of money in 1959 for a father of three.

Indeed, 1959 was a pretty good year all around. My first book came out, a history of the Queen's Plate commemorating the 100th year of this country's most notable horse race. The book was commissioned by Jim Coleman, the public relations boss at the Ontario Jockey Club. Coleman had dropped his sports column in the *Globe* partly on impulse one night at the Paddock Tavern in Toronto, a favourite haunt of his in his drinking days. This night, he had received permission from the proprietor, a horse owner named Morris Fishman, to go behind the bar and mix drinks for himself and his good friend Jack (Deacon) Allen, a fight promoter and bon vivant in his 70s or thereabouts. After several champagne cocktails Coleman decided he had written enough columns in the *Globe* so he phoned the paper and told the city editor, Tommy Munns, he had decided to retire. The following morning, watching his two children wolf down their corn flakes, he wondered if he had been a trifle premature in abandoning steady employment. He placed an advertisement in the *Globe* announcing that he was looking for work. The field he turned to was thoroughbred racing, his first love, as a Jockey Club executive.

Prior to commissioning me to put together the Queen's Plate book Coleman had hired me in another capacity. One of his jobs was handling thoroughbred publicity, but when E.P. Taylor, who was revolutionizing the racing industry in Ontario, decided to take on harness racing as well, Coleman rebelled. His lifelong devotion to racing began and ended at the thoroughbred tracks; he had no real affection for the "jugheads," as scornful running-horse people call the trotters. Still, their annual two-month summer meeting had to be publicized.

I was walking along King Street one afternoon in June of 1951 when I heard someone call my name. It was Coleman. "You're just the man," he said with what I took to be unusual enthusiasm. "Stand still."

He said that during July and August, when thoroughbreds were racing at the Fort Erie track across the Niagara River from Buffalo, he needed someone to look after publicity for the trotters in Toronto. A half-mile track had been carved inside the one-mile thoroughbred track at Woodbine in Toronto's east end. Coleman's enthusiasm upon spotting me, I now perceived, wasn't so much a product of my vast charm and good looks as that I represented a means of his avoiding the harness horses.

I protested that I knew nothing about horses of any description, never mind trotters and pacers, but he was a hard man to dissuade.

"It doesn't matter," he urged. "You've worked on papers. You can write releases. You can get the odd plug from the radio guys. This is the opportunity of a lifetime."

"Gee, I don't know," I said.

"It's three hundred a week," he said.

"On second thought, why not?" I said.

And that was how I got into the horse-racing game.

At first the provincial government refused to sanction charters that permitted racing under lights. Accordingly, harness racing in Toronto was confined to the daylight hours while the thoroughbreds were out of town racing at Fort Erie. That was perfect for me. I did my usual freelance magazine stuff at home in the mornings and went to the track in mid-afternoon. Post-time was five o'clock during July and August, with the last race completed by sundown. George Hendrie, the Jockey Club's managing director, was the only member of the board who showed the slightest interest in the trotters. None of the other pillars of racing society – Charles F.W. Burns, Harry Carmichael, Viscount Hardinge, Malcolm Richardson, Frowde Seagram, Allen Case, and Conn Smythe, among others – deigned to show up at the jugs.

But, oh, what they missed. There was a wonderful old two-storey house just off the clubhouse turn, white and square with a wide balcony across the front on the second floor overlooking the track, and it served as the directors' lounge during thoroughbred meetings. Of course, with no directors ever turning up for the, ugh, harness races, it was a private sanctuary for George Hendrie and me during the long summer evenings. My wife June came down the odd evening and we'd sit on the balcony for a while having an occasional drink, looking across the track at Lake Ontario's calm waters reflecting the dying day. Every 20 minutes or so the horses would go clop-clop-clop-clop-clopping by, pulling drivers hunched above the spinning wheels, rushing past in the gathering twilight.

There was something basic and earthy and genuine about the trotting-horse people. They really did have a deep-rooted affection for their horses. As often as not the driver was the owner and trainer and he tended to his stable from dawn to dusk and then some. Thoroughbred owners weren't like that, not many of them. You'd seldom see one who trained his horses and, indeed, they had no real contact with them at any time. They'd stand by the rail in the mornings seeing them work or, in the afternoons, watch through binoculars from on high in the clubhouse. Occasionally they'd drop past the barn and proffer the odd carrot, but their kids certainly never got to ride them. On the other hand, the kids of harness guys grew up with horses, worked around them, and even before school age drove them.

In the late 1950s when night racing was legalized, harness racing expanded rapidly on the Jockey Club circuit. Two new tracks were built, one at St. Catharines called Garden City Raceway, and the other, Mohawk Raceway, 30 miles west of Toronto near Guelph. Also, a new thoroughbred track on Toronto's northwestern outskirts was completed in 1956 and was opened with a flourish. The Queen herself was there, elegant in a frock of cerise and white printed silk with a cerise silk coat lined with print. Her hat was a toque of white organza petals covered in pink tulle. The whisper came down that she bet with both hands. Her husband, the Prince, was in his sailor suit and had his hands behind his back.

This new track was called Woodbine, and for a couple of

years the old track in Toronto's east end was called Old Woodbine. But that was too confusing so the name Greenwood replaced it. The racing surfaces were reshaped and resurfaced and the runners and trotters began alternating meetings around the calendar.

Six years after the big new Woodbine's opening, Jim Coleman decided to go back to working for a living, undertaking a sports column for Southam's national chain of newspapers. That meant the Jockey Club was looking for someone to oversee publicity and advertising for both the thoroughbreds and the trotters. I could see that my p.r. days were dwindling because harness racing was soon to be a year-round business. As long as the season was confined to two months in midsummer I enjoyed combining it with freelance work. But I couldn't see horse racing as my game on a year-round basis.

But one day in November I got a telephone call from John Mooney, who had succeeded George Hendrie as the managing director (Hendrie had become president). Mooney said he'd like to meet me for a drink and a chat.

"I know what he wants," I said to my wife.

"Coleman's job?" June said.

"Sure. The guys they want have turned it down and they've turned down the guys who want it."

A freelancer lives in a half-world between freedom and security. No boss nags you, you don't punch a clock, but if your stuff doesn't sell regularly you have to abandon this habit of eating. And by 1962, June and I had four kids and a mortgage.

"I figure the job pays maybe $15,000," I said. "I'll tell Mooney I want 17. If he says no, well, I really don't want the job, do I?"

So I met John in the downstairs bar at the Royal York Hotel and he said the OJC needed somebody to oversee the harness and thoroughbred publicity and advertising.

"Sort of a public relations director," Mooney said.

"What's the money?" I said.

"Twenty thousand," he said.

"I'll take it," I said.

But over the next six years, until the summer of 1968, I wasn't a very good public relations man. I could deal with the media people, of course, because I'd been one of them and knew their needs. The people on the backstretch – jockeys, trainers, grooms on the thoroughbred tracks, and the owners and drivers and trainers with the trotters – were friendly and co-operative and dedicated to their unique lives. No problem there. But I found the Jockey Club directors to be remote and self-centred for the most part. The majority of them remained aloof to the harness horsemen and, I felt, tolerated the lowly jugheads simply because they were making money for them.

However, my main problem was that I was in the wrong line of work. I wasn't a bettor, wasn't interested in improving the breed, and underwent long periods in the endless seasons when I was plain bored. Connie Smythe must have sensed this, though in my six years at the track we didn't exchange five words. But he delivered a significant little jibe just before the 1968 Queen's Plate while making a presentation at the Constellation Hotel.

The occasion was the Joe Perlove dinner. Joe had been a turf writer for the *Star* for many years, a charming, wise, witty, dapper man of wide popularity. When he died of cancer his close friend Ray Timson, later the *Star*'s managing editor, organized a bursary in Joe's name to be presented annually to the top graduate at the Ryerson journalism school in Toronto. So in presenting this prize in a ballroom crowded with horsemen, Smythe said he had no idea in what direction the young recipient might be headed. "But if you'd like a job in the publicity department at Woodbine you'd be welcome. The guy we've got in there now doesn't know a stud from a collar button." Ah, yes, dear old Conn. We'll not soon see his like again (I hope).

No one at the Jockey Club personified the spirit of harness racing better than a warm, merry-eyed, quick-witted native of St. Catharines named Jim Lampman, who came to work in the publicity department in 1962. He had no experience and he couldn't type a line but he had an unrestrained affection for the game and an abiding enthusiasm for the work. He owned a pacing mare, too, called Lexie Herbert. I don't know if she ever won a race but you'd have thought when Jim talked about her that she'd never known a losing stride.

Lampman came to the Jockey Club after E.P. Taylor bought the land for the Garden City track on the St. Catharines outskirts. Jim and two friends had an option on the property and when they sold it, part of the deal was that if they wanted to work for the OJC, Taylor would employ them. One of Jim's partners was a lawyer whose office was thriving and the other owned a prospering dairy. Neither gave a second thought to the offer.

But Jim, who was in his early 30s, had been running his father's feed company since he was 18, when his father died of a heart attack at 45. He wanted a change of scene. When the harness-racing publicity department was suggested Jim leaped. His counterpart with the thoroughbreds was Bruce Walker, who is still the p.r. boss there, and I was their overseer in this job John Mooney had hired me for over our Royal York drink.

Lampman was a hit from the start and he remained one long after I left the OJC even though he still couldn't type a news release and mispronounced the names of half the horses on the OJC circuit. But when a harness-racing strike ended at Toronto's Greenwood track in 1985, Jim was standing at the entrance gate on the first night back handing free past-performance programs to fans tumbling from the streetcars. On the back of the programs, which are the life's blood of a bettor's calculations, were two large black words and one exclamation mark, Welcome Back!

When another strike ended a year or so later Jim wasn't standing anywhere. He was lying in the Toronto General Hospital having a malignant tumour removed. Still, when the strike ended he sent word that the fans should be welcomed back appropriately – free parking, free admission, and a free past-performance program.

Publicity guys aren't quite as well known as the people who score 60 goals or belt 50 home runs but for 25 years Jim found ways to make harness fans feel good. He'd have a band leader named Bobby Gimby bouncing through the stands with his band playing trumpets and clarinets and saxophones, and he'd have gorgeous creatures modelling fur coats or short dresses or skimpy blouses on an infield podium or he'd have young kids from a nearby boys' boxing club stage amateur bouts for prizes between races. One night just before the Blue Jays won their first AL East pennant in 1985, Jim presented manager Bobby Cox and his wife Pam to a big crowd at Greenwood when the whole town was Blue Jay daffy. Reggie Jackson was there in the winner's enclosure one night and George Brett another and Lou Piniella and King Clancy and Serge Savard – anybody Jim thought the fans might enjoy seeing.

One night Frank Drea, the chairman of the Ontario Racing Commission, visited the Mohawk track. That day one of the papers had run a favourable profile of Drea, a former cabinet minister in the government of William Davis. Drea had once worked for the *Toronto Telegram*.

"That was a terrific story about you today," Jim said. "You can still type, I see."

When I left the Jockey Club Jim went to a lot of trouble to get me a beautiful marble-based pen and pencil set inscribed with enormous sentiment in white gold: *Keep It in Your Knickers*.

With his vast enthusiasms, lusty language, and broad humour, Jim represented the very antithesis of the stuffed-shirt atmosphere of the OJC's directors' lounge that provoked the earthy and genuine horsemen of harness racing in the early years. Lampman's presence on the side of management helped preserve the uneasy peace between the harnessmen and the track operators. What a blow it was for harness fans when cancer killed him in July of 1987.

By then I'd been gone from the OJC for nearly 20 years. One afternoon in 1968 I ran into Ray Gardner, the editor of the newly created Insight section at the *Star*, who asked me how I'd like to jump back into the newspaper business. I jumped, and after six years of writing features on politicians and business-men and movie stars and cities and neighbourhoods and the

1972 Olympics in Munich and the closing four games of the September Summit between the Soviets and Team Canada in Moscow I jumped again, this time to the little paper that grew, the wacky *Toronto Sun*, and began writing a sports column, which I did for nine years, and then went to the *Globe* for six more.

Chapter 10

Colourless Canadians? Who says so?

Often the complaint is made that a characteristic Canadian restraint prevents our hockey players from becoming the flamboyant and memorable and even legendary people that, say, ballplayers become in the U.S. We have no loudmouth Reggie Jacksons or Dizzy Deans or Babe Ruths. Instead, we're a country of quiet heroes, such as Bobby Orr and Gordie Howe and Wayne Gretzky, young men who soared in Canada's game, yet remained modest and earth-bound.

This is a bunch of baloney. Our national game has been turning out extroverts almost since the invention of the puck, though it's a fact we don't celebrate them as persistently or as blatantly as the scribes and broadcasters do south of here. What's true is that we don't *preserve* the memory of our big stars as the Americans do. Their broadcasters will talk about Ol' Diz and Yogi and Schoolboy Rowe as though those players performed in the 1980s rather than generations ago, and millions of fans immediately recognize who the announcers mean. Everybody in the Great White North knows about Paul Henderson's goal in Moscow in 1972, of course, but you never hear a broadcaster say, for instance, "Hey, this reminds me of the night Clancy drove Shore crazy and the Leafs eliminated the Bruins, right, Chuck?" Yet this was one of the highlight moments in hockey history.

Hockey is an exhilarating game that stirs the blood, and it has produced more than its share of loudmouths – the unmatched buffoon Ballard, Conn Smythe, Eddie Shore, Babe Pratt, King Clancy, Grapes Cherry, Punch Imlach, to mention a few. And the game itself packs a unique historical wallop. One of my all-time favourite quotations about hockey belongs to one of this country's most revered novelists, Hugh MacLennan. The U.S. magazine *Holiday* devoted an issue to Canada many years ago and asked MacLennan, a professor at McGill University at the time, to write a piece about hockey, and he wrote a beauty.

"To spectator and player alike, hockey gives the release that strong liquor gives to a repressed man," he began. "It is the counterpoint of the Canadian self-restraint, it takes us back to the fiery blood of Gallic and Celtic ancestors who found themselves minorities in a cold, new environment and had to discipline themselves as all minorities must. But Canadians take the ferocity of their national game so much for granted that when an American visitor makes polite mention of it, they look at him in astonishment. Hockey violent? Well, perhaps it is a little. But hockey was always like that."

And old Connie Smythe had a thing or two to say about hockey apart from that one classic line of his, "If you can't beat 'em outside in the alley, you won't beat 'em inside on the ice." One night at Maple Leaf Gardens Smythe, flushed in excitement, blue eyes blazing, ran into Scott Young, then writing a sports column at the *Globe*. There had just been a chilling fight on the ice between Rocket Richard and a tough Leaf youngster named Bob Bailey, and Smythe said to Young, "We've got to stamp out that kind of thing or people are going to keep on buying tickets."

Young, incidentally, wrote Smythe's memoirs in 1980 when the old man was 85 and literally on his deathbed. As Scott finished each chapter he'd take the manuscript to Smythe for his approval. In what turned out to be the last visit, the Leaf founder lay silent, eyes closed, the skin drawn taut on his face and bald head. He waved aside the chapter Young proffered and told him to read it aloud instead.

"But first he wanted me to put on a recording of 'The White Cliffs of Dover,'" Scott told me not long ago. "I did that, and then coming to a funny part that I particularly wanted him to hear I raised my voice. It must have made the damnedest scene, me standing and shouting above 'The White Cliffs of Dover' and Smythe lying there with his eyes closed and this mask of his slowly taking on a broad smile."

Numerous critics believed Smythe suffered a mild attack of paranoia when he got back from World War Two and expressed a conviction that Frank Selke, among others, had tried to oust him from his Gardens position in his absence. Selke had worked with Smythe from the time the Gardens first was conceived and he ran the hockey club while Smythe was overseas. Smythe says in his memoirs that Selke left the Leafs in May of 1946 "because I was making things tough for him." Selke subsequently was hired by the Canadiens and he put together championship teams in 1953 and for five straight springs from 1956 through 1960.

In my earliest dealings with Selke I wrote short pieces on hockey nights for the Gardens program, which he edited. For this I was rewarded handsomely – two seats in the rink's Blue section valued at $2.50 each (by 1990 kindly old H. Ballard had painted those seats red and was charging $35 for each). One afternoon after Smythe returned from overseas I got a call from Selke telling me he didn't want my program stuff any more. I was working for the *Globe* then, making $45 a week, and using the tickets to take out June on Saturday nights. So I was slightly crestfallen, losing the seats, and phoned Selke and told him I'd like to see him. In his Gardens office I asked him why I'd been dropped without explanation. He wanted to know what difference it made.

"If you were sending Sweeney Schriner to Syracuse you'd give him a reason, wouldn't you?" I said. "So why don't I get a reason?"

Selke was a runt of about 5-foot-4 with a thin crewcut, rimless glasses, and a habit of clasping and then revolving his hands as he talked.

"You just have no idea what it's like working for this man Smythe," he said. "Things happen without rhyme or reason. I'll see what I can do."

That afternoon he called me at the *Globe* and said he'd managed to straighten out the matter; I could continue to write for the program.

Not long after that I was working on a magazine piece for *Maclean's* on Rocket Richard and I phoned Selke to ask him for an assessment of this great scorer's ability. Selke wasn't working at this time, having recently parted company with Smythe, and said he'd be visiting his married daughter and if I wanted to talk to him at her home he'd meet me. I lived nearby in the Leaside area of Toronto and readily agreed. We sat on the veranda of his daughter's home as he told me what he thought of the Rocket, and then he launched into a long account of how impossible it had been to work any longer for an irascible boss like Smythe.

A couple of months later the Canadiens hired Selke as their general manager and soon afterwards, in the fall, I ran into him at a hockey luncheon in the Royal York Hotel.

"Oh, Frank, Ralph Allen has assigned me to do a two-parter on Smythe in *Maclean's*," I said. "Will it be okay if I use the stuff you've told me about him?"

"I really have nothing to say about Major Smythe," Selke responded stiffly. "He is one of the pillars of our game. If you write anything more than that I'll deny it." And he walked away.

No question about it, though, Smythe was a bombastic and sarcastic martinet with a riveting personality. In truth, his teams weren't nearly as good as he touted them to be. For instance, in his 30 years of active involvement at Maple Leaf Gardens from 1931, when he built the rink, until 1960 when he sold his interest to his son Stafford, the team topped the standings only three times – in 1934, '35, and '48. In the six-team league of the

1950s they finished as high as second only once. A decade earlier, in the 1940s, the team won the Stanley Cup five times but finished on top of the standings only once.

Those Stanley Cup wins and the veneration for the team created by Foster Hewitt's broadcasts gave the Leafs stature far beyond their station. Even in the early 1990s crowds in Winnipeg and Edmonton and Calgary still were heaping applause upon the Maple Leafs during Toronto visits that must have reflected nostalgia for the Hewitt times.

Hap Day, who coached the five Cup winners in the 1940s, once told me that he began preparing his teams for the playoffs soon after midseason. The three top teams of that six-team era perennially were Detroit, Montreal, and Toronto. Two of the other three were terrible, usually the Rangers and Chicago but occasionally Boston, as well. So Day, assured of a playoff position, would utilize the season's second half to get his troops healthy and rested and organized. In four of the Cup finals they beat Detroit and in the fifth Montreal.

Jack Adams, the Detroit boss, was particularly incensed following the 1942 series, the one in which the Maple Leafs became the only team to lose the first three games of the Stanley Cup final and come back with four straight wins, a record still unmatched.

The Red Wings were 15 minutes away from a four-game sweep, but they lost that fourth game by a goal after what Adams called the most irresponsible refereeing he'd ever seen, a succession of penalty calls that bewildered him. Adams rushed, livid, onto the ice to confront the referee, Mel Harwood. He was later charged with punching the referee and was suspended by NHL president Frank Calder for the rest of the series.

He called the comeback that won the Cup for Toronto a farce. "The Toronto newspapers and that little son of a bitch Smythe controlled the whole thing," he told me once in his office in the Olympia. "Their influence on Calder provided me with the darkest moment I ever knew in this game." At the next governors' meeting a month later he turned to Calder and barked, "You're through persecuting me, my boy. I'm through being your patsy."

Adams and Smythe were the most flamboyant operators of those years, but far more spectacular than either of them was the Boston defenceman Eddie Shore. Shore is mostly remembered as the tight-fisted, insensitive, even cruel owner of the Springfield Indians, whose antics were so bizarre that the players secretly contacted a Toronto lawyer, Alan Eagleson, to represent them in their complaints against him. That was the genesis of the National Hockey League Players' Association.

But Shore was a great player in every sense of that adjective long before he became a despised owner. And he was one of the most colourful players of all. He was an actor with a flair for the spectacular. When he was knocked down he arose like an Olivier and appealed to the referee for justice while Boston crowds brayed their approval and fans on the road booed the showoff.

"He could do a dying-swan act that would have aroused the envy of Margot Fonteyn," Baz O'Meara wrote in the *Montreal Star*. "He knew every nuance." A feature writer for the old *Collier's* magazine, Kyle Crichton, said Eddie was hockey's leading drawing card. "What makes him that way is the hope, entertained by spectators in all cities but Boston, that he will some night be severely killed."

All of this was in the mid- to late 1920s after the Bruins entered the expanding NHL along with teams in Pittsburgh, Chicago, and Detroit. There was one particular Shore act that can be seen in retrospect as successful in attracting the unwashed as it is in the pro rassles today.

Before a game the Bruins would skate onto the ice without Shore or fanfare. Then the lights would dim and a band would burst forth with "Hail to the Chief," and Shore would emerge in a spotlight, skating furiously and wearing a toreador's cape flowing from his shoulders. When he came to a halt in a spray of ice chips, a trailing valet would slowly remove the cape and the lights would go up, sending the crowd into paroxysms (if not the street).

Unfortunately, the act had to be scratched permanently one night when the crazy New York Americans came into the Boston Garden. After Shore had gone through his number, Amerk players skated to mid-ice carrying a rolled-up rug. When they unfolded it, who should be reclining there on one elbow – not Cleopatra, but little Rabbit McVeigh, an Amerk forward, who leaped to his feet, performed a pirouette on the points of his skates, and blew kisses to the crowd.

In Toronto, Smythe didn't need this sort of lunacy to attract crowds to the new rink for which he'd scrambled to raise a million dollars at the beginning of the Depression in 1931. Hockey had a built-in interest there, particularly after Smythe bought the contract of 27-year-old King Clancy, a dashing, jaunty, even ingenuous motivator, from the Ottawa Senators.

It was King Clancy's spirit, his happy outlook, his warmth, his decency, his enthusiasm, even his prodigious profanity that made you always glad you hadn't missed him. For 83 years he was a kid at heart. If anything hurt, he didn't bother telling anyone. He didn't carry grudges. He made people feel good.

Smythe was able to get him away from Ottawa because the Senators were failing financially, and it was the best hockey deal Smythe ever made – $35,000 in cash and a couple of players. In a three-volume series of books called *The Trail of the Stanley Cup*, Charles Coleman, a most conservative and factual writer, says of Clancy's seven-year hitch in the Maple Leaf lineup:

"He became the inspirational leader of a team that won the Stanley Cup in his second year with them. They were always contenders while he was around. His defence partners were Hap Day, Red Horner and Alex Levinsky but he outshone them all. He received many cuts and bruises that would have forced other players out, but not this indomitable man."

Clancy was only 5-foot-7 and 155 pounds but every inch and each pound exuded energy and even *joie de vivre*. When he retired as a player in his seventh year with Toronto he turned to coaching and refereeing and then settled into a lifetime job as vice-president of whatever happened to come up at Maple Leaf Gardens. It was a job he suited perfectly – and vice versa. One morning when King was well into his 70s I was in a Gardens snack bar waiting to interview somebody amid a scattering of people – secretaries from the offices upstairs, scouts, maintenance men. At about 10:30, in bounced himself, King Clancy, rugged features alive in a grin, and when he spotted the secretaries, he cried, "Ah, good mornin' to ye, ye lovely ladies," and he did a little jig, ending it by jumping off his left foot and clicking his heels, then off his right foot and clicking them again. The young women, as with everyone in the place, burst into delighted laughter.

Once, sitting at a table in this coffee shop, we talked about the enormous changes hockey had undergone since his boyhood days in Ottawa when all that mattered was playing the game, and concerns over money and renegotiated contracts and agents and travel and time zones were rare if not non-existent. I wrote what he said in the introduction of a book I'd been working on, and here is what it was:

"I was 17 when I turned pro. Before that, I played for St. Brigid's. We were the raggedy-ass Canal boys who played on the Rideau Canal in 25 degrees below zero. We used to play the Model School, kids of wealthy parents. They'd come in all dressed up in hockey uniforms an' we didn't have anything but the clothes we wore in school an' it didn't make any difference. They played just as hard as we did an' they could fight *almost* as good.

"Andy Blair was the first fellah I ever played with who had an education. Jesus, he was a graduate of the University of Manitoba when he played with us on the Leafs. He could fight pretty good, too, come to think of it. Before that, when I was with the Senators, the practices were as tough as the games. That Sprague Cleghorn, why, he'd cut your heart out.

"Everybody had hard men. Like Sylvio Mantha; I remember one night with the Leafs we were playin' the Canadiens and Sylvio Mantha was the key to their defence. Dick Irvin was coach for us then, an' he called me over to the bench. 'Get that Mantha,' he told me. First chance I got I caught him with a cross-check an' broke his jaw – I didn't mean to *break* it – an' we beat them.

"A couple of nights later little Artie Somers who was with the Rangers gave me a butt-end in the face. It split my tongue halfway back and knocked out four teeth. The part that bothered me the most was the gum that stuck in the teeth. That was sore for a long time. It was all part of the game. I loved it all, ye know?"

For Toronto, Clancy was a marvelously spirited player in a colourful setting, but what really made the Maple Leafs Canada's team back then were the broadcasts of Foster Hewitt. Many of us who grew up on the Prairies will go to our graves with a vivid recollection of Hewitt's slightly nasal greeting to us every Saturday night, "Hello Canada, and hockey fans in the United States and Newfoundland. The score at the end of the first period is . . . " The games used to come on the air at nine o'clock in Toronto after an 8:30 start and that brought them to us in Winnipeg at 8 p.m. That's when we'd find out how the home team, *our* team, was doing.

Those pre-television broadcasts of Hewitt's had an enormous impact, one of the great advantages being that Foster's voice ignited a listener's imagination. There was no picture tube to bring in the game's warts. Foster continued to sit in his famous gondola doing his unique play-by-play for a couple of decades after his radio days, but the era before television enabled us listeners to see our heroes in the eyes of our minds and all of them were nine feet tall. They grew smaller on television.

Speaking for myself, I'd hear him in the early 1940s when I was working on the *Winnipeg Tribune* and living at 55 Donald Street. There, I shared a large comfortable room with a young broadcaster recently arrived from Saskatoon, Jack Wells, who became the celebrated Cactus Jack, the voice of the West. Around 1980 or so, some of Jack's friends organized a testimonial dinner for him in Winnipeg and *everybody* came, the lieutenant-governor, the mayor, stars of sports and entertainment. Speakers praised the contribution of Cactus Jack to sports in western Canada, but then it was the turn of a next-door neighbour to get to his feet at the head table, the token neighbourhood friend. This fellow praised Jack's humility in the face of his fame and lauded his earthiness. It became a trifle embarrassing. "All these famous people come to Jack's home but it doesn't change him," the man droned on. "Nothing has turned Jack's head through all these years. He's just a guy who treats everyone the same, rich or poor, unknown or famous – *shitty!*"

Jack and Foster became firm friends, as people will in the same line of work, but there was nothing about their personalities to suggest they should have followed similar paths. Wells was outgoing and gregarious, a golfer, a curler, a drinker of awesome capacity, fame, and longevity. Foster was a shy, conservative, reclusive man of celebrated parsimony. He spoke quietly with a soft lilt. It seemed incongruous that he was the owner of this powerful, resonant broadcast voice. Socially, he was pleasant and polite, with never a trace of self-importance. Wells used to go around at parties patting ladies' bottoms, then muttering, "Hells bells, they expect it. What can you do?" Foster would blush at the mere thought of such a gesture.

No broadcaster has yet invented a better way of saying that the puck has gone into the net than Foster's famous "He shoots! He scores!" but he maintained there was nothing dramatic about how he came by it. "It just seemed the easiest way to describe it," he'd say over and over. He was 83 when he died in April of 1985.

On another April afternoon, this one in 1978, in the lobby of the Inter-Continental Hotel in Prague, word of an upset back home reached a cluster of Canadian hockey scouts and scribes: the Toronto Maple Leafs had won the seventh and deciding game of a Stanley Cup playoff with the New York Islanders.

"Good for them," applauded Babe Pratt, an old Leaf

defenceman scouting for the Vancouver Canucks. "Who do they meet now?"

I leaned across the arm of my chair and told him, "The Canadiens."

"The *Canadiens*!" cried the Babe. "Holy shit, that's like bustin' your ass to get on the *Titanic*."

The Babe was no introvert. In his latter years he became a sort of tall King Clancy for the Canucks, not doing much but doing it with great enthusiasm. He didn't walk into any coffee bars and click his heels for the secretaries, but he might have had he not been 6-foot-4 and around 230. For a fact, he cheered everybody up with his adroit one-liners.

In his years with the Maple Leafs Babe worked in the off-season in the CPR yards and became known as the Honest Switchman because he never stole a boxcar. In his late teens he was an outstanding defence player for the Kenora Thistles in the Manitoba junior league, tall for his age and a good skater with a long reach.

The New York Rangers spotted him in 1936 when he was 20 and added him to a strong defence of Ching Johnson, Art Coulter, Ott Heller, and Joe Cooper. But these were times of two sets of defencemen, and with Johnson growing old the Ranger boss Lester Patrick felt young Pratt could be excellent insurance. Lester was right. Johnson broke down, a bald-headed thumper of 38, and the Babe moved into his position admirably. In the playoffs against Toronto that spring he was the hero of the deciding game when he scored the winner in overtime. A few nights later in Montreal he was a star again, scoring the game's only goal. In the spring of 1940 he helped the Rangers win their most recent Stanley Cup – 50 years without a drop of champagne! – and three seasons later Smythe got him in a trade. It was a trade that paid off handsomely in the spring of 1945 in the Detroit Olympia when Babe scored the goal that won the Stanley Cup in the seventh game of the final.

The goal kept the Maple Leafs in the record book for the next half-century because it prevented the Red Wings from duplicat-

ing the Toronto feat of coming back with four straight wins in
the final round after losing the first three games, the Leaf feat of
'42. In '45, with ulcer-ridden Frank McCool in goal, Toronto
won the opening three games on a mere four goals – by 1-0,
2-0, and 1-0. But back came the Wings with three wins, two of
them shutouts, so that the deciding game, in Detroit, owed its
outcome to Pratt's goal in a 2-1 win.

During this series Babe made his celebrated assessment of
King Clancy's skills as a referee. For a decade Clancy was
regarded as the NHL's most efficient referee. "Nobody can kid
me, I know all the tricks," Clancy used to say. "The ones I
didn't invent I stole."

But on this night Clancy seemed to be detecting far more
Toronto infringements than Detroit infractions, and on one
occasion with two Leafs occupying penalty-box pews and the
Wings none, Pratt happened to back hard into Referee Clancy,
sending him skidding across the ice.

"You long-legged son of a bitch," barked Clancy. "I'd like to
be playin' against you tonight!"

"Well," said Pratt, glancing at the penalty box, "ain't you?"

A year later the Babe was in deep trouble when NHL president Red Dutton suspended him on a charge of betting on
games. There was no evidence that Pratt had bet on Leaf games
but he writhed under a dark cloud until, after an appeal and a
further investigation, Dutton reinstated him.

So Babe traipsed through the days of retirement with an easy,
raised-eyebrows look at life. Anytime I ran into him in the
Pacific Coliseum out on North Renfrew Street or, if he was on
the road, at the cash box at Church and Carlton, his face would
light up and he'd grin and holler, "He-e-e-y, how you do-o-o-
in'?" and stick out a big mitt. He was like that with everybody
and then one night in the autumn of 1989 in the rink in
Vancouver he had a heart attack and that was that for the Babe.

When the novelist Hugh MacLennan wrote of hockey's ferocity
he may have had in mind the six-team league when defensive
play was rigorously emphasized. Body checking was in vogue,

fights were not uncommon, and the teams played in a hard, rugged manner but did very little hemstitching.

"No, not violent; that isn't the word," Sweeney Schriner told me in Calgary during the Winter Olympics in February of 1988. The old Leaf star settled there when he retired from hockey. He said the word he'd use to describe the play back then would be "chippy."

"You had to know how to use your elbows in the corners. But not the sticks. They were on the ice for the puck. You'd hear the referees say, 'If you raise that stick, you're gone.' So if it got a little rough in there, you'd bring up the elbows."

Hockey is the hardest game, nobody disputes that. It has the most collisions and, along with that, the players are armed with three lethal weapons – those sticks, razored skates, and flying frozen pucks. Accordingly, the game's normal flow produces its share of mayhem, and of course the gladiators are wearing equipment now that protects their heads, eyes, and teeth, something they seldom bothered with until the 1980s.

But the goons haven't disappeared. It doesn't seem to matter what new ways the rule-makers dream up to punish the miscreants, every team still has its roving brutes. Excesses creep in, too, the cross-checking from behind that pitchforks players into the boards, the high sticks that probe for openings, the blindside butt-ends that threaten the jawbones.

Outside Canada the game's critics still call hockey the dumbest game and the classic player image is that of a toothless oaf. In 1978, two years before the Atlanta Flames transferred to Calgary (they spent eight seasons in Georgia), a southern old boy named Paul Hemphill wrote in *Inside Sport* magazine of the game's appeal.

"The indigenous sports in the South have been football and stock-car racing and professional wrestling and, more recently, the roller derby. Each has two major ingredients, speed and unmitigated violence, whether genuine or orchestrated, and that is exactly what ice hockey has to offer. The Southern sports fan, steeped as he is in violence that goes all the way back to the Civil War and lynchings and such, eats it up."

Lynchings, yet.

The average American's curious view of hockey was one of the first things Wayne Gretzky noticed when he moved to the L.A. Kings. "It's very disappointing to see how the sportscasts and sports pages mock hockey down there," Wayne said in Toronto after a season in California.

The unmatched Bobby Orr, who appeared to have lost none of his public appeal approaching his 42nd birthday in March of 1990, was another who was dismayed by the developing excessive violence. Appearing at a sports symposium at the Ontario Science Centre in Toronto, Orr happened to arrive a few days after Vancouver's Rich Sutter was catapulted into the boards by a vicious cross-check from behind delivered by Philadelphia's youthful defence hulk, Craig Berube, in a game in Vancouver. To illustrate how Berube plays the game, as a rookie in Hershey in the 1986-87 season he played 63 games during which he scored seven goals and accumulated 325 minutes in penalties.

"If the NHL people can't see what's happening in hockey, then shame on them," Orr told a packed auditorium, amid cheers. "That check in Vancouver, that shouldn't be. That guy should go for a long time."

Sutter, who with his twin brother Ron is the youngest of the six NHL brothers from Viking, Alberta, narrowly avoided serious injury by bracing his crash with his left arm. He was taken from the ice on a stretcher, always a chilling sight.

Orr and Gretzky weren't the only highly regarded hockey figures concerned about the game's newly minted viciousness. Mike Bossy, the retired sharpshooter of the New York Islanders, produced a video in 1989 in which he called cross-checking from behind gutless and dangerous, and in Orr's appearance at the Ontario Science Centre the former Boston star gave total agreement.

At 42 Bobby Orr is the self-effacing fellow he was at half that age, one of those reticent Canadians. You never catch him looking anything but dapper, his mood ebullient. For the Science Centre he wore a dark grey suit, laundry-fresh white shirt, and narrow dark tie. His sandy hair was thick and groomed, his grin infectious as he answered questions from the floor with the joking modesty he carried through the 13-year career that was terminated by injured knees (six operations on his left one, one on the right). These days he lives in a Boston suburb with his wife Peggy and two teen-age sons, Darren and Brent, and dashes about seemingly oblivious to a slight limp.

"You want my biography?" he repeated a question from the throng. "You got a minute?" he grinned.

"Am I busy? Yes, I'm involved in some real estate, I do work for RJR Nabisco, I sit on the board of a bank, and I just made a nice arrangement with General Motors of Canada. The great thing is" – the grin again – "I don't get beat up any more."

"Do I have a secretary? Yes, only don't call her that. She's an administrative assistant, right?"

"No, I can't skate. I hurt my knee and I can't run. I'm hoping I can play a little golf." He grins. "I'm hoping I can break 100."

The smile left his pleasant face when he talked about hockey and he showed a real concern that the kids who play it nowadays don't get fun from it.

"Sometimes people will say, 'Oh, your sons don't play hockey. What a pity.' But I don't see it like that. My boys play baseball and football and they wrestle and they're doing okay in school. They're good kids."

I've known Bobby since he was a shy, earnest kid of 16 setting junior A scoring records for defencemen in the Ontario Hockey Association (later the OHL) for the Oshawa Generals. I went to see him to do a story for *Maclean's* and we sat in a booth in a coffee shop on the main drag and after about 20 minutes I'd run out of things to ask him. I mean, what *do* you talk about with an untroubled, modest lad of 16? He said he didn't read any of the things that were being written about him, he didn't want to get a swelled head.

I talked to his mom, Arva, and his dad, Doug, and a couple of the siblings at the family home in Parry Sound, a brother and three sisters as I remember, a warm, close family. One time when he was still a junior Bob got in a fight along the boards with a tough kid who played for Hamilton. While they tugged and heaved, a young woman scurried over the rows of seats down to the boards and walloped the Hamilton player across the head with her purse.

"You big brute," cried Bobby Orr's sister. "You leave Bobby alone!"

His sisters visited Bob occasionally when he went to Boston at 18 to play for the Bruins and lived in the house in the winter that the Red Sox manager, Dick Williams, rented in the summer.

Gerry Cheevers, the Boston goaltender, told me many times that Orr was a fiery competitor, an inspiration to the players. They knew how he suffered as the knee surgery mounted but he rarely showed it and never on purpose. "He'd go around the room before a game tapping each guy with a hockey stick, on the shin or the thigh, and say a couple of words. Guys would look at him and think, 'Okay, okay, let's go.' And we'd *go*."

How good was Bobby Orr?

"The best, the best ever," Phil Esposito used to say when they were teammates.

"He was in a class above the superstars," said John Ferguson, the Montreal enforcer.

"I played in the Orr era," said Don Awrey, who played beside him in Boston. "These other defencemen, like Denis Potvin, Brad Park, Larry Robinson, Serge Savard, Borje Salming, good as they were, they couldn't carry his skates."

Because the game took them down widely divergent paths, it usually comes as a surprise to hockey fans to learn that in the autumn of 1966 when Bobby Orr attended his first training camp with the Bruins, another rookie bent on cracking the lineup was Glen Sather.

Sather, known as Slats, has been the force that drives the Edmonton Oilers for so long that the fact he toiled for a decade in many NHL vineyards is all but forgotten. Come to think of it, apart from the Edmonton involvement his career was hardly memorable. Slats was five years older than the precocious Orr at the 1966 Bruin camp and after five games was dispatched to the

Oklahoma City farm. Then he bounced back for two seasons with Boston. Whereupon he was launched on sojourns with the Pittsburgh Penguins, the New York Rangers, the St. Louis Blues, the Montreal Canadiens, and the Minnesota North Stars, and then Peter Pocklington made him coach and vice-president of operations of the old World Hockey Association Edmonton Oilers in January of 1977.

Later on he became president and general manager of the Oilers and for a while he let his old sidekick, boisterous Bryan Watson, coach the team. As a couple of pugnacious NHL journeymen, Sather and Watson once were described by Gary Ronberg as "relatively small rogues." Ronberg, a cheerful blond fellow who worked for *Sports Illustrated*, an American weekly publication, before going straight and joining the *Philadelphia Inquirer*, also noted that this pair of sawed-off furniture movers "do not intimidate players but they have a knack of unnerving them with an impertinent word or gesture, an annoying slash or cross-check."

However, when his buddy Watson was unable to satisfy Sather as a coach, Slats fired him. "He figured his close and cherished friend wasn't ruthless enough," Peter Gzowski wrote in his 1981 book, *The Game of Our Lives*. "If my own brother was coaching this club, or playing on it, and it wasn't working out, I'd let him go, too," Gzowski quoted him. He took on the coaching job himself since he had a lot of free time when he wasn't doing whatever it is that presidents and general managers do, and held the three jobs until the 1989-90 season when he let his longtime assistant, snowcapped John Muckler, take over as the coach.

Sather made a nice move when Muckler won the Stanley Cup for the Oilers in his first try. This was in the spring of 1990, and Sather stayed completely in the background, letting his coach take the bows as the team returned to the pinnacle with a great playoff splurge after being down three games to one to the high-spirited Winnipeg Jets in the opening round. Then they rattled off 15 wins in their next 18 games, burying the Jets, Los Angeles, Chicago, and Boston along the way.

This came two years after the electrifying deal by which Oiler owner Peter Pocklington got $18 million from the Kings for Gretzky. This great player's departure was a traumatic experience for fans and teammates alike, but Sather, his hockey brain whirring, patiently filled the gap and saved the hide of the despised Pocklington. The bearded owner stayed largely out of sight as Sather slowly brought the team back to an even keel, but not surprisingly he was right there in the dressing room after the final victory over the Bruins. He was even interviewed on television by a *Hockey Night in Canada* announcer, who should have known better than to invite him on. I have no idea what he said; I nearly dislocated my thumb reaching for the off switch when he hove into view. Whatever he's paying Sather these days, it isn't enough.

In his playing days Slats had trouble scoring (80 goals in 10 seasons) but that fact never inhibited his confidence. His demeanour remains one of calm assurance. Sometimes you get the feeling you should make an appointment to say hello. He is enormously competitive and he is *good*.

For instance, back in 1984 when the very thought of a Russia-Canada hockey series gave people goose-bumps, Sather was the man picked by Alan Eagleson and Sam Pollock to lead the Canadian all-stars in the Canada Cup, a quadrennial six-country round-robin devised by Eagleson. It was a hairy moment for Canadian pride because in the final of the previous clash between the best hockey players in these two great hockey-playing countries, the Soviets had slammed the pride of Canada by 8-1 in a turkey in New York's Madison Square Garden.

Thus, when the giants clashed in Calgary's Saddledome in 1984 Sather's neck was in the noose because he had insisted on doing things his way – selection of players, style of play, the works. He took half a dozen guys from his Oilers as the nucleus and in the game that mattered most to Canada's hockey pride since away back in 1972 in Moscow, the Canadians beat the invaders by 3-2 in what some people were calling the game of all time.

With that victory Sather climbed up beside the hockey giants. In the spring of '84 his Oilers had ended the four-year reign of the New York Islanders in the Stanley Cup final and in September his hand-picked team had regained Canada's international prestige. By the time the summer of 1987 rolled around the Oilers had won the Stanley Cup twice more (they won a fourth in five years in the spring of '88) and it was obviously time that Sather be made immortal between hard covers.

It turned out that more than one genius besides me had come up with the idea – and much sooner. Unaware of this, I thought that before contacting Sather I'd better have something concrete to offer him so I called a publisher in Toronto and asked if he'd be interested in a book under Sather's name written by me. In due course my suggestion of an advance of $50,000 was agreed upon and I set out to enlist Sather's concurrence.

He was not an easy person to track down that summer but eventually I caught up to him on the phone in a high-priced Vancouver hotel and laid out the plan. I would visit Edmonton periodically through the fall and winter of 1987-88, taping material in sessions with him, and the book would be published in the fall of '88. He didn't say yes and he didn't say no. What he did say was that he had read his share of this kind of sports autobiography and he didn't think much of it. Besides, he added, he didn't think what he had to say was particularly interesting anyway.

I suggested he mull it over and I'd call him in a week. By this time, early autumn had arrived and NHL teams had begun training. It happened that Edmonton was opening the exhibition season in Maple Leaf Gardens and when I called Sather for a decision he said he'd let me know when he arrived in Toronto. I caught up to him at a screening of a film that had been made of the Oilers by Bob McKeown called *Boys on the Bus*.

"Well, what do you think?" I asked.

"Oh, I don't know," he answered in his laid-back way. "It's not much of an idea."

"I think it would make a pretty good book," I said.

"Other guys have mentioned it," he said. "Gzowski mentioned it. Scott Young mentioned it."

"Nothing but the best," I said. "And now me."

"And the money isn't much," he said. "I'm not knocked out by it."

"Okay then," I said. "We can drop it."

"I haven't said I'm dropping it," he said. "Are you going to the game tomorrow night?"

Good God, I hadn't been in Maple Leaf Gardens for two years with the team so lousy and the owner such a windbag, and now I'd have to go to watch an exhibition to placate this guy.

"I *can* go," I said.

"Okay, I'll see you at the game tomorrow and let you know."

So I went to the Gardens the next night and from a perch in the press box up near the ceiling I scanned the Oiler bench but couldn't see Sather. John Muckler was there, but no Sather.

I walked along the press box to find Bill Tuele, the Oilers' public relations director.

"Bill," I said, "where's Slats sitting? I don't see him at the bench."

"He's in Indianapolis," Tuele said.

"Indian*apolis*?"

"Yeah, we're going there from here. He went at four o'clock."

"I was supposed to see him here. Did he leave a message?"

"Nope. Didn't say anything to me. I can give you his number in Indianapolis."

I called the publisher the next day and told him to forget the Sather book.

"He's declined to be immortalized," I said.

As it turned out, it's just as well Slats took off for Indianapolis. If we'd done the book I'd have finished the manuscript in the spring of 1988 and it would have been on the presses in the late summer. There would not have been a thing in it about a trade the Oilers made on August 9 that involved a skinny centre named, er, I had it right here. Ah yes, Gretzky.

Chapter 11

The gentlemen's game

Golf can be a humbling game, no question about that, but it is a marvelous game for the egos of champions. All their lives they hear the roar of the crowd, for no crowds are more appreciative of their heroes than golf crowds.

Gene Sarazen slowly climbs the hill that leads to the ninth green at the Augusta National Golf Club. Gene Sarazen is 82 years old at this time. Forty-nine years earlier he holed a 220-yard 4-wood for double eagle on the last day of the Masters tournament and then he beat Craig Wood in a playoff.

That was in 1935 and now here he comes puffing up the hill, a roly-poly little fellow looking wonderfully dapper in a white porkpie hat, a white V-neck sweater over a dark turtleneck, the plus fours he is famous for in a light shade of brown, dark brown woollen stockings, and brown and white golf shoes. On both sides of the fairway people are acknowledging him, smiling in warm affection and clapping their hands. His dark features brighten into a wide grin and he touches the brim of his porkpie, an old, *old* man still hearing that lovely applause.

It happens every spring, if not to Gene Sarazen then to some other legendary names in golf, such as Byron Nelson or Sam

Snead or Arnold Palmer or Jack Nicklaus, players who have either tottered into the PGA Senior Tour or, like Sarazen and Nelson and Snead, have retreated to the shadows. It doesn't matter how they're hitting them now, the applause is there whenever they lace up their golf shoes and venture out of doors.

The Masters may be the most elegant tournament on earth, and it is assuredly played amid the most breathtakingly beautiful floral surroundings. The first Masters was contested there in 1934 on property picked out by the master, Bobby Jones, on the outskirts of the sleepy little Georgia town of Augusta. But even with so brief a history it has accumulated a rich sheen of tradition.

Each spring, for instance, two or three of yesteryear's luminaries are accorded the honour of teeing off first and playing nine holes to launch the tournament. Twice when I was at the Masters Sarazen and Snead were the twosome, another time it was Snead and Nelson, and the fourth time there were all three of them.

Sharp at 8:30 on the morning of the first round the crowds have already formed a multicoloured avenue all the way to the first green, nestled 425 yards from the elevated tee in a horseshoe of tall pines. Indeed, there have been lineups at area restaurants as early as 7 a.m.

On this particular cloudless morning, Sarazen is partnered by Snead. He doffs that porkpie hat to acknowledge his introduction, tees up his ball, steps back, and hits it. No practice swing, no waggle, just bang. And off the ball climbs, 190 yards, maybe 200, down the middle.

Now Snead steps up. He is wearing a light brown straw hat with a wide flowered band, the sort of hat that has been his trademark since at least 1939. That was the year I saw him first at the Spring Mill course outside Philadelphia leading the field at the 72nd hole of the United States Open. I still have the clipping from the *Winnipeg Tribune* of the piece I wrote of Sam's celebrated disaster.

He needed only a par five on the final hole for a 283 total and the championship (we'll be back at the Masters in a moment) and instead he took an eight. "More than 10,000 witnessed the catastrophe," penned the *Tribune*'s man on the scene. "Sam's drive hooked to a trap 250 yards out. He blasted with a 7-iron from there and topped the ball, staying in the trap. Then he tried again. The pellet soared into another beach near the green. Sam finally reached the carpet and then three-putted, failing on his seventh shot from two feet.

"'It's just like Bobby Jones once remarked,' said the dethroned champion, Ralph Guldahl. 'The Open isn't won, it's lost. I've seen a lot of blowups in my time but none so complete as that. Recollection of that 18th hole will always be a mental hazard to Sam.'"

Guldahl turned out to be a pretty good prophet. Sam won 84 tournaments in his years on tour, including the British Open, the Masters three times, the PGA three times, and the Canadian Open three times, but, though he was four times the runner-up in the U.S. Open, he never did manage to win it. (By the way, Byron Nelson won that 1939 Open and first prize of $1,000. The runner-up, Craig Wood, earned $800. These days, caddies make 10 times as much.)

However, in spite of Snead's failure in his own country's Open, it's always said that no golfer owned a sweeter swing. And on this morning at Augusta when he played the ceremonial nine with Sarazen, he swung his arms past an imposing front porch in a slowed replica of his once matchless driving form and knocked his ball well past Sarazen's.

"When I was 75," Sarazen said drily, "I could do that, too."

Few players were more competitive than Eugene Saraceni, who once said he renamed himself so he wouldn't be mistaken for a violinist. People who knew him when say his game was more an expression of emotion than technique. He was aggressive and challenging, even pugnacious.

I found that out. I spotted him early one afternoon on a clubhouse balcony and in an impulsive instant asked him if he'd spare a few moments.

He scowled. "I've just had my lunch, I want to sit quiet," he said crustily. Then, perhaps hearing his tone, he smiled the smile that transforms his leathery kisser. "I'm 82," he said softly.

Later that day he felt rested and talked with a large circle of scribes. He said he was amazed by the size of the purses these days. He remembered winning the British Open at the Prince's course in England in 1932 and collecting $500. We restrained ourselves from passing a hat for the little man in the knowledge that golf has made his life warm and comfortable. He lives in Florida and plays a leisurely nine holes a couple of times a week (or was doing so, anyway, when he hit 85). In the mid-1960s he was a television host for a golf series for Shell Oil that was enormously popular, taking him to courses around the world and rekindling his celebrity.

"Hosting that show exposed me to the world for 10 years and gave me great business contacts," he told us. "I never thought I'd be paying the income taxes I'm paying today. In the old days we didn't pay *any* taxes." He brought out that wry smile again. "Of course," he added, "we didn't make any money, either."

Another of the traditions of the Masters is the annual par-three competition that falls on the Wednesday before Thursday's opening round. The event is played on what surely must be the most picturesque par-three course on God's green footstool. And if the weather happens to be a trifle on the cool side, the pros slip into something comfortable, such as $400 cashmere sweaters in pastels of every hue. Imagine them strolling from tee to green beside lovely outcroppings of azaleas, shoulder high bushes of exploding colour in three blazing shades of pink – hot pink, orange pink, and plain old pink pink.

The par-three course borders two man-made ponds, the nine greens banked high with spectators, most of them sprawled comfortably on the manicured grass. Here, too, are Georgia dogwoods, slender boughs adorned in white and pale pink blossoms. And intermittently there are clumps of towering pines, straight as telephone poles and three times taller, their lower branches stripped away so that from a distance they resemble a forest of giant mushrooms.

I was sitting on a little hillock beside Rick Fraser of the

Toronto Star on one of the cool Wednesdays and we decided to document the colours of the strolling peacocks. Here was Arnold Palmer in Augusta's traditional green, sweater and slacks, there was Seve Ballesteros, the caballero from Spain, a vision in brown fitted slacks and a salmon cashmere V-neck.

The conservative Tom Watson predictably wore a navy blue sweater, Ray Floyd glowed in flamingo, and Hale Irwin was buoyant in burgundy. Jack Nicklaus, who at age 46 won his sixth Masters title in 1986, nodded and smiled to repeated applause as he moved along the water's brim from hole to hole in navy shirt, navy V-neck, and navy slacks, flaxen hair falling in careful disarray across the deep, sun-kissed furrows of his forehead. This day, though, Rick and I decided the prize had to go to Fuzzy Zoeller and Hubert Green, both former Masters winners, resplendent in yellow V-neck cashmeres, paddy-green plus fours, and yellow ribbed stockings.

One of the things that makes the Masters special, at least for snow-blinded Canadians, is its timing. It is a kiss of spring, a bursting reminder early each April that winter has made its overdue exit. Within the high fences and dense hedges that surround what Alistair Cooke has called "the most majestic inland course on earth," the springtime tapestry of tall pines and bursting flowers arrives straight from heaven.

Within this 365-acre enclosure a northern visitor is sure to take an extra deep breath coming upon a tiny cluster of holes on the back nine called Amen Corner. It is a nesting ground for the magnolia blossoms and flowery popcorn of azaleas that comprise the bottom half of the 11th hole, the short 12th over the bluest of streams (the water is dyed for TV), and the first half of the dogleg 13th. The middle hole, the par-three 12th, has a green that is banked to the sky in flowers and fern, a veritable rajah's bier. Nicklaus once called it "the hardest tournament hole in golf." Fuzzy Zoeller said it was "the spookiest little par-3 we play." It's a gorgeous 155-yarder with this babbling brook in front and a grove of tall pines swaying behind. Of it, sportswriter Rick Reilly once said that more green jackets have been lost at the 12th than at the Augusta City Dry Cleaners.

At the Masters you hear a great deal about Amen Corner because it's a segment that can decide championships. What you don't often hear is why the demanding holes are called Amen Corner. Lorne Rubenstein, who may be the best golf writer on earth – books, magazines, and a twice-weekly column in the *Globe* – wrote once that "the famous three holes were so named, according to legend, because the golfer who gets through the stretch safely believes a little more in God."

Rube could have gone farther, had he chosen, because of a circumstance that followed the 1986 Masters, the one in which Nicklaus, a ripe 46, scored his surprising victory. On Sunday evening Lorne and I, having finished our work, drove into slumbering Augusta for dinner and settled in the dining room of the Hilton Hotel. There, a few tables away, sat the golf sage of *The New Yorker*, Herbert Warren Wind, whom both of us knew. When we saw he was alone we invited him to join us.

There is no more modest or courtly man on earth than Herb Wind, a sort of tweedy, pipe-smoking fellow, the kind of person central casting would send over to play the headmaster of a private school. I'd read somewhere that he was the first to call the three holes Amen Corner, and he confirmed after we'd ordered our dinner that he'd done so in 1958. The outcome that year had hinged, in Wind's mind, on how Arnold Palmer played the 12th and 13th holes on the final day.

After heavy rain, Palmer's tee shot at the 12th was embedded in a muddy bank. A local rule permitted him to lift the ball and drop it clear but the official at the hole, apparently unfamiliar with the newly instituted rule, told Palmer to play the embedded ball. He did, had difficulty, and took a five. Then, on his own, he dropped a ball, played it, and made three. Later, his second ball was ruled legal for a three, and on the next hole, the 13th, he made eagle three.

"Those two holes, and a well-played par at 11, were the keys to his victory," Wind told us, dabbing the corners of his mouth with a linen napkin. "I felt I should come up with an appropriate name for the three holes."

He quickly discarded coffin corner and hot corner and then,

searching his brain, he remembered the title of a song on an old Bluebird 78-rpm record by a clarinetist named Mezz Mezzrow. The song was "Shouting in the Amen Corner." In this fashion, legendary names are born.

At any rate, the beauty of Amen Corner and the rest of the course, together with the relaxed and soft-voiced ambiance of the Deep South, are attractions in themselves in springtime. I suddenly remember how I jumped at a Rubenstein suggestion that he and I walk the course in the early morning of Sunday's final round. It was a day that broke cloudless and windless, the air fresh as new-mown hay. We walked every yard of the undulating, 6,905-yard landscape, and on almost every hole, especially on the back nine, Rube had a tale to tell. He is a black-bearded giant in his early 40s, a golf scholar and former curator of the Royal Canadian Golf Association's museum at the Glen Abbey course near Oakville, Ontario. He knew that Arnold Palmer had once described his favourite hole, the 13th in the Amen trio, as "a joy to behold and a challenge to play" – a dogleg left where the drive must skim tall pines and clear a winding brook for the short route home. A duffer can play his tee shot safely to the right, lay up short of the brook as it passes in front of the green, then, on a good day, hit the green in three, giving him a fighting chance at a bird by one-putting.

"Palmer calls this hole the strategic design of Bobby Jones at his best," Lorne said. "It rewards the gambler while giving the average guy a chance."

In 1930 when Bobby Jones won golf's Grand Slam – the British Open and Amateur and the U.S. Open and Amateur – he and an assortment of friends purchased these 365 acres we were walking. They then hired a Scottish golf architect, Dr. Alister Mackenzie, and assigned him to build this course under the pines.

To ward off riff-raff such as real-estate developers and sports scribes, Jones and friends turned their course into a private club. Once a year, beginning in 1934, a select number of touring professional golfers and deserving amateurs and past champions were (and are) invited to play the course. Unwashed outsiders are allowed past the gate guards and behind a tall green fence that surrounds the property for this one week a year to watch the tournament.

Strictly speaking, fans come by invitation only. They're called patrons and each January an application for tickets is mailed to them, thousands of them. In 1971 the list of patrons was closed and a waiting list begun. When the waiting list reached 5,000 in 1978 it was closed. Now the only way a newcomer gets in is if a patron expires or otherwise relinquishes his grip. Patrons pay $60 for the four days of the tournament. Ordinary mortals can watch practice rounds Monday and Tuesday for $10 each; they can watch the par-three event on Wednesday for $15.

Scribes get in because from the beginning the Masters catered to print guys. I love the place because it's the only sports event left on earth where the sponsors don't faint at the sight of a television camera. At Augusta we have our own press building where tournament leaders or guys who shoot hot rounds are brought for interviews. Television people wait their turn in their own cubbyhole. Radio guys aren't allowed in our work area, either. It's wonderful.

In spite of the exclusive nature of the Masters toward the general public, there's a courtesy about the tournament that's damned near unreal. Even the marshals are polite. The ambiance is epitomized by a message from the master himself, Bobby Jones, reprinted on the back of each Masters ticket:

"Most distressing to those who love the game of golf is the applauding or cheering of misplays or misfortunes of a player. Such occurrences have been rare but we must eliminate them entirely if our patrons are to continue to merit their reputations as the most knowledgeable and considerate in the world."

While the Jones civility doesn't precisely permeate golf, golfers as a group are the most rewarding athletes to interview (ballplayers are the worst). World-class performers such as Nicklaus, Curtis Strange, Tom Watson, Greg Norman, Jeff Sluman, and Paul Azinger, to name a handful, go to pains to present comprehensive answers to often vague questions. Once, at the Masters, I had this idea of writing a piece about choking, not an easy topic to bring up before a player who's just apt to.

Tom Watson, winner of the British Open five times, the Masters twice, and the U.S. Open once, was seated on the podium before the general questioning began. I scurried up beside him and said quietly, "I don't like to ask this out loud, but I was wondering if you have any thoughts on, you know, how golfers sometimes tighten up."

"You mean choke?" he said, grinning.

"Well, yeah."

"That's a good topic. Do you mind waiting until we're through here and then we can talk about it?"

I was astonished by the consideration this champion was showing a stranger. I said I'd wait, all right.

The thing is, in the big games the easy part is playing well when you're behind. What's there to lose? The hard part is doing it when you're narrowly ahead. Learning to win is a difficult process. Choke is a word that carries the unsavoury connotation of crumbling under pressure, of failing when tested, of quitting under fire.

But Tom Watson said this day that the definition is unfair. He said everybody chokes. He said choking is a hazard to be acknowledged on the road to the winner's enclosure. Choking is anxiety, and until a person learns to deal with this anxiety it causes tension and costs composure.

So, since he was a champion, I asked him how he deals with it.

"Well, physically, by breathing deeply, for one thing," he said. Rising, he placed his arms wide, hands limp, and waggled them. "I shake my arms. I literally try to shake myself calm."

He sat again, looking thoughtful. "Mentally, it's another matter. I'm not into Zen but I imagine that something like it would help. The best I can do is try to have positive thoughts and realize in critical situations that the adrenalin is pumping, and profit by it. Like, I'll switch to a shorter club. If I'd normally take a 5-iron I'll switch to a 6. Things like that. Does that help you any?"

Did Curtis Strange choke in the 1985 Masters? Probably not, for it was in the opening round, not in the tense moments of the finishing holes (though that came later) that Curtis shot a round that endeared him to all the world's hackers – an 80.

He booked a ticket home, then had to cancel it when he came back with 65 on the Friday. By Sunday at the 13th tee on Amen Corner, Curtis had a three-shot lead on the field. Then the sky began falling.

I don't know where you'll find a more personable fellow than Curtis. He seems genuinely glad to see you. He smiles, showing a great set of teeth, and runs a hand awkwardly across crisp, greying hair. By the time he reached the Glen Abbey course for the Canadian Open three months after his disaster at Augusta, Curtis was ready to talk in his soft Virginia accent about how he blew the Masters he had in his calloused mitts.

At that 13th hole he had pasted a drive high across the trees on the left that create the dogleg. So with his three-shot lead he didn't need to make the long, accurate shot required to cross a stream fronting on the green. He could have laid up short, then pitched on and made his par with two putts.

But, no, Curtis had done a lot of gambling recovering from that opening-round 80 so he wasn't about to quit now. He hauled out a 4-wood and *whack*! soon followed by *splash*! He pulled on his rain suit, waded into the stream, and, with a brilliant foray into the deep, made the green and wound up with a bogey.

Two holes later he was back in the drink, this time miscalculating his second shot, landing on the far bank of a pond, then slithering back into the water. This time he lifted the ball, taking a penalty stroke, and lost his lead to the eventual winner, Bernhard Langer, the German.

Discussing this downfall later at Glen Abbey, Curtis was philosophical, the smile back in place, the accent a lilt. "What a story it would have been, coming back from 80," he enthused.

"That would have been kind of neat. For you guys, for me, for everybody."

Would he make the same club selection if he could play the two shots again.

"Hey," Curtis Strange chuckled. "Hindsight is 20/20. That's where you guys shine."

Far, far from the Masters or Glen Abbey or any North American course, for that matter, golf is a vastly different game in the British Open, the granddaddy of all the classic tournaments. It's played on links, the wild area that actually "links" coastal land with the sea. Courses in many parts of England, Ireland, and Scotland are built on seaside links.

Some say that St. Andrews, with its majestic royal and ancient clubhouse, is the most loved British course and some say Prestwick is the quaintest. Storied Muirfield, 20 miles outside Edinburgh, is often described simply as the finest course, but this doesn't mean that there's a similarity between it and anything on this side of the Atlantic.

Talk about history. I got to Muirfield in July of 1987 for the 116th British Open to learn that the club, whose full title is the Honourable Company of Edinburgh Golfers, is recognized as the oldest in the world, with records that date back continuously to 1744, the year the very first rules of golf were laid down.

If this title conjures up visions of plumed knights in shining breastplates defending great stone castles in battle against infidels, forget it. Muirfield lies on the fringes of the little town of Gullane on the North Sea and there's not a castle or a moat or even a guy waving a pennant for miles around.

As you approach the course in a rented car and bumpety-bump-bump across a parking lot of deep, tangled grass you're confronted by a tent village bordering the length of the 445-yard first hole. Once, the tents were confined to sponsors displaying golf equipment. Now, with flags and canvas snapping in a stiff wind, the tent village resembles a huge country fair, with everything available from Scotch whisky to large succulent baked potatoes, their middles lavished with chunks of butter or garnished with cheese or brown beans or chili or kernels of yellow corn.

The tents form a long avenue paralleling that first hole, and I was a trifle startled to observe that the first five display tents across from the baked-potato window were banks – the Royal Bank of Scotland, the Trustee Savings Bank, the National Westminster Bank, the Bank of Scotland, and the Clydesdale Bank. The Trustee Savings Bank featured a walkway bordered by pink and red geraniums, so I went in and asked a tall young woman greeting visitors what it said about Scotland that *five* display tents in a row were banks.

"Why, it says that we're tight with our money!" laughed this dark-haired woman, who said her name was Jacqui McFarlane. And then her compatriot, John Tynen, spelled his name and poured a wee jigger of Bell's Scotch for the visitor. "Aye, laddie," he said, "Jacqui's right. Here, wet yer whistle."

Back of the tent village and beyond the golf course, the North Sea lay flat and grey in the distance. The course itself was a billowing confusion of dunes, thickly grown with shrubbery and tall coarse grass except where the architects had cut out fairways. I trudged along a path where the grass seemed relatively short, smelling the frying onions wafting from a concession tent, when suddenly a voice cried, "Git off the fairway, ye! There's golfers comin'!"

Banking left, I could see spectators in the distance climbing through the gorse and thistle of a hillock and as they crossed the crest they slowly disappeared, their legs, their waists, their shoulders, their heads dropping from view.

And surely in no other land are there such bunkers. These aren't the sloped mini-Saharas that North Americans are accustomed to; these are bomb craters with sheer walls, 10 feet and more in diameter and four or five feet deep. A guy as tall as the skinny American Paul Azinger, 6-foot-2, goes down there to whack out a ball and all you can see of him is his head. And there are 165 of these craters at Muirfield.

In the second round Arnold Palmer dropped into one at the 449-yard 14th hole and by the time he surfaced and at last got his ball into the cup he'd made 10. Arnie's Army, U.K. division, winced as he dug at his ball four times in this bunker. When he emerged he was wearing a sheepish grin that appeared and quickly disappeared.

On the third day, the Saturday, the celebrated wind off the North Sea struck. Wind, especially North Sea wind, is one of the classic obstacles of life in the British Open. This day a fierce northeast wind came in off the sea carrying vicious slanting rain and an icy chill. The players wore woollen toques and shiny rain-suits and between shots they pulled on thick mitts and leaned against the wind walking to the balls. Sometimes in the shooting they'd see a ball start off well and suddenly be whooshed away by sudden gusts and slammed into the clutching grass and gorse of the rough or into one of the dreaded bunkers. I saw the great iron player, Greg Norman, hack at his ball three times to get it onto the fairway from hips-high blowing grass.

But the Scots have an astonishing dedication to the game. Driving from Edinburgh to Muirfield that wet wild Saturday morning I passed a public course and out on the fairways, leaning into the wind, golfers were trudging along, tugging their carts, actually playing recreational rounds and obviously not discouraged by the wet gale.

Days this ferocious are rare, surely, but on the links courses that border the sea there is almost always wind. Indeed, there's the story of a Muirfield member playing one rare calm day, having a bad round, and being overheard to mutter, "How the devil can a man be expected to swing a club when there's nothing to lean against?"

So, as I say, golf is a different game in the British Open, a point that was made by Tom Watson, who started off with a pair of 69s before fading at this 116th Open.

"I not only learned to love the linksland courses, I learned how to play them," said the man who has won this classic five times. "I had always hit the ball like this (sweeping his right arm, he indicated the top half of a Ferris-wheel arc), while the British players were hitting it like this (now, palm down, he sweeps the arm straight and low). You have to play it under the wind and let it hit and bounce to the green. If you try to bounce it up on American grass, it stops."

This time, a native son won the tournament. Nick Faldo hit 18 straight pars on the final day. The lean American, Azinger, needed only two pars on the last two holes to turn the trick but he drove into a fairway bunker on the 17th and caught a manhole beside the green on the 18th. Each time he lost a shot, and Faldo did exactly what was printed on the Muirfield scorecard – 36 out, 35 in, par 71.

Was Azinger crestfallen? No. He didn't jump up and cheer by any means, but he said something that every golfer, even the hackers, has thought at one time or another: "It was a learning experience."

That's how most golfers feel, for golf is one game that induces the notion that the next round will be a better round. It encourages a dreamer to relive his fantasies, even *old* dreamers. An old pitcher finds that his changeup has become his fastball, an old defenceman trips on the blueline, and an old quarterback can only remember when. But golfers, well, now that they've found this new bonanza, the PGA Senior Tour, they've discovered that fans are demanding they return for a curtain call.

Their prime time may be behind them but these over-50s continue to amaze and astound the galleries with their shot-making. "Hitting the ball doesn't change," George Knudson observed one afternoon in the summer of 1987. "Once you know how to hit it, you can hit it."

George Knudson, now there was a player. George was probably the best Canada has had, George and Stan Leonard and the current star, bulky Dave Barr. None of them, as far as I know, ever got to the British Open, but certainly Knudson's eight tournament wins on the U.S. Tour were the best by any Canadian. Back in the late 1960s, look out for George. He won the New Orleans Classic in 1967 and then back-to-back titles in the spring of '68 in the Phoenix Open and the Tucson Open. A year later he was in a four-way closing thriller at the Masters with Tom Weiskopf, Billy Casper, and George Archer. Archer beat George by one shot to win it.

George had the cheery, optimistic philosophy that belongs to good golfers but he differed from most of them in that he felt the game was an end in itself. I mean, winning wasn't everything; hitting properly was. People used to stop and stare when George addressed a golf ball. Jack Nicklaus once told Lorne Rubenstein that George owned a million-dollar swing and Rube wrote in the foreword of a book he wrote with George, *The Natural Golf Swing*, that many knowledgeable people told him George swung the club better than anybody since Ben Hogan.

But therein lay the strength and the weakness in George's game: he loved to swing the club but he hated the drudgery of putting. He was a guy who pursued a flawless golf swing with passion but had no time for prodding a ball along a carpet with a boring little pat.

Perhaps George could have made that million Nicklaus saw in his swing if he'd had the patience to study the putt, but, since he hadn't, he didn't brood about it. "I got what I deserved," George conceded once at a golf school he'd set up at the Buttonville course on Toronto's northeastern fringes.

Anyway, when George hit 50 in June of 1987 he planned heading out on that Senior Tour that was catching on with golf fans. His three boys were grown, Kevin, who was 25 then, Paul, 22, and Dean, 17, so George and his strawberry-haired wife Shirley were on their way, he figured.

But what he didn't figure on – who does? – was lung cancer. I met with him and Lorne and a couple of others one noon-time in a Japanese restaurant called Sasaya in Toronto, a restaurant that George claimed served sushi almost as good as he had enjoyed many times during his 13 visits to Japan as a pro golfer. This day, he ordered for all of us, surrounding us with little cylinders of rice and cucumber that featured shrimp, trout, tuna, yellowtail, and salmon.

"Hm-m-m, hm-m-m, good!" George purred, the ivory chopsticks clicking. All through lunch George had this optimistic attitude I've mentioned as being normal for good golfers, this positive outlook.

"I'm feeling fine now," George said. "Some people say the disease is in recession. I don't believe that recession crap. If you've got cancer, you've got cancer. You get checkups for the rest of your life to see how you're doing."

I remembered the first time I saw George, maybe 25 years earlier at the practice field of the Oakdale Golf Club in Toronto. I'd gone there to do a piece about this slim, freckled, young guy who'd arrived from Winnipeg with magic in his woods and irons. Even then he was puffing these damned cigarettes he never seemed to be without. You'd see him on the golf course between shots, hurrying along the fairway in quick, short strides, smoke streaming out behind from a cigarette in the middle of his mouth.

This day at Oakdale he might have hit a thousand shots. Truthfully, his fingers were wrapped in white strips of tape through which blood had seeped in four or five places.

"Watch this," he said once. He hit 12 balls in a row with a 4-wood, alternately hooking one and fading one, all of them taking off in a high curving line to the left or to the right and six on each side winding up reasonably close to each other.

George made one trip to the Senior Tour when he partnered Johnny Pott in a two-man best-ball event called the Legends in Texas in April of 1988, and he planned returning to the tour in the fall. But he didn't feel well enough to go, and on January 24, 1989, that was it for George.

Not all the guys in golf are Mr. Nice Guy, of course, and not all the Mr. Nice Guys are *terrific* nice guys. In the summer of 1989 when the game's caravan reached Glen Abbey for the Canadian Open, Ken Green, the defending champion, and Curtis Strange, who had just won his second U.S. Open in a row, grew a trifle miffed facing a quizzical assortment of Canadian scribes (and a handful of blank-faced American ones) when called to account for playing in a highly controversial event in South Africa.

Green, who is a chubby bespectacled chatterbox, said he'd enjoyed the experience. "I met a couple of baboons and had a great time," he reported. For his part, Strange pointed a finger at the guy who'd posed the question.

"We are here to play golf, not involve ourselves in politics," lectured Curtis. "I have won your national championship twice and I'm proud of it. That's all I'm going to say." A little later he had a little more to say. "I do what's best for Curtis Strange," said Curtis Strange.

Not involving themselves in politics, eh? Like many others, Curtis seemed to have the notion that there is no place for politics in sports. But what sense does that make? This tournament in South Africa, called the Sun City Invitational, is an annual affair on a course designed by Gary Player, the South African golfer, at Sun City, a sports and gambling resort in the tribal homeland of Bophuthatswana. The total purse in 1989 was $1,650,000 in U.S. funds, a nice round one million of it for the winner. If there is nothing so crass as politics in this four-day event, why do you suppose there's a spectacular first prize in a meaningless exhibition? Surely it isn't to draw the names that can attract attention to a country slavering for international acceptance. No indeedy.

Ken Green chimed in with his two cents' worth (if I'm not over-pricing his contribution) by whining, "Up here seems to be the only place anybody's worrying about political implications. Nobody in the States is worked up about it."

Maybe that's the fault, in part at least, of disinterested U.S. golf-writing camp followers who write of nothing but birdies and eagles. However, there's no question that some American athletes are concerned, such as the bushy-browed, conscientious tennis player, Tim Mayotte. In December of 1987 Mayotte missed out on the rich Masters tournament in New York open to only the top eight money winners on the Grand Prix circuit. He missed because he refused to play an event in South Africa, sacrificing a chance to win a quarter of a million dollars.

Writing about Mayotte in the *New York Times* a year later, columnist Ira Berkow described a thoughtful man. "Maybe the only person who cares that I didn't go was me," Mayotte was quoted. "But I went once, in 1983, and felt pretty bad about it afterward. I decided I'd never go again, no matter what. It may only be a small way but it's the only way I know that I can protest."

Mayotte was a student at Stanford University looking for money and experience when he went to South Africa in 1983. What bothered him once he got there, among other things, were signs on the washroom doors, Coloured Only and White Only.

"Everyone knows that blacks simply have no control over their future there," he told Berkow. "All you have to do is put yourself in their shoes to feel the disgust and rage that they must feel. The reason South Africa wants to hold sports events is to try to be a part of the international political community. They seek stature in those tournaments that they don't get in other areas." This was true even after the release of Nelson Mandela after 27 years in prison, for following the early euphoria that greeted his release riots and the subjugation of blacks continued.

Obviously, the chance of winning a million dollars while playing golf and being treated like a visiting potentate for a week are attractions a lowly scribe can only imagine, but the golfers who have been lured to that Godforsaken country are wealthy people already – Mark O'Meara, Lee Trevino, Seve Ballesteros, Lanny Wadkins, David Graham, Hubert Green, Sandy Lyle, T.C. Chen, Chip Beck, Don Pooley, Bernhard Langer, scarcely a man among them who hasn't won his million by now. Pro golfers are a bright and articulate lot so you have to assume it is through indifference or selfishness that some of them go on traipsing off to South Africa to brighten the darkest tournament on earth with scant concern for the harm they do.

Some golfers question the impact an individual can make on an issue so widespread and fundamental, so I took the matter to

Michael Valpy, who returned to the *Globe and Mail* after a four-year stint as the paper's correspondent in Johannesburg and then returned for a six-week tour in April of 1990. I asked him if sports matters over there and Mike said nothing touches the average South African quicker. "Sports can put more pressure on the government than any other outside influence," he said. "That's why they're desegregating sports now. The people are sports mad. There's no question the whites prosper if name golfers go there."

For a long time many people argued that as long as repressive Soviet troops occupied Afghanistan it was inconsistent for Canada to ban competition with South Africans while applauding it with hockey-playing Soviets. That argument turned to smoke when the Soviet troops went home.

I can look back 25 years or so to an afternoon I stood in the locker room at the Scarborough Golf Club in Toronto and listened to Gary Player talking about something called apartheid, a word I'd only vaguely heard. He explained with an air of resignation that it was pointless to go into a discussion of the topic because Canadians simply didn't understand anything about the situation in or politics of South Africa.

A quarter of a century later, many South Africans were uttering the same complaint. In the late 1980s the Canadian government began a policy of refusing to issue visas to South African athletes, which meant that a fine golfer from there, David Frost, couldn't cross the border from the U.S. to play in the 1988 Canadian Open. Similarly, if Gary Player had wanted to come to this country, as he had many times before, he wouldn't have qualified for a visa.

The South African tennis star Kevin Curren, now an American citizen, told us scribes who were critics of apartheid that we were "ignorant." This was in 1988 when we'd had time to think about it. He said the visa law made no sense. "It makes no impact whatsoever on South African policy."

So for 25 years, from Player to Curren, South African athletes have been telling us how misunderstanding we are. The way they see it, the rest of the world has been wrong about a system in which 4 million whites dominate and subjugate 18 million blacks. It never seems to occur to these wealthy tourists that maybe the rest of the world is right now and then. They pay lip service to the injustice of apartheid but they do nothing about it except criticize the efforts of people such as Tim Mayotte who try.

Based on the law forbidding visas, a point I used to try to make in the *Globe* was that if an accident of birth keeps the David Frosts and the Gary Players out of Canada, it should also deny visas to non-South Africans such as the wealthy Ken Greens who blithely go over there to play, attracting favourable attention from whatever segment of the universe follows sports.

Oddly enough, although prime ministers from the time of Sir John A. Macdonald have leaped to attention whenever I've rattled my spoon on my high-chair, the current legislators in Ottawa haven't yet embarked upon this typically brilliant suggestion.

Chapter 12

The not-so-sweet science

As a guy who abhors the sight of two adult males earnestly seeking to scramble one another's brains, I've sat in on too many championship fights. Still, it's a hard game not to like. The people and the atmosphere that surround what A.J. Leibling chose to call The Sweet Science in his fight stuff in *The New Yorker* are the next thing to irresistible.

Let's see, the first time I saw a real live boxing champion was back in the dark ages of September 29, 1941, in the old Polo Grounds in New York, Joe Louis over Lou Nova on a sixth-round knockout. The ring was built over second base and I had a seat in the baseball press box back of home plate. It was a warm sultry night; I remember the bugs zooming around the light bulbs over my head and the ring a tiny bright glow in the near distance. In 1941 Louis was at his peak, or right near there – 200 pounds, 6-foot-1½, 27 years old. He had won the title four years earlier by knocking out James J. Braddock, a pedestrian champion at best, in the eighth round of a quiet affair in Chicago.

In this fight with Nova, the Brown Bomber, as Louis was known, was making his 19th successful title defence, all but two by knockouts. The way I remember it, the hard-thinking publicity department that toiled in the Madison Square Garden office of Mike Jacobs, the game's foremost promoter, revealed that Nova had unearthed a cosmic truth about the planet, which enabled him to deliver his punches in the direction the earth was turning. This gave them such force, it was said, that all of his opponents cringed at the thought of facing him and, more to the immediate point, had the Brown Bomber quaking in apprehension. Luckily for Joe, by the sixth round he had figured out for himself which way the earth was orbiting, and first thing you know Nova is travelling in the same direction, feet first.

Twenty-five years slipped past before I saw another champion in the flesh, and this one turned out to be the most remarkable athlete God ever placed on this turbulent soil. The name? Muhammad Ali, of course. I saw him in six fights, the first pair in his feisty and unquenchable youth, against the veteran Toronto heavyweight, George Chuvalo, his absolute opposite as a fighter, and the last four on the down side of his life in the ring but at his zenith as an unrelenting foe of silence. Talk? When the mood was on him, Ali's voice was unstoppable.

There are those who feel that Chuvalo was not a legitimate heavyweight contender, claiming he was allowed to climb between the ropes with his betters because he was white. But this isn't so. At his best Chuvalo was ranked No. 3 in the world in the mid-1960s by the game's accepted authority, Nat Fleischer, editor of *Ring* magazine. One afternoon in 1970 or thereabouts I visited with Fleischer in his office on the sixth floor of a faded-brick building at 120 West 31st Street in New York when he was an old, old man sitting in a big leather chair surrounded by pictures of surely a couple of hundred fighters, a little bird of a man in a knitted vest and a bow tie and rimless glasses who said he'd been watching fights and fighters for 64 of his 84 years. And he said that in the period when he ranked Chuvalo third in the world he was impressed by the manner in which George could follow up his punches and land powerful damaging punches. "He could leap at an opening like a jockey taking a good horse through a hole in front of him," the little fellow said. "But now he has lost that ability to follow up his punches and he is no longer in my top 10."

Chuvalo was an ebullient and effervescent guy who created excitement outside the ring. This surprised many people on meeting him because in the ring he was an impassive plodder, a stoic, always moving ahead whether he was absorbing four tons of leather a drop at a time over 15 rounds with Ali, or a frightening left hook that almost ripped out his right eye in the shocking climax to four rounds with Joe Frazier, or taking 20-odd withering, pile-driving punches along the ropes without a single response in the third, and last, round from a young George Foreman; just moving ahead, unblinking, into this dreadful barrage, fighting, as New York writer Jimmy Breslin once put it, with his face, an automaton impossible to topple and for this reason one of the most remarkable heavyweight fighters, in a left-footed, back-handed way, who ever lived.

In 83 professional fights Chuvalo was never knocked off his feet. Some very good men made mincemeat of his face, raised bumps the size of robins' eggs over his eyes, bent and bloodied his high-bridged nose, but none of the world's champions he fought – Ali and Frazier and Foreman and Floyd Patterson – and none of the top contenders – Jerry Quarry and Buster Mathis and Jimmy Ellis and Doug Jones – ever found a way to floor him. This would be an entirely negative achievement if it were not for the fact that some of them weren't able to beat him, either, such as Quarry, whom George knocked out in seven, and Jones, in 11, and also that his fights with Ali and Patterson were beautiful fights that went the limit. He was the first man to go 15 with Ali.

Because his face became misshapen in many of his fights the impression was created that Chuvalo was a punching bag with a concrete skull. Like so many things about George, this wasn't true either. He was not the world's best heavyweight and he was far from the worst. He won 64 of those 83 fights, 55 of them by knockouts, and there was one draw, a 10-rounder I well remember in Maple Leaf Gardens against a good South American,

Alex Miteff, who handled George through nine rounds, and then was planted with a long left hook high on the head that knocked him out of the ring. Miteff struggled back, barely weathered the avalanche that greeted him, got away and got a draw.

But by 1970 the game was full of people, including Nat Fleischer, advising George to hang 'em up, partly because of the Frazier beating in mid-1967 and more so after Foreman destructed George's battered kisser in three rounds in August of 1970. Still, if George had listened to all the free advice he got in those years from fight promoters and fight managers and doctors and his wife Lynne and sportswriters and all the other people who lurked on the periphery of the fight game, he'd have retired long before he did. And, anyway, he laughed at all of them following a 12-round crowd-pleaser in May of 1972 against the dancing Ali.

It was four years after that that I sat in on the first of Ali's final four fights, against Ken Norton in Yankee Stadium in September of 1976 when he was growing a trifle worn. Then came two fights with Leon Spinks, first in Las Vegas in February of 1978 when Ali was relieved of his crown in an unrelieved upset, and the second seven months later in the Superdome in New Orleans when he completely flummoxed young Spinks and won it back. My sixth and final exposure to Ali arrived in October of 1980 when as an old *old* campaigner of 38 he presented his hollow shell of a body to the defending champion, Larry Holmes, on a sorry night in Las Vegas.

I saw him one more time, but not at work, and this was the saddest sight of all. Here he was on a blistering street in Miami, walking woodenly in the searing sun, dressed incongruously in a navy-blue flannel suit, a dark tie on a light blue shirt, and black patent-leather shoes. He was suffering Parkinson's syndrome then, as he is to this day, and the disease had sapped the wondrous expressiveness from his round features and left him impassive and wooden, blinking rapidly and endlessly in this blaze of noon. He was on his way to talk in a raspy, high-pitched whisper to some school children who had assembled in a midtown park.

Not all of the observed champions were heavyweights. Between Ali fights there was Sugar Ray Leonard, a performer who finds himself incapable of standing outside the spotlight. The rain drizzled down on him and Roberto Duran in Montreal's Olympic Stadium as the little warhorse from Panama dismantled him. But I missed the return bout in New York ("No mas, no mas") when Duran quit cold before Leonard's taunts and punches.

Then there followed a luncheon in a smallish upstairs dining room in the Friar's Club, normally a showbiz eatery on 55th Street in New York but given over this day to a handful of ravenous scribes and a grumpy middleweight champion, Marvelous Marvin Hagler. Not long afterwards Hagler was in a Las Vegas ring with Thomas Hearns and almost before we had settled in pews set in the parking lot at Caesars Palace the rout was on. The bell rang, Hagler leaped from his corner and looped a crazy swinging right hand at Thomas's curly black head, and for the next eight minutes of breathtaking, sustained, unrelenting fury nobody sat down in the screaming multimillion-dollar crowd. At the end of eight minutes, one guy did: Thomas Hearns.

That was in April of 1985. Before that, Ray Leonard had narrowly escaped an ambush by a predator named Ayuibi Kalule from Uganda via Denmark, an unusual route to take to be rewarded by a punch in the nose. Next was a collision in beautiful Buffalo in which the reigning lightweight champion, Ray (Boom Boom) Mancini, ran into unexpected disaster against an uncaged tiger named Livingstone Bramble. (His manager, Lou Duva, said of Livingstone that "he does everything wrong but it comes out right. He has a dog named Snake and a snake named Dog.") Livingstone, a brooding, dark-visaged fellow in a baggy, brightly coloured, knitted tuque, had expressed undying distaste for Boom Boom on the grounds that Boom Boom had an Italian heritage and Livingstone was a member of the Rastafarian mystical sect from the Virgin Islands. Livingstone claimed he was dedicating the fight to the memory of Ethopian freedom fighters who died in two wars with Italy. There was a suspicion that this praiseworthy dedication was the work of a man named Irving Rudd, who was and at last report is the non-stop publicity man for Top Rank Inc., a fight-promotion corporation headed by Bob Arum.

Irving is a throwback. He is not your modern, three-piece-suited, richly cologned public-relations counsellor. No, Irving is a bustling, scurrying, unbridled press agent, seeking lapels and ears wherever they come to rest. In July of 1990 Irving hit 73, white-haired, earnest, restless. Irving worked for the old Brooklyn Dodgers for six years until they moved to Los Angeles. Whereupon he described their owner, Walter O'Malley, as "a man with deep pockets and short arms."

Irving and I had breakfast one morning in the Hilton Hotel in Buffalo when Irving said that after the Dodgers left Brooklyn he went to work at Yonkers Raceway outside New York. Driving to the track one day he saw workmen putting up a new sign over the entrance, and he suddenly found his fist banging into his own forehead. He stopped his car, jumped out, and sped to the side of the foreman of the work crew. The two men argued briefly and then the sign was hung according to Irving's instructions.

YONKERS RACEWYA, the sign said in letters three and a half feet high.

"In no time the track's telephone switchboard was exploding as people called to tell the track operators they were idiots," Irving recalled fondly. "We sold the joint out opening night. Wire-service pictures of our sign were flashed across the country and appeared in newspapers from coast to coast."

Irving is a short, bustling, warm, and enthusiastic man with wide blue eyes, a ruddy complexion, and a few stray hairs caressing the top of his head. He was born in Brooklyn's Brownsville section that spawned Murder Inc., Danny Kaye, Steve Lawrence, and Shelley Winters, among others. Of his schooling, Irving said between mouthfuls of an English muffin that "I wasn't graduated, I was acquitted." He went to commercial school and learned to type. "I was the smartest boy in my class of 24," Irving said. "There were 23 girls." He was a friend of Al (Bummy) Davis, a tough young fighter from Brooklyn. "Bummy tried to break up a holdup in a gin mill one night and he got shot in the neck. He chased his assailant for two blocks before he collapsed and died. Do I remember when it was? Yes, I remember. It was November 21, 1946, just past midnight."

Irving publicized many of Muhammad Ali's fights though he is the first to acknowledge that Ali didn't need a hell of a lot of help in this department. Ali's later years were so woeful, what with his doleful final bout with Larry Holmes and the subsequent onset of Parkinson's syndrome, that it is sometimes overlooked not just that he was a moody man but that in his antic periods he was capable of being a colossal bore, a man in charge of the most overworked larynx in the known galaxy.

I remember catching a view of Ali one afternoon in Montreal in a large convention room in the Bonaventure Hotel a couple of days before Roberto Duran taught Ray Leonard that life is not always beautiful. This was after Ali had gone into retirement though before he'd decided to unretire and fight Holmes. He had been brought to a luncheon meeting of some organization or other. He was enormously overweight, in the 250s somewhere. His face was rounder than seven zeros. But the old larynx was in fine fettle when its owner placed it in front of a microphone and turned it loose. It went on and on. The thing was, though, nobody listened. In this vast room in the Bonaventure Hotel where people were tearing into the hors d'oeuvres and the free booze nobody was listening to the world's most experienced voice box. You could not make out what he was saying even over the magnified metallic sound of the p.a. system.

He wasn't sick then, or if he was the public hadn't heard of it. I think the reason he was ignored was that he was no longer in action. He had retired from his position as the world's heavyweight champion. There isn't much that the public turns away from faster than an ex-star, a former performer. People listened while he was champ. But this day in Montreal he was simply a fat, boastful bore, ranting on about past triumphs.

It was later, when the illness got to him and he became truly a sad figure, hesitant in his walk, whispering in his talk, unanimated, careful, it was then that people's hearts went out to Muhammad Ali. And nowadays when he shows up at the big fights, moving slowly down an aisle amid half a dozen close acquaintances to his ringside seat, the chant goes up, "A-li, A-li, A-li," and grows and swells until it fills the arena.

There were so many Alis, each of them so different, and I am not sure I ever saw the same one twice. In New York before the Norton fight in 1976 there he was on the stage of a large convention room called the Casino Ballroom in the Essex House, beaming, frowning, mugging, scowling, waving his arms, leaping to his feet, talking endlessly, and announcing that a movie was going to be made of his life. (The film, naturally called *The Greatest*, was released in 1977 and critics raved about Ali's performance in it; then they panned him in a 1979 TV movie, *Freedom Road*.)

All the biggies were there at this Essex House press conference, the chairman of the board and the president of Columbia Pictures, the producer and the director of the picture, and the writer was there, too, Ring Lardner, Jr., assuring the film a brilliant script. Ali sat basking among this galaxy only briefly. He was up and down from his chair, unable to just sit. He was dressed in a black velour outfit, loose-fitting pants and pullover top with black-and-white knitted collar and cuffs. And on his feet were big black army boots halfway up his calves. He began the morning quietly enough but, as seemed to happen so often with him, the more he heard himself talk the more antic he became, his words feeding upon themselves.

"I remind me of Moses," he declared at one point, jumping behind a microphone. "Moses open up the ocean. He turn the waters to blood. Sometimes people doubt me and that make me think of Moses. How can people doubt me? I'm too big for boxing. Think of that, *I . . . am . . . too . . . big . . . for . . . boxing!* They're lucky to get me in Yankee Stadium tomorrow night to fight this Norton. Columbia Pictures is lucky to get me in this picture about me."

He broke into a wide boyish grin and rolled his eyes toward the Columbia board chairman, Alan Hirschfield, and the president, Sidney Jaffe, who both smiled dutifully.

Continuing this examination of his favourite human being, Ali said, "It is amazin' how big I have become. They talk about Barbra Striesand bein' a big hit in her first movie. She is an American symbol, a European symbol. I am a *world* symbol. I am gonna defeat all of 'em after I destroy this Norton in the ring. I'm goin' into the movies and I'm gonna defeat all of 'em, Charlton Heston, John Wayne, all of them big men."

A voice from the middle of a couple of hundred scribes at Ali's feet wanted to know what happens to the movie if he loses to Norton.

Ali went into a mock faint. He threw the back of his hand against his forehead. He stared with an incredulous smile at the multitude.

"Why," he cooed, ever so polite. "Me? Lose? You must be funnin'."

The following night after Ali won a 15-round decision, Ken Norton was crying, not from anything Ali had done in the Yankee Stadium ring but from what two judges and a referee had decided was justice. There was an enormous stampede of scribes rushing to Norton's dressing room in the concrete corridor under the stands. Joe Frazier was making his way there and I hustled beside this former champ who had battled Ali in three blood-curdling fights and shouted, "What'd yuh think, Joe?"

"A terrible decision, just terrible," Frazier said. "It look like you don't knock a man out, you don't win his title."

The papers were echoing the same cry next day. WHAT'S ALI GOT LEFT? NOT MUCH, yelped the tabloid *New York Post* all over its back page.

What clings to my memory was going back onto the ball field after listening to the disconsolate Norton and standing in the milling crowd on the infield grass, people talking and laughing, not wanting to leave or maybe just waiting for the throng to thin. Suddenly, a kid of about 16 came zigzagging through the cluster of people and a cry went up from a slim, nicely groomed, middle-aged woman in a long blond mink coat.

"Oh my God!" she cried. "He's got my purse!" She looked down at her empty hands. Then, noticing, "And my *rings*!"

I turned as quickly as I could but the kid had flashed from view through the crowd as fast as he'd arrived.

Back then there was something special about the outdoor fights in the big ballparks. The night sky in a city gave the fights an atmosphere all their own, a canopy for a constant stir of excitement and anticipation and, for some, even apprehension. Me, for one. I said earlier I disliked the sight of two guys hammering one another; I can refine that a little. What I can't handle is what follows when one guy has been tagged and his opponent leaps in to finish him, when this helpless hulk is trying to cover his vulnerable chin but can't and everyone knows the devastating finishing punch is coming in this terrifying and sometimes lethal hail of blows.

Well, anyway, that's the apprehension some of us feel. But in the moments before the bell rings at a summer fight outdoors there's an adrenalin let loose that sends shivers along your spine. And that night in Yankee Stadium was the first outdoor championship fight I'd seen since one late July night in 1956 when the elegant Archie Moore splattered the blood of James J. Parker across the rented white dinner jackets of newshounds and other swells at ringside in the old Maple Leaf Stadium in Toronto.

Nineteen thousand people had assembled there, partly as a result of the sterling promotion job done by Jack Kearns and Bill Daly in the weeks leading to the affair. Kearns, called Doc, had been Jack Dempsey's manager generations earlier when Dempsey was the heavyweight king in the early 1920s. Daly was a guy known as Honest Bill, though Rocky Graziano once said of him that he never stole anything unless it started with the letter "a" – a diamond necklace, a Rolls-Royce, a Brinks truck.

Kearns and Daly held a cocktail party in the old Prince George Hotel, from which Kearns disappeared briefly to make an appearance on the Jim Coleman television show, a popular interview program. There, he talked at length of the skill of his man Archie Moore, the world's light-heavyweight champion and a man who had laid claim to Rocky Marciano's heavyweight crown. A few months earlier Moore, who labelled himself the Mongoose, had dropped the undefeated Marciano for a count of two before being knocked out in the ninth round. Not long afterwards, Marciano retired, still unbeaten.

Moore, of course, was prohibitively favoured to destroy James J. Parker, an untutored heavyweight from Barrie, Ontario, but this was not a point upon which Kearns chose to dwell in his interview with Coleman. "Archie Moore is a magnificent specimen," the Doc intoned. "The only man on earth he fears is" . . . there was a pregnant pause . . . "James J. Parker."

Recalling the moment, Coleman said later, "I broke into a fit of astonished laughter. I couldn't control it. It's remarkable that the show wasn't cancelled then and there."

The imaginative Moore said he held the highest regard for James J., but that he himself was unbeatable. "Did you ever watch a mongoose at work?" he asked. "He waits and waits and then he strikes, swallowing his adversary."

For his part Kearns, returning to his party in the crowded room in the Prince George Hotel, had apparently merely been warming up in his visit with Coleman. He concurred with Moore that Parker had impressed him. "He reminds me a good deal of Dempsey," the Doc said, as the audience blanched. Then he added. "Except he don't hit quite like Jack."

Some $150,000 was in the till at the ballpark on fight night, where a red carpet bordered the ring for $20 seat holders at ringside. The retired king, Marciano, was there, the barrel torso stuffed into a white dinner jacket, as were the flabby hides of the working press, garbed by the Syd Silver rental clothiers at the expense of the promoters. Later, reports circulated that scribes had made off with the fancy haberdashery following the fight, but the niggardly charges were never substantiated, and cooler heads presented a logical demurrer. "What would one of those ink-stained ne'er-do-wells do with a white dinner jacket?"

Nothing so good-natured had transpired in Yankee Stadium during the Ali-Norton unpleasantness. The following morning the two fighters sat at a conference table in the Essex House with their managers and a couple of handlers for a post-mortem. Fanned out before them was the usual array of newspeople in a windowless meeting room where floor-to-ceiling, maroon, velour drapes hid the walls and windows, if any. The room was dimly lit except for this table bathed in bright light for the TV cameras.

There was a subdued ambiance. The questions came softly from the floor and the fighters responded in quiet tones, the letdown following the tension and excitement of the past week. Ali was all in black – black slacks, black loafers, black silk shirt open at the neck. There were welts beside one eye and under it and the bridge of his nose was pinkish.

"Yeah, sure, I know I'm marked," he said, fingering his nose tenderly. "I got hit two or three good right hands. Ken Norton was 'way better than he's bin against them guys he's bin fightin' lately. I'm takin' nuthin' away from him."

For his part Norton was solemn and withdrawn, a tall, broad-shouldered, handsome man now wearing modish rimless shades perhaps to cover a pink welt around his right eye. He said he didn't want to knock boxing but that he'd received a shabby decision from two judges and a referee mesmerized by the Ali mystique. "Boxing has turned sour in my mouth," Norton said somberly.

With everybody quiet, looking at their hands or staring off into space, a wonderful moment arrived, one I always think of when I think of Muhammad Ali, this astonishing man of so many moods. At the back of the room there was a mild commotion as someone moving outside the seated rows of newspeople banged into a hard-backed wooden chair in the darkened room and sent it skidding across the polished floor, a man with a little girl. Then they moved into the light at the front of the room and it turned out that the man was Ali's brother Rahman and his daughter, Ali's niece Satina, a child of perhaps five. She moved shyly to Ali sitting in the lights answering the questions. Not interrupting himself, he lifted her easily into his lap. He stopped talking and looked smilingly down at Satina.

"Hello sweetheart," Ali whispered, barely audibly. "How's my sweetheart?" He opened his lips slightly and pressed them against her cheek and squeezed her as she looked up at him with adoring eyes. Then he went on answering the questions, rubbing her arm gently with his great right paw, and for the rest of the interview, perhaps another half hour of questions and answers, they sat like this, the child snuggled against him, her head against his chest, her legs stretched across his thighs, her big dark eyes watching the people, her face still. And all this time there was about Ali an unforgettable poignance.

Nearly two years later, in February of 1978, Ali was to meet an inexperienced newcomer of 24, Leon Spinks, a professional for all of a year. Fight fans had seen Leon on the tiny screen from Montreal during the 1976 Olympic Games where his swarm-of-bees style had carried him to a gold medal in the light-heavyweight division. (His brother Michael won the middleweight gold.) Practically no one expected Leon to bother Ali, who had just turned 36, because while he had a nonstop, exciting style, what did he know? One of the tigers he had met on his way to this fight, Scott LeDoux, butted him, elbowed him, hit him on the break and below the belt and after the bell and so distressed him that Leon had asked, "Why you got to cheat to win?"

This so amused the veteran LeDoux that he said, "Because this isn't for the gold medal, this is for your living." And reflecting on Leon's boxing naiveté later, LeDoux observed, "He eats the jab real good."

But such is the nature of the fight game that upsets never cease (think of Buster Douglas destructing the indestructible Mike Tyson in Tokyo in February of 1990). In Vegas this night Spinks became the world's heavyweight champion by a split decision over Ali and immediately agreed to a rematch in New Orleans in September.

The Spinks brothers had survived a hard, hard upbringing. Their parents split up when they were youngsters. Leon's relationship with his father was sometimes frightening, and writing of it in the *New York Times Magazine* Phil Berger quoted the hurried speech and jammed sentences of Leon on that topic:

"I remember I stayed with him one time and I did something. What I did? I did something. But when I did it, he hung me on a nail and hit me across the face with some cord of some kind. A cord or belt. It put a long mark on my face. He told me he was sorry. But ever since then I didn't like him. Okay, I had done wrong. But why'd he have to scar me up? I mean, I can take a butt-whippin'. But you don't have to scar me."

When the fighters reached New Orleans in September to put the finishing touches to their training, a new Ali emerged, a new one on me, at any rate. To receive the press in a small dressing room backstage in a civic auditorium where a ring had been set up on the stage itself, Ali arranged himself on a chair and a footstool as though reclining on a divan. He placed a wide white towel over his crossed legs and allowed his head to tilt back so that he could observe the ceiling. Except that from the waist up he was naked as the day he was born, Muhammad Ali could have passed for Cleopatra floating down the Nile.

This was on the first day of the final week before the world's greatest talker exposed his restless chin to the bustling mittens of Leon, the champ. Ali hadn't worked very hard in the ring on the stage that day. He had broken a sweat but it was more from the heat and humidity of the place than from hard labour.

For New Orleans was hot – hot, hot, hot. The heat rose in little wiggling waves from the sidewalks and people moved from air-conditioned store to air-conditioned store along Canal Street, not shopping, just cooling off. And in this auditorium where the fighters trained it was cooler only to the extent that there was no sunshine.

Newshounds ebbed and surged close to Ali as he reclined on

his chair with his legs crossed on the footstool, trying to catch the pearls as they emerged from his lips. But he had chosen as his mood a low-key and unresponsive one, his voice so soft that no one more than five feet from him could hear a word he said. He didn't raise his voice or change his expression. If he didn't hear a question he inclined his head slightly, indicating that if an answer were expected he would entertain a repeated question. There should have been a canopy above his head. Slaves should have been stirring the heavy air with giant fans.

The next day – it was September 13, my birthday – who should I run into but my little friend from the bowels of Yankee Stadium during the World Series of 1977, Sam Taub. That very day in New Orleans, Sam turned 92 and weighed 106. He was not on a diet; he was merely his normal fighting weight for a guy approximately the size of a large hummingbird. I mentioned in this book's opening chapter that Sam had been around since just this side of forever. Boxing was his game. He was the blow-by-blow announcer on radio when Tunney beat Dempsey in the rain of Philadelphia in 1926. He was there in 1910 in Reno when James J. Jeffries failed to win back the heavyweight title from Jack Johnson, the first White Hope bout ever. Five years later, at age 29, Sam was in Havana when Jess Willard knocked out the great Johnson in the 26th round. He remembered that Johnson lay on his back in the brilliant afternoon sun shielding his eyes from the glare with a raised arm while the referee counted him out.

All right. As a man who had seen almost everything, Sam said he had never seen anything like Muhammad Ali. "He hypnotizes yuh," Sam said. "At his age Spinks should beat him but this guy hypnotizes yuh. Whattayuh gonna do?" Sam was wearing his cigar. Well, in truth, he had removed it from his spry little mug to talk, and then he had stuffed it back in after he'd made his pronouncement. It might have been the same heater he was wearing that night in Yankee Stadium, still unlit but somewhat chewed and damp.

As for Ali, following the torpor of his Cleopatra stage he had become a raving maniac after his workouts when exposed to the folks sitting out front at $3 a head. He would finish his sparring and then walk to the front of the stage in a white terrycloth robe and take the p.a. announcer's mike and start talking. Look out below.

He'd talk for half an hour, occasionally pausing to breathe, once he got that mike. He'd ramble on about the state of the world and his place in it, about how he was the most famous man on earth and how he was bigger than boxing. "I am like oxygen," he announced one afternoon. "I am all over the world."

The guy was incredible. "It's my personality that attracts people," he said another time. "It's not that I am much greater than Joe Louis or Sugar Ray Robinson or Jack Dempsey. It's just that they couldn't talk. They didn't have my wisdom. Very few can handle the mentality of the world. The wise man can act the fool but the fool cannot act wise."

The crowd's response was like revival night in an evangelist's tent. Ali repeated the line and tore on. "People listen to me because I have imagination. Sonny Liston was the Bear and I set traps for him. George Foreman was the Mummy, Floyd Patterson the Rabbit. Spinks is the Vampire. You seen them teeth? I'll beat that vampire if I stay out of the clinches and don't let him bite my neck."

The crowd adored him. People rushed to the metal barricades placed by police at the front of the hall and called to him, popped flashbulbs at him, waved paper and programs for him to sign.

"The man who has no imagination stands on the earth, he cannot fly," Ali thundered on. "I am a man who flies. I am bigger than boxing. Add all this up and I'm the greatest of all time."

The people cheered and banged their hands. Sam Taub, who had made it to 92 that day, who could remember James J. Corbett and Bob Fitzsimmons, shook his head and stared in wonder.

A couple of nights later Ali had no trouble regaining his title. It may have been the first heavyweight championship fight between a novice and a champion in which the champion was the novice. Leon Spinks was far beyond his depth against a man 12 years his senior. Ali never stood still. He used the entire ring, backing, side-stepping, circling. When a hint of trouble came from onrushing Leon, Ali flitted or tied him up or held him.

The next morning not long before noon I happened to see half a dozen scribes entering an elevator in the lobby of the New Orleans Hilton, so I jumped in beside them. They turned out to be heading for Ali's 17th-floor suite where the champ was resplendent in a light blue zippered jacket, navy blue slacks, and a pair of those black calf-high work boots of his. He was seated on a divan behind a wide coffee table. Somebody tossed him a big red apple, which he slowly munched while revealing that he uses his head for something more than a place to run a comb.

"Boxing's a mental exercise," Ali told us. "I know if I win eight rounds the other guy can't beat me unless he knock me out. I know I'm good for eight at my age but I don't know how many more, but I know eight. If I win the first three my opponent got to win the next four to get ahead, so last night I went out to get the jump. The last time, in Vegas, I gave him the first jump. This time I keep movin', keep makin' him miss, keep jabbin' him."

He chewed on his apple, sitting deep in the divan, his knees pressing against the coffee table.

"Funny thing," he continued, "before, like in the other fight, if I win it's nuthin'. People say, 'Why shouldn't Ali beat the kid?' But this time, comin' in in such great shape and goin' the full 15, people say, 'Hey, that Ali great.' Before, it would've been nuthin'. Now, I'm the greatest again. The first loss was a blessin' in disguise."

Suddenly he grew enormously animated, his face aglow as he cried out, "Hey now, there's that Jimmy Grippo! Wait'll you see this. Hey Jimmy Grippo, let's go!"

Jimmy Grippo, it developed, was a magician, a guy doing card and coin tricks, and in no time he was turning the heavyweight champion of the universe into a child of eight. I was standing next to the coffee table in front of Ali's sofa and Jimmy Grippo reached behind my left ear and came away with a silver dollar. Ali was ecstatic.

"Man-n-n, did you *see* what he did?" he cried, eyes sparkling. "He took that coin right off that man's ear! An' lookit him now! Why, he made that card come right out of that fella's pocket. Man-n-n, that card can't be in there, we're all lookin'. Why, that man ain't real."

The Spinks fight marked the third time Muhammad Ali had won the world's heavyweight title. The first time was when he kayoed Sonny Liston in Miami Beach in 1964, the second time was when he kayoed George Foreman in Kinshasa, Zaire, in 1974 (remember, the rope-a-dope tactic), and now Spinks. He retired then, but two years later, closing on 39 years of age, he decided he wanted to be history's first four-time holder of the crown and challenged Larry Holmes, the incumbent.

Larry Holmes had to be the dullest heavyweight champion since James J. Braddock. Back then, in October of 1980, Holmes had won 35 successive pro fights, unbeaten since the very first one, in March of 1973, and people were still calling him Ernie or Garry or they'd say, "Hey, isn't that, uh, you know?" There were only two names this Holmes hardly ever heard, Larry and Sherlock.

But taking on Ali was making him famous. "I never saw so many people," Holmes said this day in suite 4520 in Caesars Palace, which just happened to have wall-to-wall fire-engine red carpeting, two purple divans that joined at a 90-degree angle, one entire wall of mirrors, and various other outcroppings of typical Las Vegas bad taste.

An English scribe, presumably from London, wanted to know rather haughtily why Holmes, the champion, was accepting a paltry $4 million for this fight while Ali, the challenger, was collecting twice that.

"Who you, anyways?" Holmes wanted to know. "I never see you before, man. You here because Ali's here, that right? You never come aroun' before because you feel I wasn't worthy. But now, because of Ali, you know me. He's makin' you *know* me. Tha's why he getting the money, man."

Holmes seemed amused by all the attention. "All you people bein' here, that's why I got to knock the sucker out, because I like it, I *like* it. Ask me some more, hear?"

Holmes had a gap-tooth hiss in his speech. He sounded like that British actor, Terry Thomas, who had the same upper-tooth space that gave an airy quality to the s's.

The promoter of this bout was a newcomer to the fight scene who later took it over, Don King, the guy with the fright-wig haircut, a straight-up hairdo that makes him look like he is in the process of being electrocuted. Don said that he'd decided to make a symbolic gift to Holmes to honour his station as the world's heavyweight champion. It was a belt studded with diamonds and rubies and emeralds and valued at $38,000.

The thought naturally arose since Don King was giving away $38,000 belts and was promoting a fight that would be seen around the world on closed-circuit television by millions of people, did he receive enough credit for his remarkable success?

Yes.

Yes, he received enough credit and, as it happened, he was not reluctant to lead the chorus of yays. Don King's thoughts on the matter were contained in a 12-page colour booklet on classy paper circulated by none other than Don King in association with the Caesars Palace Hotel, Clifford Perlman, chairman of the board.

Whenever Don spoke of Clifford in the booklet he was not given to understatement. "Cliff Perlman is the guiding genius who created the mold that brought Caesars Palace to international heights. A perfectionist he had made the bold-daring decisions to pave the way for Caesars greatness," is how Don described his partner.

Warming to the task, Don said of this promotion of his that it was more than just a fight. "It is a true epic," Don said. "It puts into one ring every known skill in fistiana. It has captured the imagination of the world." Moving right along, Don King had a few more warm words for Don King. "Few men in the history of mortals become living legends. Don King is one of them. Don King is many people and even those who work with and for this 49-year-old master of words from Cleveland, Ohio, have difficulty fully understanding this sometimes complex man. And yet, in many ways, Don King is predictable. Don King loves America."

The way things turned out, Ali had nothing to offer Holmes. In some miraculous way he had lost 37 pounds from a blubbery 254 for this engagement, and while he *looked* great at 217 pounds he was a shell. For $5 at a gift shop in the hotel, fight fans were picking up rubber punching bags about four feet high with a picture of Ali painted on them. For $4 million in the ring on the parking lot out back, Larry Holmes made a punching bag of the real thing. Ali's whim to become the four-time champion vanished in a cloud of lumps, a technical knockout for Holmes when Ali did not get up from his stool for the 11th round.

This was one I scarcely watched. I left my seat in the second press row at ringside after the third round and watched the rest intermittently on the closed-circuit screen in the press trailer. Ali took a continuous pounding from the first round on. He tried psychological ploys – talking, gesturing, mugging – to distract Holmes but the champion stuck strictly to the task, jamming his pile-driver left jab into Ali's face in every round, chasing him constantly, cornering him occasionally, and never giving him a breather.

I didn't see Ali again for six years. Then one morning in March of 1986 when I was in Florida doing the east coast ball clubs around Fort Lauderdale, I saw a piece in the *Miami Herald* that Ali was going to talk to some kids at a fitness seminar sponsored by the Miami-Dade Community College that day at noon. I drove the 20-odd miles to watch and it was there on this very hot day that I saw him in his dark blue business suit, moving as though in a trance toward a ring set up in the middle of a street in the middle of Miami.

It was a long narrow pedestrian mall, lined on one side by the windowless wall of the community college and on the other by the trees and landscaping of a small park. On a rise of ground, seated in neat rows on the grass, school kids aged 7 to 15 squealed and cheered when Ali hove into view, black kids, white kids, tall kids, short kids, girl kids, boy kids.

There were two young men with him, guiding him, one with his hand gently on Ali's broad shoulder. The old champ put his hand slowly into the left pocket of his jacket and brought out a pair of sunglasses. But then, reaching to brush something from his forehead, he knocked off the glasses. The interesting thing was that this didn't dismay him or upset him. I've read since that nothing about his illness does, that he accepts it with equanimity, that while it affects his neurological function, there's nothing wrong with his thinking, only with his motor responses.

Now he climbed some steps into the ring and a tiny smile suddenly appeared on his round features that had been utterly impassive. In a very soft voice, high pitched, he told the kids to be sure to stay in school. He said he'd been successful as a fighter with very little formal education but that his wasn't a good example for youngsters to follow. "I was lucky," Ali said, his speech slurred a little and slow. "I happened to be in the right place at the right time. Get your education. It's more important than staying in the streets and fighting."

None of Ali's former vast entourage was with him. In the old days, the days of the Essex House and Caesars and the New Orleans Hilton, he was surrounded by what used to be known as cats and foxes in marvelously assembled garb, everybody grinning and patting his back, champ this and champ that.

This day there were just the two young guys. I spoke to one of them who said he was Scott Weinberger and described himself as Ali's investment adviser. He said Ali's illness wasn't degenerative. "It isn't boxing related, either, although the over-extension of his workouts brought it on earlier than would have been the case for a non-fighter."

Up in the ring back of Ali was a small scrawny seven-year-old boy wearing a yellow headgear, red boxing gloves, and red-and-yellow gym clothes, a little fellow who had been lifted into the ring and had begun shadow boxing with an instructor. When Ali saw them he dropped into the classic boxing stance, left hand high and extended, right cocked, facing the boy. The lad, his yellow headgear scarcely reaching Ali's waist, flailed away at the man who once floated like a butterfly, stung like a bee, flinging his mitts into Ali's thigh. "Say now," Ali said, almost in a whisper. A slow smile invaded the puffy cheeks and, very gently, the old champ patted the yellow headgear.

Muhammad Ali may have been the best *boxer* to become the heavyweight champion. More often than not those fellows are nose-flattened thunderous punchers in the mould of Jack Dempsey, Jack Johnson, Max Baer, Ingemar Johansson, Joe Louis, Rocky Marciano, and Mike Tyson. But Ali could flit like a welterweight and until late in his career he was a relatively hard man to hit.

Among smaller men there were many of whom it was said that pound for pound they were the best. Such as the Toy Bulldog, Mickey Walker, and the Human Windmill, Harry Greb. Also there were Billy Conn and Stanley Ketchell, Barney Ross and Henry Armstrong, and the one most often cited, the dazzling Sugar Ray Robinson.

But before any of these there was a dark terror from Weymouth, Nova Scotia, who wasn't just hypothetically ranked with the greats but who actually fought the giants of his time and was acclaimed by numerous expert witnesses as, pound for pound, possibly the greatest. This was Sam Langford, born some time around 1880 but not sure of the year when I spent an afternoon with him upstairs in a venerable old boarding house in Boston in 1955. Ralph Allen, the *Maclean's* editor, sent me there to do a piece on the legendary character from the bad old days of boxing.

I found Sam rocking in a creaking wooden chair, a pair of scratched sunglasses propped over his sightless eyes, a faded maroon baseball cap on his head, and his thin body wrapped in a nondescript flannel bathrobe. This was at 136 Townsend Street in an old 15-room house from which the paint was peeling and the shutters were hanging at odd angles. There, smiling and uncomplaining, sat this bent old man whose fists had carried him through hundreds of fights around the world.

I'd gone to Boston via New York, where I talked about Sam with my all-time favourite sportswriter, John Lardner, whose advice to me was to go to the New York Public Library to read about Sam. There, I found the words of Hype Igoe of the *New York Journal-American*, the best-known boxing writer of the era, and Hype didn't bother groping for obscure superlatives. "Langford is the greatest fighter, pound for pound, who ever lived," he wrote.

Joe Williams in his column in the *World-Telegram* concurred: "Langford was probably the best the ring ever saw." And the sage Grantland Rice described Sam as "about the best fighting man I've ever watched."

Going on to Boston I located Langford's former manager, a peppery fellow named Joe Woodman. "At '72," he said, meaning 172 pounds, "he'd have eaten Joe Louis."

Sam was only 5-foot-6 but he had shoulders on him wide as a boxcar and his arms were a couple of oak trees. He fought guys 10 inches taller and 60 pounds heavier and he chased Jack Johnson all over the world trying to get a rematch after Johnson had squeaked a 15-round decision over him in 1906. Johnson didn't become the heavyweight champion for another two years – he beat up on Tommy Burns in Sydney, Australia – but until 1915, when he lost the title to Jess Willard in Havana, he steadfastly avoided Sam.

"On a good night Sam is just liable to beat me or make it close," Johnson said once. "And what's the sense of that for the kind of money we'd draw?"

The Johnson victory over Tommy Burns launched the White Hope industry. Burns, whose square name was Noah Brusso, was born in Hanover, Ontario, the only Canadian ever to hold the heavyweight title, which he did for almost three years.

Beating him, Johnson became the first man to cross the so-called colour line invoked by John L. Sullivan in the 1880s and perpetuated by succeeding champions for nearly 30 years until Burns agreed to give Johnson a shot.

Because Sam was black – and good – he had trouble getting fights except against other black men, and he took on and usually beat all the best of those, large and larger. Near the end of his long, peripatetic career he made his only appearance in Toronto, where he met Young Peter Jackson on October 18, 1921. Newspaper clippings paint a sordid racial picture of the era. The *Toronto Star* carried this advance notice on October 14:

"Nothing is too good for Sam Langford, the King of Smoky Swat, according to local colored folk. One grand reception has been arranged for Hon. Sam by Toronto people of his race. . . . After a downtown parade King Sam Swat is going to dine somewhere but just where has not been decided. About every colored man in town who has a spare room and credit for a pair of chickens or a collection of pork chops wants to have Sam's knees under his mahogany."

On October 19 the story of the fight in which Langford knocked out Jackson in the second round appeared under the byline of Lou Marsh, the *Star* sports editor, who is honoured annually to this day by a trophy in his name for Canada's most outstanding athlete.

"A pickaninny has as much chance in a rassling match with a gorilla as Young Peter Jackson had with Sam Langford," Marsh wrote. "They say Langford trained on pork chops. Well! if he did he done gobbled up Mistah Y.P. Jackson in two bites like any other pork chop."

Langford's sight was failing by then but fighting was all he knew so he kept going. Late in 1923 he had three fights in Mexico City and then he had to quit the ring.

"He couldn't *see*," his old manager, Joe Woodman, told me in 1955. "He and I broke up six years before he finally quit. He'd already lost the sight of his left eye then."

Sam actually fought an exhibition in Texas in 1929 when he

might have been 49 years old. He told me that he'd stayed in Mexico City six or seven years and then got tired of it and went to San Antonio, where he watched a fight card.

"Both my eyes were bad then but I could see a little bit," he said, smiling and rocking in his wooden chair. "I knew I could lick the whole bunch put together. So when I got in there, this fella started swingin' that left hand and I blocked it and he swung again and I blocked it. An' then I knocked him out."

In 1945 Al Laney was writing a series of articles on old fighters in the *New York Herald-Tribune* and went looking in Harlem for the all-but-forgotten Sam Langford. After a two-week search he found him "in a dingy hall bedroom on 139th Street down a corridor so dark you had to feel your way."

By then Sam was broke and totally blind, but Laney's piece marked the beginning of a fund that enabled Sam to return to Boston, where he lived with his sister until 1954. Boston writers raised a few thousand dollars in a benefit boxing card but the money had just about run out when Sam's sister died. A woman named Mrs. Grace Wilkins, who ran this somewhat dilapidated house on Townsend Street, agreed to look after Sam. When I saw her she said she got occasional cheques of $49.18 from the New York fund and an infrequent $60 from Boston's.

That was 35 years ago. I don't know when or in what circumstances Sam died. What I remember was Mrs. Wilkins telling me as I was leaving her house that she'd asked Sam once what he'd like to do if he could do anything he wanted. And what the man who may have been the greatest fighter, pound for pound, who ever lived said was this:

"Missus, I've been everywhere I wanted to go, I've seen everything I wanted to see, and I guess I've eaten just about everything there is to eat. Now I just want to sit here in my room and not cause you any trouble."

Chapter 13

The CFL is better than you think

Bud Grant never tired of telling Canadian fans that they didn't know how good their brand of football really was. Bud coached the Winnipeg Blue Bombers for 10 years but he was no prejudiced witness: even after he went to Minnesota and led the Vikings into the Super Bowl four times in the 1970s he'd reflect on the well-known Canadian inferiority complex.

"Canadians have a very negative attitude when it comes to football, or anything else for that matter," he told Paul Rimstead in *Weekend Magazine* in 1971. "They underestimate themselves. The football in Canada, in the West anyway, can't be improved on as entertainment. The public doesn't realize how good the CFL is."

Years later, when Bud came out of retirement to help straighten out the floundering Vikings in 1985, I phoned him at his summer camp in Wisconsin to talk about his return. Then the topic got onto the decline in CFL attendance, and he mentioned again the lack of fan appreciation of the game up here.

Once in a magazine piece under his name Grant had written: "There is nothing else in football like the Grey Cup. The excitement surrounding the game is probably even greater, per capita, than the Super Bowl." Of course, going four for four in the loss department, as the Vikes did, could colour a guy's judgement.

But other people who've been around the block and back share Grant's notion. For one, Hugh Campbell, a sort of Bud Grant of the 1980s, who in six seasons as Edmonton's coach made six trips to the Grey Cup game and won five of them before becoming the head coach of the NFL's Houston Oilers.

"People who put down the Canadian game should attend the annual American coaches' convention," Hughie noted one time. "At it, everybody watching the CFL's highlight film is hootin' and hollerin' and often even cheering, they enjoy it so much – only 20 seconds in the huddle, the ball always in the air, the fast turnovers of the kicking game, American coaches think it's great."

Lending a voice to the chorus was Joe Theismann, the Super Bowl quarterback of the Washington Redskins. "I don't think American fans appreciate the entertainment factor of the CFL," said Joe, who left Notre Dame in 1971 to play three seasons with Toronto. "People think the CFL is a lesser league but I say that's wrong. It's definitely a different style of football."

Curiously, even vehement critics of the Canadian variety agree there's something special about the Grey Cup. The annual rite is a lot of things to a lot of people. Dick (the Hat) Beddoes, an irreverent broadcaster, called it the Grand National Drunk. From the other side of the football Jake Gaudaur, the former CFL commissioner, said it was the last great unifying force in the country. Either way, a unique Canadian flavour continued to surround the Grey Cup game, which during the final three years of the 1980s put the extravagantly hyped Super Bowl to shame.

Grand National Drunk? Of course. Five-gallon hats used to float from the mezzanine of the Royal York Hotel annually during Grey Cup Week, sometimes with people wearing them. Unity? That, too. The commissioner used to sit between Pierre Elliott Trudeau, noted nationalist, and René Lévesque, renowned separatist, at the Grey Cup game. For three hours they'd huddle there shivering, occasionally smiling, and never an unkind word in any language.

It's hard to know how much longer there will be a Grey Cup game for fans to cheer about or drink to. Hamilton and Ottawa and Calgary went into the 1990s sparring with financial disaster. Still, history says there'll always be a CFL and, with it, a Grey Cup game. I sat in Jake Gaudaur's office many a time when he was the commissioner, listening to him anoint the owners. Jake would insist they were motivated by a desire to preserve the game, not make a buck, a philosophy that grew progressively quaint as inflation took over pro sports.

Television largesse threatened to make money meaningless. When the NFL added two wild-card teams to its playoff format for the 1990 season the added TV rights for those games increased revenue for each team to $30 million for television alone. That's $30 million for each owner, fans, before a single ticket or hot dog was sold. The final television tab for the first four years of the 1990s reached $3.3 *billion*, equally divided among the 28 teams. Baseball's take was just as juicy and even in individual sports the payoffs became a trifle mind-boggling. For instance, the Australian golfer Greg Norman banked $252,000 in March of 1990 the morning after the Doral Open in Miami for his four days of golf.

Obviously then, regardless of how spectacular and crowd-pleasing the Grey Cup game is, it can't compete on an economic basis with those numbers. Accordingly, talented players weren't as available as they were in pre-television times when Canadian teams could compete with American owners for occasional headliners. For a long time, though, Gaudaur's theories held up.

"Football is part of our heritage," he'd proclaim whenever he found a pair of receptive ears. "The game originated in Canada and was picked up from us by the Americans. It was played here as an organized sport in 1882 and it retains its distinctive Canadian rules on a distinctive Canadian field. Owners know

Canadian football will never be better than a break-even proposition but they're in it because it's a piece of our culture."

But gradually a kind of major-league mentality attached itself to sports fans in some Canadian cities – the Expos and the Blue Jays in baseball, the Oilers, the Flames, the Canucks, and the Jets in hockey. It became fashionable for football fans to put down the CFL and blindly applaud the game south of here played by behemoths of 300 pounds on postage-stamp fields. The CFL was perceived as minor league in towns suddenly exposed to the major-league labels (the Flames, the Oilers, *et al.*). What so many people didn't choose to consider was that the rules and the field's dimensions accorded Canada a unique game that put different demands on its players.

Gaudaur, as with anybody else who thought about it, was aware that far too many Canadians were awed by the affluence (and baloney) of the United States, in football as in so much else. "On TV we see their parks filled with 50,000 or 60,000 people, and since we draw half that many we're mightily impressed," Jake expanded on this theme one time as we drank coffee from CFL mugs in his Toronto office. "But why? Their population is 10 times ours; why shouldn't they draw twice as many?"

Of course, crisis is no new predicament for the CFL. Scarcely a decade has passed since World War Two that hasn't produced a chaotic situation threatening the Canadian league's life. Indeed, right after the end of that war the All-America Conference was born in the U.S., a league embracing the Cleveland Rams, the Buffalo Bills, the Brooklyn Dodgers, and others. The doom-and-gloomers predicted it would kill the CFL. Where would the talent come from to accommodate us now? Well, where a lot of it came from, soon enough, was the All-American Conference, which went belly up in 1949.

In the 1960s, Canadian fans got a taste of the four downs and 100-yard fields many of them clamour for now. It was a league called the Continental, bringing forth the supreme talker Leo Cahill and the wonderfully folksy quarterback Tom Wilkinson, among others practically as immortal. The Canadian entry in that league, the Montreal Rifles, flopped at the gate so the franchise was switched to Toronto where it flopped at the gate.

In the same decade in the U.S. the NFL expanded on its mounds of television money, and Lamar Hunt, a Texas billionaire, founded the American Football League. Obviously, the CFL couldn't survive *that*, the thinking went, a wealthy league competing with the NFL for talent. But somehow the CFL endured. The U.S. rivals knocked each other's wallets off and when both were gasping they merged.

Nothing more of a two-league concept was heard down there until the U.S. Football League emerged in 1982. It produced inflated salaries that reflected on the CFL and put a severe strain on Canadian budgets. Some owners up here had already gone overboard. In 1981 Nelson Skalbania, who briefly (but not briefly enough) owned the Alouettes in Montreal, brought in a handful of name players at exorbitant prices, among them Vince Ferragamo, the first-string quarterback of the Los Angeles Rams, Billy (White Shoes) Johnson, an established wide receiver from the Houston Oilers, and David Overstreet, a first-round draft pick of the Miami Dolphins that year, a running back from the University of Oklahoma.

Maybe the infusion of such players would have made a difference in Montreal if the Alouettes had made any kind of positive impression. Instead, they went 3–13 in 1981 and 2–14 in 1982. Indeed, they didn't have a winning season through 1986, when they were 4–14, and by then they had only a couple of thousand fans rattling around in the vastness of Olympic Stadium. Moments prior to the start of the 1987 season, they folded.

If that didn't terminate life in the CFL, you'd suspect the solution to Montreal's departure would turn the trick: the Winnipeg Blue Bombers (the *Winnipeg Blue Bombers!*) were shipped east to replace the Alouettes. Historically, the Bombers were one of the great western teams. But instead of rigor mortis setting in right there, the CFL came up with the three most exciting Grey Cup games in its recent history. In 1987 under the bedsheet in Vancouver's B.C. Place Stadium, Jerry Kauric kicked a last-second 49-yard field goal to give the Edmonton Eskimos a chilling 38–36 win over the Argonauts just when the Argonauts were counting the money. A year later in Ottawa, the Blue Bombers slipped past the highly favoured B.C. Lions by 22–21 to bring the Grey Cup to the East, and the topper arrived in the 1989 game in Toronto's new dome when, with two seconds showing on the clock, Dave Ridgway kicked a 35-yard field goal for Saskatchewan's 43–40 victory over Hamilton while a throng of 54,088 went slightly daffy.

Daffy? Yes, that's the word. People from the towns that most epitomize football in this country, Regina and Hamilton, set a wild and happy tone in the opulent new playpen almost from the beginning. Waves of Saskatchewan's green-and-white filled whole sections brandishing pennants and banners, and they were matched by the yellow-and-black legions from down the road in Hamilton, hoarse mobs from this country's grain and steel capitals. Blue-collar football, Hamilton coach Al Bruno had called it.

It was a marvelous couple of hours in the Canadian game, 83 points from two teams acclaimed for their defences. They set a Grey Cup record for points in the second quarter when the westerners outscored the Tiger-Cats 21–14, a 35-point exchange in 15 practically end-to-end minutes. The quarterbacks, Hamilton's Mike Kerrigan and Regina's Kent Austin, a couple of clean-cut Canadian boys from Illinois and Mississippi, were firing the football with startling velocity and location, the two favourite words in the vocabulary of any big-league baseball pitcher.

But whether it was enough to bring fans to their senses in the 1990s, who could guess? The Argonauts pulled off a couple of attention-grabbing swaps with the B.C. Lions that brought them the experienced scrambling quarterback Matt Dunigan and a veteran battering-ram lineman, James (Quick) Parker, but there still was conjecture about the future, a conjecture unknown in earlier decades when new American leagues kept folding and the CFL kept blithely sailing from crisis to crisis. It was right after the All-America Conference's bankruptcy that American players – imports, we called them – flooded across the border into eastern Canada. The Tiger-Cats and the Argos loaded up on them.

Back then, the Double Blue Argonauts were the best team on this side of the border, so good that *Maclean's* magazine ran a piece about them titled "Break Up the Argos!" One of their new arrivals was an assistant coach named John Kerns, who also played tackle. Kerns had come north from the Buffalo Bills, a bear of a man of 6-foot-4 and 250 pounds with a wry sense of humour.

This was in the early 1950s when Toronto newspapers ran late-afternoon editions. On Saturdays the front pages carried late scores and play-by-play accounts of that day's football games, the *Telegram's* on pink paper, inducing the owners with rare perception to call the edition *The Pink Tely*. I was working there then, covering the baseball Maple Leafs until the season expired and then switching to football.

One afternoon the Argos were far ahead of the Tiger-Cats and late in the game added a meaningless touchdown, so meaningless that the regular kicker didn't bother going out for the ensuing kickoff. John Kerns took it, and booted a puny kick of maybe 20 yards.

Writing running copy for the *Tely's* night edition I filed, "Kerns kicked off miserably for the Boatmen, 20 yards to Carpenter at the Hamilton 53."

On the following Monday the scribes assembled in the Varsity Stadium quarters of Argo coach Frank Clair for the usual quotes and misquotes. As the team's assistant coach, Kerns shared Clair's digs, and he was there slowly tugging off his sweaty gear for a post-practice shower. Then he trudged, stripped, toward the shower-stall and as he neared my chair he stopped, put his ham hands under my armpits, and hoisted me level with his eyes.

As my feet dangled somewhere just below his knees he said to me, amiably enough, "Listen, you little bastard, for all you know, people might be reading that stuff."

Then he set me down and continued wearily on his way to the shower.

Kerns and Clair arrived in Toronto in 1950 and it wasn't long before Clair was known as the Professor. He was a lanky, studious-looking fellow wearing shell-rimmed glasses and given to staring off into space during conversations with us newshounds. Frank had played end for one season for the Washington Redskins after coming out of Ohio State University and then he went into the army and played football under the legendary Paul Brown. Coaching fascinated him. He joined the staff of another acclaimed brain, Sid Gillman, at the University of Miami of Ohio upon leaving the army, and then spent two years at the University of Buffalo.

I remember him early in his Argonaut career searching for a suitable fullback and trying a slender Canadian named Teddy Toogood, who immediately scored two touchdowns, including the winner on a long, twisting 40-yard run, against the high-powered Alouettes of Sam Etcheverry, Hal Patterson, Tex Coulter, and so forth.

"Well, Coach, I guess you've found your fullback," proffered one of us afterwards.

"Oh, I don't know," Frank said, peering narrow-eyed at the concrete wall. "Have to wait till Monday and look at the films."

"But he ran 40 yards," exclaimed his questioner.

"He did, didn't he," muttered Frank. "But can he block?"

This sort of thinking was far too advanced for the scribes of the day. Frank was the Professor from then on.

Frank may have been the only man in the country prepared to combat the dreadful field conditions for the 1950 Grey Cup game, the famous Mud Bowl. Snow had fallen in Toronto early in the week and again on the night before the big game between the Argos and the Blue Bombers whose quarterback, Indian Jack Jacobs, had been setting standards for passers in the West.

But Clair, knowing the Varsity Stadium field had no tarpaulin, wondered in midweek about the sort of field a sudden thaw might produce. He went to various sports stores and high school gyms and found what he sought in the athletic department at the University of Toronto – football shoes with extra long cleats.

The weather dutifully climbed into the 40s the night before the game, and when the fans and players arrived at the Bloor Street stadium on Saturday afternoon they were confronted by rows and rows of seats covered in melting snow and by an unbelievable quagmire of mud and dead grass and thawing ice and gooey puddles on the field. The cleats gave the Argos passable footing and the team got a lift, too, from the sure-handed ball control of Al Dekdebrun, a quarterback from Buffalo recruited by Clair. Dekdebrun, no dummy, taped thumb tacks to the fingers of his throwing hand. His quarterback adversary, Indian Jack, was unprepared for the footing or the slithery ball and endured a hopeless afternoon.

This was the game in which the import tackle of the Blue Bombers, Buddy Tinsley, was saved from drowning by Hec Crighton, the referee. Tinsley maintained that reports of his imminent demise were grossly exaggerated (he was a Mark Twain lookalike) but Crighton insisted in many a visit to the old Toronto Men's Press Club upstairs over a barber shop on Yonge Street that Tinsley had been knocked down while chasing an Argo ball-carrier on an end sweep. "He landed face down and slid into a hole," Crighton told us often. "He was definitely breathing water when I turned him over and he was *out*."

So was Clair, sooner than anticipated. His team won another Grey Cup in 1952, missed in 1953 and 1954, and then there began 30 years of weird hirings and firings of Double Blue coaches. A former player, Harry Sonshine, fat and rich, sat on the board for the team's owner, the Argonaut Rowing Club, itching to get his hands on the tiller. In 1955 he forced Clair out by writing ludicrous stipulations into Clair's new contract, declaring that Sonshine would name the starting lineup for each game and have authority to phone from the spotter's box what Canadian players Clair could send on the field. So Clair quit, went to the University of Cincinnati for a year, and then joined the Ottawa Rough Riders as head coach and later general manager for a long career during which his teams made seven Grey Cup appearances, five of them victorious.

Meantime, the rowing club was divesting itself of the football connection, selling out to John Bassett, publisher of the *Telegram*, and a group of his cronies that included Lew Hayman, who had been a winning coach for the Argos and later the Alouettes. This was in 1956, whereupon the Argos finished dead last for four straight seasons with identical records of four wins and 10 losses. There was a glorious (and brief) respite when Hayman landed a tall, aging NFL quarterback, Tobin Rote, a classic drop-back passer, a star for the Green Bay Packers and later the Detroit Lions, and who turned out to have a few throws left.

Tobin looked like the guy central casting would send over to play the hit man in a Mafia flick. He was 6-foot-4 or so with thinning black hair, black eyes, a laid-back manner, and the sort of black beard that made him look like a guy needing a shave right after he'd shaved. Jay Teitel, in *The Argo Bounce*, wrote of Rote's penchant for nighttime prowling, of a Sunday game in Montreal in 1960 when Tobin stayed up all night Saturday touring bistros. When halfback Dick Shatto arrived for the game he found Rote stretched on his back on a bench, an arm covering his eyes.

"I'm not sure I can get through the game, Dick," Rote confessed, and Shatto replied hopefully, "Sure you can, Tobin, sure you can."

That afternoon Rote threw 22 passes and completed 19 for an 84.6 percentage. Another time he threw seven touchdown passes, and another he tossed 38 completions. In three seasons he set records that endured for 20 years and more – until Warren Moon and Dieter Brock began flinging footballs all across the western steppes.

Rote was an innocent bystander in the craziest football game ever played north or south of the border, the eastern final of 1961 between the Argos and the Tiger-Cats in an era of two-game total-points series. The Boatmen won the first game at home by 25–7, an insurmountable advantage that proved sur-mountable and was mounted. Early in the fourth quarter of the return game in Hamilton the Tiger-Cats had sprung ahead by 20–0, a two-point edge overall. The Argonauts came back on two long singles off punts by Dave Mann, the league's top kicker, and with a minute and a half to play they forced a break when defensive safety Stan Wallace intercepted a pass by Bernie Faloney at Hamilton's 27-yard line. The way Dave Mann could punt, another single was a cinch to send the Double Blue into the Grey Cup game.

But what to do? Should Mann kick immediately and thereby not risk a fumble or should Rote use up some clock with a couple of careful ground plays? The Argonaut coach, Lou Agase, decided to play the latter hand.

Rote cradled the ball on a sneak on the first play but the Argos were offside. The five-yard penalty put the ball on the Hamilton 32, still first down. Tobin carried again and made three yards. Second and 12 from the 29. Next, a draw play, one very similar to a quarterback sneak, which the Tiger-Cats sniffed out for a two-yard loss. That put the ball on the 31, a distance Mann could handle standing on his head.

He should have stood on his head. He hit a 39-yarder eight yards deep in the end zone. Don Sutherin caught the ball and booted it out, nearly 40 yards to Hamilton's 30 where Mann, the peerless punter, caught it. And what did he do with it? Why, unloaded his worst punt of the day. This one landed on the goal-line and bounced to Bernie Faloney, who ran and ran and *ran* all the way to the Argonaut end zone 111 yards away.

This should have sent the Tiger-Cats to the Grey Cup, but it didn't. On Faloney's run a Hamilton guy illegally blocked an Argonaut guy and the penalty wiped out Faloney's gallop. Thus, regulation time expired with the teams at 27 points each. They went into a 30-minute overtime period, not sudden-death, and for the Argonauts the 30 minutes lasted for genera-tions. The Tiger-Cats scored four touchdowns and won the game by 48–2. That's 48–2.

What a blow. The next year, even with Tobin firing again, the team reverted to its 4-10 record and Rote went back home to Detroit. Then the bottomless Boatmen sank to 3-11 in 1963, then to 4-12 in 1964, back to 3-11 in 1965, and a barely respectable 5-9 in 1966, nailing down last place in the East for the ninth time in 11 seasons. Whereupon there arrived the unforgettable, the singular Leo Cahill.

In retrospect here in the 1990s, when you consider that football is a very emotional game and that Leo is an emotional fellow, you really must wonder why he hasn't become a mental basket case. No one in the CFL endured more real heartache – I'm serious – while contributing to the lore of the Canadian game than Leo.

The Argonauts hired him three times and fired him three times and firing is very hard on any man's ego. Running a football team may not be quite as vital a contribution to mankind as, say, cardiac surgery, but when it is the biggest thing in a person's life it carries a tall impact. On at least two of the three occasions when the Argonauts told Leo to get lost there was little justification for it apart from the time-worn business of firing one coach because it's simpler than firing half the players. But Leo has handled it, each time coming up stubborn, and even in the summer of 1990, age 62 and unemployed, he was game and cheery and optimistic.

As a football coach Leo was a delight for newshounds, a talkative, impulsive, uncomplicated, controversial, outgoing person who wore his emotions on his chubby kisser. He was solidly built, a man who had played guard at the University of Illinois, a big-boned bespectacled fellow who may or may not have been a good coach but was an outstanding recruiter of talent. He enticed several players to Toronto who were being wooed by NFL teams, notably Joe Theismann, Tim Anderson, Jim Stillwagon, Leon McQuay, Noah Jackson, an alphabetic aberration named Ron Mikoljczyk, and a pair of stars from the University of Georgia, Mike Wilson and Joel Parrish. Later, Leo was the general manager of Johnny Bassett's World Football League team, the Toronto Northmen, who became the Memphis Southmen when the Canadian government decided that this country was too small for the CFL *and* an American invader. Leo helped Bassett lure three stars from the Miami Dolphins, Larry Csonka, Jim Kiick, and Paul Warfield, an enormous coup in 1973.

Ironically, Bassett's father, John, Sr., the Argonaut chairman, had handed Leo his first shock as a football coach. In 1971 Leo had guided the Argonauts to their first Grey Cup appearance in 19 seasons. There, a fumble by Leon McQuay did them in. McQuay was one of Leo's favourite players, a dashing waterbug of a halfback. Late in the game against the Calgary Stampeders in gentle rain in Vancouver's ancient Empire Stadium, McQuay took a handoff from Theismann deep in Calgary's end and was on his way to the winning touchdown. But he dropped the wet ball and Calgary won the Grey Cup.

Years later Leo looked philosophically on the McQuay goof, but he felt no such compassion for his firing in 1972 when the Argonauts won three games and dropped 11. One morning in the spring of 1990 Leo and I gulped coffee and ate a couple of English muffins in Toronto's Skyline Hotel coffee shop while Leo reflected on the trauma of that first firing.

"In the four years '68 through '71 I won 37 games and lost 19," Leo said. "Then we had a million injuries in 1972 and I'm gone. What kind of justice is that? Geez, even Bud Grant went 1-and-15 at Winnipeg one year and wasn't given the boot. You remember '72, don't you? Joe Theismann went down in the opening game with a broken leg. Jim Corrigal, our top lineman, went down with a broken leg. Tim Anderson, the best defensive back we ever had, went down with a broken leg. Dave Cranmer, our best runner, had abdominal surgery and almost died. Dave Raimey broke his thumb. I remember after Corrigal bust his leg in the all-star game, Blackie Johnston, who was one of the assistant coaches, came over to me and said, 'Leo, you ain't gonna believe this but John Trainor has maybe ripped off his kneecap and he's gone for the season.' And then when the season was over with us 3-and-13, *with cause*, Bassett called me in and fired me. I couldn't believe it."

Chances are, Leo had an inkling. Halfway through that 1972 season the fans had begun to chorus "Goodbye, Leo" to the tune of "Good Night, Ladies." There was nothing original about the chant. New York Giants fans were already serenading the Giants coach, Allie Sherman, a former Winnipeg thinker, with "Goodbye, Allie."

More woe loomed for Leo, but in the meantime Bassett sold the Argos in 1974 to an innkeeper named Bill Hodgson, a lifelong Argo fan (fans make terrible bosses; they think because they've made money in business that they know sports). John Rauch, an experienced NFL coach, was the Argonaut incumbent but the new owner grew increasingly disenchanted with Rauch as the season dragged along. Playing in Montreal the Argos were trailing by 14–0 but were threatening at the Alouette 5-yard line. Two incomplete passes put them in difficulty so they tried a halfback option. That's where the quarterback pitches out to a halfback who either runs with the ball or throws it. This halfback, Ernie Carnegie, made a sort of loaf-of-bread push and the ball was intercepted.

The owner, like any devout fan, was furious. He descended from his box to the Argonaut room the instant the game ended and fired John Rauch. That winter, again like any devout fan, he hired his personal football hero, Russ Jackson, as the new head coach. Russ, at quarterback for the Ottawa Rough Riders, may have been the best football player ever born and bred in Canada, but he'd had no coaching experience, none at any level.

Still, he had great confidence in his football sense and knowledge, and the demeanour he chose to present to the public and his players was of a man confident and in charge. I remember one game, after a tough loss, when we descended on Russ in the sweaty Argonaut dressing room and, as usual, there was a brilliant opening question.

"Well, Coach, what do you think?"

"Won't know till we see the films," Russ said cryptically.

On Monday after practice, there was the question, "Well, Russ, what did the films show?"

"Nothing we didn't already know," Russ replied, big jaw outthrust.

Russ had two years at the helm, by which time the owner's hero worship had petered out. Now who do you suppose Hodgson hired as his new head coach? Correct, Leo the Larynx.

However, there was a tiny hitch: Leo had agreed during a meeting a short time earlier with Bobby Ackles, the Vancouver general manager, to coach the B.C. Lions. Oops.

Leo was available because the World Football League had folded, pulling the Memphis Southmen down with it. Leo's wife and family had settled into life in Memphis so Leo's Toronto lawyer, Herb Solway, advised Bobby Ackles that she refused to uproot the family again for a move to Vancouver. To resolve a looming crisis, Leo paid the B.C. Lions $10,000 for release from his Vancouver commitment and rejoined the Argonauts. The kindly owner waited a season and a half before firing him.

During that 18 months Leo's record was unimpressive, 5–11 in 1977 and the groundwork for a 4–12 disaster in 1979 when Hodgson elevated an Argonaut assistant, Bud Riley. Even so, the owner was still thinking like a fan. Before the axe settled on Leo's neck I happened to run into Hodgson one afternoon at the first tee of the St. George's golf club and he asked me if I thought he ought to make a coaching switch – me, a lowly newshound. Without benefit of a second guess, what'd I know?

Also, one early evening before a game Leo had walked into the Argo room and spotted an unfamiliar face. It belonged to Ken Clark, the Hamilton punter.

"Hey, Clarkie, what are you doing in here?" Leo asked.

"You got me," Clark replied. "They told me in Hamilton to get over here. Said I'd been traded."

Upon investigation Leo was advised that Owner Hodgson, the fan, had read in a newspaper that the Tiger-Cats were disappointed in Clark's recent work. The owner had picked up a telephone and traded for him, not bothering to consult with his coach.

Years later over that breakfast at the Skyline Hotel Leo confessed that the firing was not entirely unjustified. "I had an awful lot on my mind that fall," Leo said. "And not a hell of a lot of it was football." Soon after his move back to Toronto, Leo was divorced.

Whatever equanimity Leo felt about his dismissal by Hodgson, he had no such compassion for the newest of Argonaut owners, Harry Ornest, or for the Argo president, Ralph Sazio, following his third Argo dismissal. That came in the wake of the 1988 season although, strictly speaking, Leo wasn't fired. It was simply that his three-year contract as general manager wasn't renewed, the difference being a mighty fine line.

Munching his muffin, Leo said that when Sazio offered him the general manager's job his income was in six figures as a football analyst on CBC television and a daily sports commentator on a Toronto radio station. "Sazio told me he'd be retiring in two or three years and that if I kept a cool profile I'd have his job," Leo said. "And I loved the idea of being the GM because ever since I first joined the Argos 20 years ago I've figured that the front office is where I'm best. So I resigned everything I was doing and jumped at it."

After Ornest let Leo go I told the owner on three occasions that the best Argonaut years for the media had been Cahill years. "He's a natural newsmaker," I told the owner. Hard as it is to digest, the owner didn't listen.

"There was nothing I could do," Harry said each time. "It was in the works when I got here."

Which, of course, is a bunch of baloney. Owners are like newspaper publishers; they can do anything they want.

As I've indicated, Leo was a wily recruiter. One time he was in hot pursuit of Eric (the Flea) Allen, a highly rated college player whose skills were being sought by an NFL team. Leo invited Allen to visit Toronto and figured if he were impressed by his reception he might sign with the Argos. Leo phoned a news photographer friend of his and named a restaurant he'd be dining at with Allen and asked the photographer as a favour to drop by and flash a few bulbs at the player. Leo said he'd act annoyed that Allen's privacy had been invaded so that Allen wouldn't tumble to the setup. Everything went according to plan; the photographer showed up, Leo upbraided him, and the picture even appeared in the paper next day. The Flea was duly impressed; he signed with the Boatmen and gave them four strong seasons.

Even when Leo lost players his ingenuity sometimes got them back. In that disastrous season of 1972 he had released a linebacker, a southerner named Bruce Bergey, who went on to Montreal. When injuries struck, Leo needed Bergey back so he telephoned an old sidekick, J.I. Albrecht, then with the Alouettes, disguised his voice, and introduced himself as Bruce Bergey's father.

"It's urgent, suh," Leo cooed. "A family crisis."

"Y'all are in luck," replied J.I., an old southern boy himself (from upstate New York). "The lad is in my office this very minute. Ah'll put him on."

"Dad?" said the concerned player. "Is something wrong?"

"Brucie boy, it's Leo. Get your ass back here. Don't sign anything. We need you."

Bergey returned to Toronto and played two seasons for the Double Blue.

Sometimes when Leo charmed players they got carried away by his eloquence. A guy named Mario Mariani was an early victim of Leo's persuasiveness when Leo couldn't find a place for him on the roster but wanted him in the wings just in case. Talking earnestly to Mario, Leo explained that in the team's final exhibition game he wanted him to feign injury so that Leo could put him on the injured list, thus keeping him on the hook though not playing.

Performing in Montreal's Molson Stadium, Mario must have thought he was on stage at the Stratford Shakespeare Theatre. He fell to the ground after somebody mildly brushed him and lay there, rigor mortis already making inroads. A stretcher arrived and Mario was sped to the Montreal Neurological Institute next door to McGill University's football field.

When an intern began peering into his head Mariani figured

he'd gone far enough as King Lear. But it was too late for protestations. He had been wired to ominous-looking devices and his reactions to tests were being checked. He later reported to the Argonaut trainer, Merv Prophet, that the worst part of his ordeal was hunger. He hadn't eaten since noon for the night game but nurses hesitated to feed him until tests had been analysed. His complaints were dismissed as symptoms of cerebral damage (that'll happen to guys who play on dee-fence). He was retained overnight for observation. By the time Mario got back to Toronto, Leo didn't have the heart to keep him out of the lineup. Mario played two seasons for the bottomless Boatmen.

Hughie Campbell didn't have so magnetic an effect on his Edmonton players as this, but he had a certain magic as a coach that reached into his first attempt as a general manager. This point was illustrated when he returned to the Eskimos in 1987 following the aforementioned two years in Houston. All he did was win the Grey Cup that first season, finish tied for the top in the West the second, and then run up a 16–2 record in 1989 before the never-quit Roughriders of Saskatchewan undid the Eskimos in the Western final.

Coming back to Canadian football as a GM, Campbell turned out to be the same deceptively mild fellow who had won five Grey Cup titles as a coach, lanky and lean as before, with small eyes and silky hair wisping across his forehead. You might think, hearing his soft voice and observing his quiet manner, that he'd be an easy mark for the Brobdingnagians who people this game. Nope, he was fully in charge, respected for his sure grasp of football's intricacies and recognized for the skills he showed when he came north as a player. That was in 1963 from Washington State University to Regina, where for six years he built records as a wide receiver for the Roughriders.

Returning, Hugh didn't propound that the pros in the CFL matched talent with those south of here, only that their game was as entertaining. "The players here are designed to play our game. Small safeties like, say, Larry Highbaugh can't stop the power-run game of the National Football League, but conversely those big tough safeties of the NFL couldn't possibly cover the wide Canadian field; pass receivers here would eat 'em up. The thing is, we're talking two different games though fundamentally they're the same."

Still, among many fans few topics draw blood faster than the suggestion that watching NFL football is not quite as gratifying as, oh, five weeks on a tropic island or a winning lottery ticket. When I used to mutter in the *Toronto Sun* and, later, the *Globe and Mail* that the spectator got more for a dollar watching the game up here than down there, jeering letters descended. I figured television put too bright a glow on the NFL, sending a carefully selected game across the U.S. and Canada, involving a different top team every week and spending hundreds of thousands of dollars on TV production alone. The fan in a *losing* NFL town, such as Indianapolis or Seattle, certainly wasn't accorded fare like this for his season ticket in the local abattoir.

Then one day a letter with a Willowdale, Ontario, postmark arrived from a man named James Seguin. The letter suggested that as entertainment the NFL was a distant second to the CFL and it didn't stop there.

"All you have to do is look up comparable statistics for the two leagues," this man wrote. "You'll find that up here there are:

1. More points scored per game
2. More plays from scrimmage
3. More yards gained per rush
4. More yards gained per pass
5. Better punters (slightly)
6. Better field-goal kickers (by far)

"No doubt an NFL team would handily defeat a CFL squad simply because they have more quality players, but the predictability of their system or style is something else."

In the 1970s the CFL's former director of information, Gord Walker, began recording comparative statistics on the two leagues, and the practice has been maintained. Year after year James Seguin's case has been verified. I could take any year in the past decade, but here's 1989 as an illustration:

1. Points per game, 54.6 in the CFL, 41.2 in the NFL
2. Plays from scrimmage, 164.1 in the CFL, 142.2 in the NFL
3. Yards per rush, 5.0 in the CFL, 4.0 in the NFL
4. Yards per pass, 7.3 in the CFL, 6.6 in the NFL
5. Punting average, yards, 40.7 in the CFL, 40.2 in the NFL
6. Field goals per game, 4.7 in the CFL, 2.7 in the NFL

An area in which the NFL excels is percentage of pass completions. Down there during the 1989 season, rival teams threw an average of 64 passes a game and completed 55.8 per cent of them. Up here they threw 71.2 passes and completed 49.8 per cent. Throwing the ball more often, CFL quarterbacks gained more yards, 520 to 421, nearly 100 yards a game. Clearly, what all this comes down to is that fans see more of the ball up here, an agreeable yardstick year after year.

Ultimately, the things that will make or break the CFL are the product on the field and a realization by fans that it can be exciting. Often, when Canadian football is at its worst it's at its best – a wild and crazy spectacle in which mistakes can usually be amended because in the three-down game the ball is so often changing hands. Until time runs out there's always another chance and in barn-burners such as the final three Grey Cup games of the 1980s fans were rung dry emotionally by this factor.

Denny Boyd, a bespectacled sage at the *Vancouver Sun*, once wrote about a football guy who captured the essence of the Canadian game. "Bill Burrell, a big, agile linebacker from Chicago, played just three seasons for the Saskatchewan Roughriders and made the 1962 all-star team. In the off-season of 1963 he died of leukemia in Chicago. The last thing he asked for before he died was that his body be returned to Regina and that he be buried there in his Roughrider green sweater. That's what those three seasons meant to Bill Burrell."

The sentiment is marvelous and merited. Only the facts are awry. The player wasn't Bill Burrell, he was Vernon Vaughan. And Vernon's body wasn't shipped to Regina; the sweater was shipped to Vernon's American home. Apart from that, though, the tale is absolutely flawless.

Chapter 14

Northern Dancer and friends

If there is one area in which your average everyday millionaire draws an almost complete blank but about which he is prepared to blow out his brains anyway, it is the area of producing a racehorse that can travel as fast as sound. Or even win one race.

I remember going to the old Prince George Hotel in Toronto on a night many years ago when Alfred Vanderbilt addressed a group called the Canadian Thoroughbred Horse Society. Apart from being even richer than most average everyday millionaires, Alfred Vanderbilt was the owner and breeder of the marvelous grey runner, Native Dancer, winner of 21 of 22 lifetime races. The only one of the 22 outings that Native Dancer didn't win at distances ranging from five-eighths of a mile to a mile and a half was the Kentucky Derby in 1953, when he lost by a head to Dark Star.

Accordingly, if anybody knew how to breed a horse to win and win and win, it was Alfred Vanderbilt, and so he was asked from the floor this night to reveal to the audience of about a hundred owners, trainers, and racing fanatics how to do it. The tanned and handsome face of the wealthy visitor turned bleak.

"Well, now, that's a question to which I wish I had an

answer," he replied. "I'm not really sure. I guess what you have to do is breed the best to the best and hope for the best."

And that's as close as you'll ever come to a solution to the age-old question, an answer that makes no sense if you will regard the species homo sapiens as reference. Wayne Gretzky has a younger brother who has the same sire and dam as Wayne had. Some people looking at Wayne the way they look at a very fast racehorse are apt to think that Wayne's mom and dad are the perfect match to produce an unending line of hockey geniuses. But no, it hasn't turned out like that. Wayne has a young brother who is not a hockey genius. So has Bobby Orr. So has Gordie Howe. Gordie and his wife Colleen combined to produce the near superstar, Mark, of the Philadelphia Flyers. But son Marty didn't quite have it. Bobby Hull and his first wife, Joanne, have a superstar son in Brett with the St. Louis Blues but their first pair of sons, Bobby and Blake, didn't have it. As hockey players, I mean here.

Yet most people hopeful of owning a winning horse feel the best way to find a winner is by matching winners. They visit yearling sales armed with money and a program. From the program they try to figure where the best broodmare has been bred to the best stallion (the best to the best). Then they spend their money in sometimes prodigious amounts on the offspring of the union that has already proven richly productive (Mr. and Mrs. Gretzky). In 1983 in Lexington, Kentucky, history never knew such a profusion of money. The thoroughbred yearling market reached a plateau that even Charles Taylor hadn't recognized, and Charles Taylor is no stranger to money. Or vice versa.

At this Kentucky auction a single 1-year-old horse was purchased for $10.2 million in U.S. funds, and ordinary mortals reading about it wondered how in the name of Croesus could a horse, who had never raced a step, did not have a name, had never seen the lovelight in the eye of a lady horse, how a horse like this could ever bring a return commensurate with the investment.

Even Charles Taylor, who just happened to own the sire of

the yearling that had fetched this breathtaking return, had no enlightened observation to make. "I don't know," is what he said when I phoned him and asked the question.

Charles had been present that night in Lexington hearing the dizzying bids. In one particularly stunning moment bidding jumped $2 million in the space of 10 seconds. Finally, when the auctioneer banged down his hammer on this bid of more than $10 million, the new owner was Shiek Mohammed bin Rashid al Maktoum of Dubai in the United Arab Emirates.

I knew Charles because he had grown up in the newspaper business, among other dalliances, before turning most of his attention to the horse-racing business. That happened when his father, E.P. Taylor, suffered a series of strokes in the early 1980s and Charles took over the operation of Windfields Farm, the racing establishment his father had founded.

The senior Taylor, who died in 1989, had been so ill for so long that he was unaware of the extraordinary sale of one of the Windfields yearlings. He was a dynamic man before illness overtook him – tall, round-faced, bald, large-bellied, and with a brief, nervous-sounding chuckle at the end of many of his sentences. In his latter business years, probably because he was a rich tycoon, enormously successful, and an easy target, he became the symbol of a pompous and aloof segment of society. I worked for him on two occasions totalling eight years and never found him to be either pompous or aloof. I never saw him anything but courteous, excessively polite, and even a little shy. When I left the Jockey Club he wrote me a thoughtful note saying that I had done a fine job and wishing me well. One night while I was still working at the Jockey Club he made a rare visit to the harness races at Greenwood and sat in the glassed-in dining room watching the trotters. When several of us went off to our various chores he was left at the table with my wife, June, who noticed him taking a couple of aspirins.

"Excuse me," he said, "I get a lot of headaches."

"There must be considerable strain in what you do," she said.

"Yes, I suppose there is," he acknowledged.

Later, June told me their conversation had turned to a

discussion of loneliness and that he seemed to be thoroughly aware of that emotion.

At any rate, when Charles took over Windfields it meant taking over the most successful stallion in racing history, Northern Dancer. The colt was bred by E.P. – for Edward Plunkett – at Windfields and, of course, won the Queen's Plate, the Kentucky Derby, and the Preakness Stakes in 1964, the first time a Canadian-bred had won the latter two stakes races. Later, when an injury forced Northern Dancer from the race track, he became the most rewarding financial stallion anywhere on earth.

I remember the night two years prior to his peak racing season when this colt, the grandson of Vanderbilt's Native Dancer, was available to anyone who laid down $25,000 for him. Nobody did. So E.P. kept him and he became the most beloved horse in Canadian history – and beloved isn't a misplaced word. E.P. mentioned once that the response to his horse had been overwhelming in the wake of his smashing triumphs.

"Hundreds and hundreds of letters arrived from all parts of Canada, and the U.S. as well," E.P. said. "The great majority of them were from young women, girls in their early teens. I had no idea that these young people had so strong a feeling for horses."

Even horsemen who practically took a magnifying glass to their examination of Northern Dancer rejected him when he was a yearling. The story is well known how Carl Chapman and the man for whom he trained horses, Larkin Maloney, passed up Northern Dancer and decided to put their $25,000 into a colt called Brockton Boy, who never amounted to much. For years following Northern Dancer's stunning success Chappie was chided for missing out on this four-legged mint.

But then one day he found his rejoinder. "Why knock me?" chirped the ebullient Chappie. "Imagine a real smart man like Mr. E.P. Taylor making that horse available for a measly 25 big ones."

There were several near-misses along the Dancer's path to fame. Such as his very birth. Taylor and two of his lieutenants, trainer Horatio Luro and chief of operations Joe Thomas, really weren't thinking much about what might result if they were to put the racing mare Natalma in with a speedy newcomer to the stud ranks, Nearctic. For one thing, it was June of 1960 when they thought of it and, since horses have an 11-month gestation period, the foal wouldn't appear until the following May, very late in the year for racehorses, whose birthdates advance one year on the first day of January regardless of when they are born. A May birth, therefore, is already five months into the calendar.

The sire, Nearctic, was foaled at Taylor's National Stud farm near Oshawa, after having been bred in England. He turned out to be a good sprinter but ran out of gas past a mile. The dam, Natalma, was purchased by Taylor at a sale of yearlings at Saratoga. Taylor liked her because her sire was Native Dancer (the familiar theory, right?). She raced exceptionally well as a 2-year-old but broke a bone in her knee training for the Kentucky Oaks in late April of 1960 at Churchill Downs. So what to do, pondered Taylor and Thomas and Luro. An operation? They decided against one, so what was left was mating her, and available was this young stud, Nearctic.

The colt was born on May 27, 1961, and as he developed he knocked nobody's hat off. "He looked pretty good as a weanling at Natalma's side," Joe Thomas told me once, "but by the following autumn he was so short and so damned chunky that he was a real disappointment."

The next crisis arrived when it turned out that the Dancer was so strong and wilful that he caused problems for jockeys. Whenever a broodmare came within sniffing distance he'd buck and lunge, trying to get at her. The brain trust almost decided to castrate him, but in the end, Taylor chose to race him.

It was as a 2-year-old that he showed real progress as a runner. And at 3, when he won the Flamingo Stakes at the Hialeah track in Florida in 1964, he became the first Canadian-bred to win a $100,000 race. He came off that race with another significant win and in another hundred-thousand dollar event, the Florida Derby, this one at Gulfstream Park up the road from

Hialeah. After that, a veteran racewriter in the Gulfstream press box wrote this paragraph about him:

"Here is a bold colt, an impudent, eye-catching rascal. He has character and a strangely disturbing personality. If you're an admirer of thoroughbred horses you will fall in love with Northern Dancer at first glance. There's something about this colt that causes your heart to skip a beat. There's a dramatic intensity in his every restless movement. He exudes explosive excitement."

The Toronto writer Muriel Lennox made several penetrating observations in a piece in *Toronto Life* magazine many years after Northern Dancer had proven himself to be the most economically successful stallion in racing history. Two of his progeny, for instance, Nijinsky and The Minstrel, had remarkable racing records in Britain. In 1970 Nijinsky became the first English Triple Crown winner in 35 years and race writers over there called him the horse of the century. In 1977 The Minstrel won the Epsom Derby.

"Northern Dancer took to the role of stud with extraordinary enthusiasm; it appeared he wanted to service every one of the several hundred mares on the farm," Muriel Lennox wrote. "When another stallion was led past his stall on his way to the breeding shed, the Dancer flew into a rage. Rearing, bucking, he kicked over his water buckets and demolished his feed tubs."

So his handlers attached a chain to his halter to pin him down, but as Lennox noted, a lot of good that did. "There was a great crash from the Dancer's stall. The trainers rushed back to find him hanging upside down by the chain; he had decided to go over the top of his stall to the breeding sheds. When they unclipped the chain he fell to the ground with a huge thud."

This horse was an unflagging lover but not all of his partners appreciated his charms. "Flaming Page found the whole performance quite objectionable," Lennox wrote. "She kicked him soundly in the ribs." Even so, the Dancer won out in the end: it was with Flaming Page, a lovely, spirited winner of the 1962 Queen's Plate, that he produced Nijinsky five years later.

When Northern Dancer was cleaning up on all the classics

except for the Belmont Stakes, the third event in the American Triple Crown, his trainer was the debonaire Señor, Horatio Luro, and he was ridden by two of racing's most successful riders. In winning the two big stakes in Florida, the Dancer had the marvelous midget, Willie Shoemaker, along for the ride, but for the Triple Crown races and the Queen's Plate there was a switch to Bill Hartack. That was because Shoemaker was offered two mounts for the Kentucky Derby, the one on Northern Dancer and another aboard Hill Rise, the California-bred who had cleaned up on the West Coast. Riders have rarely achieved immortality for their ability to pick winners, only to ride them, and the Shoe chose Hill Rise. "I just think he's a better horse," Shoemaker said, pressed for a reason. In the Derby the Dancer beat him a neck.

The Canadian colt was even tougher in the Preakness two weeks later, and then, three weeks after that, came the grinding Belmont. At a mile and a half it's the toughest race for a 3-year-old – and actually Northern Dancer, the late foal, was barely three on the calendar. On the morning before the race there was a breakfast at the Aqueduct track where owners, trainers, and other horsey fauna assembled. Among the trainers was the wonderful gentleman, 92-year-old Sunny Jim Fitzsimmons, who had saddled some of the great horses of the American turf. In spite of arthritis that bent him severely, his blue eyes carried a twinkle, he had a ready smile. His hair was snow white and his face marvelously lined.

The topic most often heard that morning was whether there would be a Triple Crown champion. There had been only eight, going all the way back to Sir Barton (Canadian owned, by the way, by J.K.L. Ross) in 1919, and none since Citation in 1948. The question Northern Dancer would have to answer was whether he had the stamina to handle the mile and a half. With Sunny Jim Fitzsimmons in the room, who better to ask? And so I did.

"Sir, do you think Northern Dancer can go a mile and a half?"

The old gentleman looked up at me with those merry eyes and his lean face broke into a smile.

"They can all go a mile and a half, my boy," he said. "The question always is, how long is it gonna take 'em."

It seemed to a great many people in the stands the next afternoon that Northern Dancer might very well be strangled before he'd gone even a quarter of a mile. Hartack had such a hold on the reins that the colt's muscular neck was almost doubled. He wanted to run right from the start but the jock had him in a grip of steel. Alas, the Dancer's strength and enthusiasm were sapped straining to tear loose from Hartack's hold in that first half-mile or so, and when he needed something extra rolling into the stretch to overhaul two horses in front of him, Quadrangle and Roman Brother, the tank was empty.

Quadrangle won the Belmont that day, so there was no Triple Crown winner. Indeed, there was not another until Secretariat came along in 1973 under the skilled and courageous New Brunswick rider, Ron Turcotte. Turcotte, whose back was broken and riding career ended in a spill at Belmont Park in 1978, told a bunch of us at Woodbine in the autumn of 1989 when he came for the running of the Rothmans International that riding Secretariat in the Belmont was "an experience in locomotion." The day in 1973 when Ron rode him he won this gruelling mile and a half test by an astonishing 31 lengths. "There was such smooth acceleration, so much power," the former rider reflected. "It was like driving a car with a V-12 engine."

For years following Bill Hartack's curious ride on Northern Dancer in the Belmont, his strangulation tactic was blamed for the defeat. Perhaps it was but, if so, the responsibility wasn't Hartack's. One day not long ago I asked Charles Taylor about Hartack's ride and was advised that sometimes riders disregard the instructions given them in the paddock prior to the race but in this case Hartack didn't. "He followed the instructions he was given," Charles said.

So perhaps they were Horatio Luro's, arrived at alone or after consultation with Joe Thomas or with Joe and E.P., all three of them. A few weeks later the Dancer made his final racetrack appearance, coming from dead last under Hartack to win the Queen's Plate at Woodbine. The horse sustained an injury that day, or aggravated one, a bowed tendon that precipitated his trek to the stud shed. I never saw the Señor again, although he continued to train in the U.S., where I assume he remained the dashing figure he'd been in his days with the Dancer. What a suave and charming fellow he was, tall and immaculate, the Cary Grant of backstretches from Woodbine to Buenos Aires – vintage wine, candlelight, sleek women, all that.

The Señor and his wife, the elegant Frances, a familiar figure at Woodbine when the Señor was training Taylor's horses, were a dazzling couple after he came north from Argentina in 1937 following the death of his wealthy father, a founding member of the Argentine Jockey Club. The Señor cut an instant swath – polished riding boots, beige corduroy breeches or slacks, a hound's-tooth jacket, flat cashmere cap at rakish angle, an accent to knock you out of your spats, a pencil mustache. Once, he gave a South American-bred filly to the actress Lana Turner. They called her Cheryba, after Cheryl, Lana's daughter. Then he met Frances, a southern belle whose father was an Atlanta mining magnate.

A couple of decades following Northern Dancer's final race Charles Taylor was indirectly involved in the record sale of the most overrated thoroughbred in American racing history. Windfields Farm consigned the yearling son of its stallion Halo to the Lexington sale. The colt brought Taylor $325,000 at auction. His new owner, James Mills, a Virginian, called his colt Devil's Bag, and in 1983 Devil's Bag developed into the hottest 2-year-old in racing. He won everything available to him and because of it he was favoured to win the classics that lay ahead in his 3-year-old campaign. In the wake of that early success, Devil's Bag was sold by Mills to a syndicate of breeders for $36 million. Yep, $36 million.

Calm unruffled people, certified sane, said Devil's Bag might be the perfect thoroughbred. The *New York Times* dispatched its racing writer, Steven Crist, to Florida to write about this horse in long, periodic pieces all winter. Woody Stephens, the colt's trainer, stood by his stall one morning at Hialeah peering in. "Is there anything you can't do?" asked the 70-year-old master trainer.

Devil's Bag. This remarkable name was inspired by Washington Irving's *The Legend of Sleepy Hollow*, in which superstitious people believed that an evil-smelling sack called a devil's bag contained explosive and supernatural powers.

So now it was time for Charles Taylor to be chided as Carl Chapman had many moons ago. I phoned him one morning in February of 1984 and asked him if he'd considered slashing his wrists, letting a $36 million goldmine go for cigarette money.

"Good gracious, no," Charles said, a trifle ruffled. "We are commercial breeders and Windfields offers everything we breed for sale, except for the odd filly. We don't put reserve prices on our horses; they are there to be sold. This one brought $325,000. That's the breeding business."

Well, as it turned out, those experienced investors who'd put their brains and their money into this colt were left holding the Bag. For whatever reason, Devil's Bag as a 3-year-old became a major disappointment. To that burning question his trainer had asked in Florida, "Is there anything you can't do?" there was an instant answer: Yes, one thing. Win.

Nineteen years slipped past before another Canadian-bred colt pulled off Northern Dancer's coup in Kentucky, this one the chestnut Sunny's Halo. Sunny's Halo was owned by a quiet-spoken stockbroker, David (Pud) Foster, who as a kid growing up in Toronto had sold newspapers on a downtown street corner. There wasn't a lot of similarity between Pud and E.P. Taylor. Once you'd noted that both owned a Derby winner and that each bred the winner himself, you'd pretty well exhausted the topic.

Oh, on a bright day they might throw similar shadows in the walking ring at the track. They were about the same size, with about the same generous front porches. But whereas E.P. owned four or five hundred racehorses, Pud owned four or five. And in 1964 E.P. was a giant in Canadian racing whereas in 1984 Pud wasn't notably prominent, at least not in the years leading up to Sunny's Halo's victory. With Pud, horse racing was just something he dabbled in, a sideline for days when he left the office early.

There were some similarities between the two horses. Both had to overcome serious injuries to reach their lofty stations. As with Sunny's Halo 19 years later, Northern Dancer had been Canada's 2-year-old champion. The Dancer's most serious injury was a quarter crack (a tear in the hoof) that would have ended his racing had it not been for an invention by a California blacksmith named Bill Bane. It was a rubber patch under which the crack was able to heal after an eight-hour surgical operation.

Sunny's Halo lost four races on U.S. tracks as a 2-year-old before it was discovered he had stress fractures in both front shins. The way Dave Cross, Pud's trainer, fixed that was to swim Sunny every day over the winter in a training pool at Hollywood Park in California. As a side effect the colt built impressive stamina, probably accounting for his virtual wire-to-wire win in a downpour in the Derby.

One afternoon soon after Pud returned from Louisville I went to talk with him in his office in the relatively modest brokerage firm he ran in Toronto. He was freshly back from the exhilaration and excitement of accompanying his own colt in his own bright orange-and-white silks into the winner's enclosure at Churchill Downs.

Pud's name, by the way, is pronounced pud as in pudding, not pud as in puddle. He explained that kids he used to run with when he wasn't selling papers called him Puddinhead and Puddinface. He had a tiny joke for me this day, which he'd probably sprung on only seven or eight thousand people before me. "I don't care what they call me," Pud said, "as long as it isn't too late for dinner."

I already knew, as most people did who watched the Derby on television that spring, that Sunny's Halo had been named for both his sire and dam – the former being Halo and the latter being Mostly Sunny. Pud had paid a modest $3,900 for Mostly Sunny at the Canadian Thoroughbred Horse Society's annual yearling auction sale at the Woodbine track in 1972. Pud said he'd gone there just to see if something might grab him, which this filly did. He named her Mostly Sunny because of her quiet disposition.

"Bought another filly that night, too," Pud said, leaning back in his chair, fingers laced across his stomach as he reminisced. He is not a demonstrative man. His expression doesn't change much when he talks. He doesn't raise his voice.

"Called her Dup Dup, which is Pud spelled backwards. Dup Dup cost $5,000 and was a real good runner but later when I bred her she died in foal to Vice Regent."

Pud had also bred Mostly Sunny to Vice Regent that year, 1978, but ran into misfortune in this mating, as well, when the mare aborted. That really distressed him and Dave Cross, the trainer, because a year earlier Mostly Sunny's first foal, a healthy colt, had been shipped to Florida for the winter and had stepped in a hole and snapped a bone in his leg. He had to be destroyed.

"It was a very discouraging time for us," Pud said.

"Well, okay," I said, waiting a moment. "So what prompted you to try again with Halo? Why Halo?"

"The Queen did, so why not," Pud said.

"The queen? What queen?"

"The Queen of England," Pud retorted testily, as though wondering who is this oaf who doesn't know his own queen.

"You mean Queen Elizabeth?" I said in a rare flare of comprehension.

"That's the one," Pud said, his rugged face relaxing into a grin. "See, Dave Cross happened to notice in a paper somewhere that Elizabeth had sent one of her many broodmares to Halo. 'If he's good enough for the Queen of England he's good enough for us,' Dave said, and I said okay by me."

Thus, instead of forsaking breeding, Pud and his trainer decided to try again with Mostly Sunny, and sent her, as the Queen of England had done, to Halo. I mentioned earlier that Halo had a Charles Taylor connection, which was that Windfields Farm owned Halo. How that came about was that Halo had belonged to Charles Englehart, an American industrialist and a friend of E.P. Taylor's. Englehart's death precipitated E.P.'s purchase of Halo. Actually, Halo and Northern Dancer were distant relatives and, trusting it doesn't empty the room, I can relate how this came about: Halo's dam was Cosmah. Cosmah's dam was Almahmoud and Almahmoud was also the dam of Natalma. Natalma, you'll remember, was Northern Dancer's dam (breeders talk this way all the time).

At any rate, distressed as Pud Foster Had been half a dozen years earlier, he was now highly stimulated with Sunny's Halo in the spotlight and everybody wondering if Pud planned sending his horse in quest of the Triple Crown, following up his Derby win with the Preakness at Baltimore's Pimlico track two weeks hence. Dave Cross was set against going on to the Belmont if Sunny should happen to win the Preakness.

"I don't believe in sending a young horse so far so soon," Dave said. "A mile and a half is too much this early."

Dave's wife Patty already had three daughters when she and Dave were married in 1977, young women of 18, 17, and 9 from a previous marriage. Dave had met Patty in California when he had a string of horses at the Santa Anita track in Arcadia, where she lived with her girls. Southern Californians generally are hooked on Mexican food but there were very few restaurants specializing in it in the Toronto area when Dave and his ménage arrived for the racing at Woodbine and Fort Erie in 1978. Patty decided to fix that. She opened Patty C's Mexican restaurant in the quiet little village of Streetsville just beyond Toronto's western reaches where they'd settled.

Why am I telling you this? Because it was at Patty C's Mexican restaurant that I decided to spend Preakness Day when Sunny's Halo took aim on further fame and fortune. Patty was in Baltimore with Dave for the big day but her mother, a slim, merry-eyed woman with the warmest of smiles, was there running the restaurant. So was Lisa Cross, one of Patty's daughters.

Naturally, the restaurant was full of life and humming in a happy ambiance. Long before the big race the enchiladas were ready for the oven, the emparadas had been stuffed with chicken, and the frosted tulip glasses were brimful of a dynamite concoction of tequila, Amaretto, Cointreau, orange sherbet, orange juice, crushed ice, and a twist of mint. Lisa Cross, black-haired and blue-eyed, one of the bartenders this day, had dreamed up the recipe for the drink, which naturally enough was called a Sunny's Halo.

Unhappily for the totally biased sentiment inside Patty C's Mexican restaurant, Lisa's drink had considerably more kick than the horse who bore its name. Up on the big television screen rushing through the slop the colt trained by the husband of the woman who owned the restaurant had a very bad time. But when it was over, with Sunny in sixth place back of Deputed Testamony, the winner, the mood of the restaurant was not subdued for long.

"Hurray," called Lisa, behind the bar. "Mom will be home."

It turned out not to be much of a summer for Sunny's Halo after the glorious beginning. He had broken out in hives before the Preakness and then got roughed up leaving the gate. Next, racing in the Arlington Classic in Chicago, he had severely injured an ankle, causing him to miss the race in which he would have been heavily favoured, the Queen's Plate back home at Woodbine.

Even before Sunny's 3-year-old year Pud had sent Mostly Sunny back to Halo in Kentucky. The first time, when Sunny's Halo resulted from the union, Pud had paid $7,500 as Halo's stud fee. That second time, with Sunny's Halo having become the 2-year-old champion in Canada, Halo's fee had gone up to $30,000. And once again Pud's racing luck had been bad; the foal had caught a virus and died.

Not long afterwards Halo was gone from Windfields. One day late in January of 1984 Charles Taylor received a phone call from Arthur Hancock, the owner of Stone Farm in Kentucky.

"Charlie, I'm interested in Halo," he said.

"But Arthur," Charles replied, a trifle mystified, "as you well know, the breeding season is upon us. I don't see how I can work you in. I'm afraid his book is full."

"I'm not talking about a season or a service," Hancock replied. "I want the whole horse!"

So a deal was struck and Halo was shipped to Arthur Hancock in Kentucky.

By then Halo was much in demand, for in 1983 Sunny's Halo had won the Derby and Devil's Bag was the 2-year-old horse of the year, each of them a son of Halo.

I saw Pud again in the summer of 1984 at a barbecue put on by the Ontario Jockey Club to promote the forthcoming Queen's Plate. He said he was trying once more with Mostly Sunny in a visit to Halo.

"In fact," Pud said, "she's two months pregnant."

"Halo's fee go up again?" I asked.

"Some," Pud allowed, poking a fork into his potato salad. "A hundred thousand this time."

"Dollars?" I wheezed.

"Dollars," Pud Foster said.

You see, that's what happens when you breed the best to the best and hope for the best.

Chapter 15

Gold fever

If you're footloose, an advantage of writing about sports is that it lands you in a lot of places that would otherwise remain names in an atlas. For me, pursuing perspiring people led to Germany and Cuba, Australia and Russia, England and Scotland, among other faraway places.

And such sights. Here was Victor Davis kicking the water bucket in front of the Queen in the Brisbane swimming pool and there was the compound where Israeli's Olympic athletes were shot dead in Munich. Here was Jack Donohue on a beach outside Havana walking hand in hand with his lady basketball players and there in Edinburgh I stared in awe at Ben Johnson's muscles in the days before the shit hit the fan.

Nothing much about the Munich Olympics remains in my memory apart from the Israeli killings by PLO terrorists who broke into their living quarters. They killed two of them immediately and held nine others hostage while German cops tried to figure out what to do. After day-long negotiations the terrorists were allowed to take their hostages with them to the airport, where an abortive rescue attempt resulted in the murder of all nine Israelis. A helicopter was blown up, killing four terrorists, a Munich policeman, and the chopper pilot. This was the first of the European terrorist hijackings and bombings that persisted for years.

I phoned the *Star* what little I knew or could see. Not long ago in Toronto I looked up my piece. In true cinematic newspaper style the desk had given it this heading: *Star Man on the Scene in Munich*.

That day presented the bizarre combination of terror on a tranquil afternoon. Two men lay dead inside a peaceful-looking white stucco building with four neat rows of balconies and window boxes of geraniums. Outside, hundreds of people stood on a high grassy knoll overlooking the sunbathed scene. A woman strolled by on a gravel path pushing a baby in a pram and happened to stop near me.

"What is it?" she asked, in English.

"Some athletes are being held hostage," I said.

"Oh," she said, setting off with her carriage, "is that all."

What's there to remember about the Games? Oh, yes, a few days after the massacre, the Soviet basketball team beat the United States on a last-second, controversial basket to win the gold medal. With government officials still trying to fathom the reasons for the security breakdown at the Israeli compound, with people still in shock following the 17 violent deaths, a half-dozen American newspeople buttonholed an IOC official in the press centre to argue heatedly that the basketball result should be reversed on the grounds that the timekeeper had been intimidated by Soviet officials and had allowed the clock to run past full time.

Two years after the Munich Olympics I went to the *Toronto Sun* to write a sports column. An early job was to go with a group of Canadian athletes to Cuba, and there I encountered the indefatigable wordsmith, Jack Donohue, a man who never met a split infinitive he couldn't lick. Jack was the Canadian Olympic team's basketball coach.

We went to Havana in a chartered DC-8 that, according to a worn logo on the door of the men's toilet, once belonged to Orient Airlines. I figured that was back when Chiang Kai-Shek was learning to use chopsticks. Aboard were 139 athletes, a CBC television crew, CBC radio sportscaster Fred Walker, and three scribes, Mary Trueman from the *Globe and Mail*, Ian Mac-Donald from the *Montreal Gazette*, and me from the *Toronto Sun*. It was a Canadian Olympic training-and-competition junket for six disciplines – women's basketball, diving, and volleyball and men's wrestling, fencing, and water polo.

The plane bumped down in Havana late at night and we were bussed along Cuba's northern coast 45 miles east to a woodsy outpost called Jibacoa on a gorgeous Atlantic horseshoe beach. Each day various teams boarded buses into Havana to play against Cuban Olympic teams, competition for both sides.

The Cubans were good in every sport. At all the arenas and pools where the Canadians played there was this emblazoned message from Fidel Castro: *El Deporte Es un Derecho del Pueblo* – Sport is a Right of the People. Kids had a chance to reach their sports potential by exposure to skilled training and technique. Next door to one downtown school was a regulation water polo pool. Kids from 12 to 18 took their academic lessons in the school and spent two hours a day on water polo instruction 10 months of the year. There were 560 boys registered at this school, 50 in the goalkeeping class alone. It was that way in all sorts of sports – volleyball, basketball, soccer, apparently whatever a kid wanted to do.

The hour-long bus rides into Havana gave the coaches the undivided attention of the athletes. I made a couple of trips with the women's basketballers listening to Coach Donohue assault their eardrums. Jack was in his mid-40s then, a big-boned, somewhat stooped six-footer in hornrims with an accent born in the Bronx. He had been lured north from Holy Cross University in Boston where he'd coached for seven years. In his New York high-school days he'd coached a gangling seven-footer named Lew Alcindor who later joined the Los Angeles Lakers and changed his name to Kareem Abdul-Jabbar. Jack was imported to Sport Canada's Ottawa headquarters to teach basketball to the men's and women's Olympic teams.

He did a terrific job. In 1972 the men's team had not even

qualified for the Munich Olympics but at Montreal four years later they narrowly missed a bronze medal and climbed to fourth in world ranking. By 1990 when Jack had become a wry toastmaster and light-hearted television panelist on The Sports Network, the men's team was still reflecting his 15-year contribution to the roundball game invented by the Canadian Dr. James Naismith. That was some switch, Naismith for Donohue.

After the Havana junket Jack gave up coaching the women's team because running the men's global operation was full time. When I mentioned earlier that I'd seen him walking the beach hand-in-hand with women players I didn't mean by moonlight. He'd talk to them in groups and individually, strolling along on days when they didn't have games in Havana. He spent as much time on philosophical infusion as he did on basketball tactics and technique.

The women responded to him. They referred to themselves as "Jack's Goils." They listened as he talked on the bus rides (who could escape?) and so did I. "You've got to appreciate how much talent you've got," he'd tell them. "You are unique. There's nobody else in the world like you. If you want to be happy, try to make other people happy. If you want to be loved, you must love others. The way to improve is to do something you have never done. Don't be afraid of your emotions. They are your generator. The intellect is the governor." Every day and half the night Jack talked like this, and between times, when the team was training or scrimmaging, he'd pace the sidelines talking the game's nuances to his goils.

All the 139 athletes and our media bunch had New Year's Day off because Havana was shut down in celebration of the 16th anniversary of the Cuban Revolution. The Canadians greeted the new year a few miles down the road from our spartan lodgings at a resort called El Tropico, a seaside spa for package tour groups from Canada operated by a Toronto firm.

There, we joined a planeload of newly arrived tourists in a roast piglet dinner that featured a Cuban band, midnight fireworks, and enough native rum to accommodate a regatta. I had this brilliant idea for a column that I'd ask the athletes for their New Year's resolutions. It was a dumb idea on a night when they had a break from the training grind, a point made clear to me when I put the question to one of the divers, an attractive, slim, dark-haired young woman. She stared at me impassively for a moment and then she answered. "I'm thinking of giving up fucking until after the Games."

Of all the venues for the 1976 Olympics the toughest ticket in Montreal was for gymnastics in the Forum where the tiny 14-year-old Romanian gymnast, Nadia Comaneci, scored the first maximum 10 marks ever achieved in that back-bending business. By the end of it she'd piled in another six perfect scores, next thing to unbelievable.

Everybody wanted to interview this solemn, wide-eyed kid, but it was a slow and largely fruitless undertaking. One night after she'd scored a couple of 10s and the crowd was standing and shouting applause, she was caught up by a pack of news people in a corner of the Forum under the seats. I remember her huddled against a rumpled pile of old canvas coverings. A middle-aged, motherly Romanian woman sat on a chair beside her, interpreting for us and trying to give answers to the most rudimentary questions. ("Do you still go to school?" "She says yes." "How long have you trained in gymnastics?" "Nadia says since she was four." "How many hours a day do you train?" "Oh, she says many, many.") Visualizing her now, I have this picture of a pale, wary child, eyes wide, perhaps even a little frightened by so much attention.

The women who had been Jack's Goils in Havana didn't do very well in this same arena. They had a sobering experience when they faced the Soviet entry. Playing centre for the bad guys was Juliana Semenova, 7-foot-1¾ and 280 pounds. The Canadian women lost by 115–51 to the team that won the gold medal by beating the U.S. 112–77.

The monstrous cost of the Olympics far overshadowed any other Games topic apart from Nadia. Nick Auf der Maur, a

Montreal city councillor and later a columnist for the *Gazette*, brought out a book called *The Billion-Dollar Game* that documented the bungling and greed of Olympic construction, a story of incompetence, duplicity, nepotism, and corruption that sent the cost of the Montreal Games to $1.5 billion.

Auf der Maur wrote that lack of controls and unscrupulous contractors with open-ended contracts sent costs out of sight. Also, the unions took advantage of power struggles inside the organizing committee to make outrageous demands. The prima donna Parisian architect Roger Taillibert, whose every whim seemed to be a command for the wide-eyed mayor, Jean Drapeau, was slated to get a fee greater than the combined fees of all the architects in Quebec for the previous year.

"Inexorably, the city was drawn deeper and deeper into a financial morass by a mayor whose vision and dream had grown into an almost lunatic obsession," Auf der Maur wrote. Typically, the foundation for the velodrome, the bicycle track, had been estimated at $497,576. Its final cost was $7,171,876. The whole project became "a monstrous, uncontrollable nightmare with an insatiable appetite for funds."

A funny thing happened on the way to Brisbane for the 1982 Commonwealth Games in Australia. Ten or twelve thousand miles from home and what did I see? Why, I saw Wilf Paiement score for the Nordiques to pull them to within 5–3 of the Boston Bruins.

Talk about exotic. Far below, from a window on the right-hand side of the Qantas 747, was the celebrated Sydney opera house with its stunning roof of yawning, spherical shells adorned in small rectangles of shining white tile. This was early on a Sunday morning. "Wow, Australia," I thought after nearly 24 hours of flying, "halfway around the world."

I had to wait in Sydney until late afternoon for a flight to Brisbane 600 miles north so I took a cab downtown to the Menzies Hotel and turned on television to absorb some local culture.

"They're a different team since they beat the Canadiens," came the unmistakable voice of Dick Irvin.

Hey, just a gol darn minute.

"That's right, Dick" responded Mickey Redmond. "The Nordiques are on a roll. But Boston is still leading."

I want to say it's mighty disillusioning to run into an NHL broadcast when you think you're a world traveller in a faraway land. Here was a five-month-old tape of the sixth game of the previous May's Stanley Cup quarterfinal and when it was over a toothy Australian booth announcer said that next week at this time there'd be more exciting action from the North American ice hockey championships.

The guide book said that Brisbane, Australia's third-largest city (Aussies pronounce it Briz-bin), was a town of a million inhabitants but it didn't feel that big. It was more like Calgary or Ottawa. Blue hills were visible in the distance, the streets had been newly vacuumed, and the downtown area was spruced up with flags and bunting. In the main shopping area, four or five blocks of Queen Street had been turned into a pedestrian mall, alive with strollers munching ice cream or people seated at outdoor cafés under phony palm fronds and eucalyptus trees. They drank beer from tall glasses or sat at marble-top tables on white wrought-iron chairs diving into the French pastry. Kids played guitars under store awnings and sang for loose change from passersby.

On the morning of the marathon, which began at seven o'clock to avoid the sun and heat of early afternoon, I came down from my 10th floor room for breakfast and found the lobby alive with young business people. I knew they were young business people because the guys were in summer suits and ties and the women were in soft summer dresses. A couple of television sets were arranged in the lobby, the furniture had been moved aside, and everyone was seated on the carpeting to watch the marathon. The hotel was serving champagne cocktails on the house and before long this was a mighty happy crowd saluting the sweaty marathoners on the screen, growing slightly pie-eyed before whooping off to work.

One Sunday, a Games day off, I went to an exhibition of Australian football. The overall philosophy of Australian football was once best expressed by a coach in Melbourne named John Kennedy. "Australian football is a game for men," John said, "played by beasts." After watching for a while I concluded that the most important piece of equipment in Australian football is an ambulance.

Australian football, which is also called Australian rules, or simply rules, by the masses, draws crowds of 100,000 in Melbourne, the town on the south coast where the game was devised in 1858 to keep cricket players in shape in the off-season (God knows how they survived for cricket). Prince Philip showed up this Sunday in Brisbane and apparently the teams cleaned up the game somewhat as a courtesy to him, for I overheard a guy say, "There's hardly any bloody blood."

It appeared that a characteristic of Australian football is that by the end of the game true fans are drunk. It's like American football or Grey Cup day.

In Australian football, passers don't throw the ball, they kick it. Or hold it in the palm of one hand and punch it with the other. This is done on the run. And the receivers leap and pluck 'em out of the air on the run, too. Defenders try every means short of drawing loaded pistols to prevent receivers from receiving passes. Usually in advancing the ball a player kicks it on the run and when it comes down there's a crowd waiting for it, a big crowd. That's when the drivers warm up the ambulances.

And now Victor Davis – explosive, temperamental, considerate, warm, hostile, thoughtful, impulsive, a young man of 6-foot-2 and 190 pounds, aglow in good looks and energy. He always seemed to be tanned. He had short wavy brown hair, a rather imperious bearing and a big chest with a tiny maple leaf tattooed on it.

Victor was 25 in November of 1989 when his parents requested that the life-support systems be withdrawn from his body and that his vital organs be sent to donor banks. A car had hit him when he and some friends came from a surburban Montreal bar at 12:30 a.m. a couple of nights earlier. There were fractures to his spine and skull. He did not regain consciousness.

Victor (I never heard anyone call him Vic) had retired from swimming the previous July, crying openly when he announced he was through. Well, why wouldn't he? That was the kind of wide-open guy he was. He felt rotten that the game was finally over, so he cried. He was a very intense person.

Victor was a kid not yet 18 in 1982 when he set a world record for the 200-metre breaststroke in Ecuador. Before he was through he won a gold medal at the Los Angeles Olympics in that same event in world-record time. He missed a gold in the 100 by an inch or two, and got a second silver as part of the 4-by-100 medley relay team. In 1986 in the Madrid world championships he won a gold in the 100 and a silver in the 200. A picture I remember of Victor came after his record victory at the L.A. Olympics. Marching to the awards ceremony he spun Frisbees into the open-air stands. "They have the Canadian emblem on them," Victor said. "I wanted to show my appreciation to the people."

And, of course, it was at Brisbane in 1982 that he acquired a sort of backhanded immortality when he kicked that plastic chair. If Queen Elizabeth hadn't been primly seated there, chances are the incident would have been forgotten long ago. But the combination of her presence and his impulsive (and highly understandable, Victor being Victor) poolside act engraved it in stone.

It had been a tough night for Victor. First he'd narrowly lost a stroke-by-stroke duel over 100 metres with Adrian Moorhouse, England's ace. Next, the Canadian medley team was deprived of a gold medal after setting a Commonwealth record in the 4-by-100 final. A newly installed electric timing device indicated that butterflier Dan Thompson had left the blocks a split second before Victor touched the wall. Of course when Alex Baumann wrapped up the final lap several lengths ahead of the arch-rival Australians, the Canadian swimmers had leaped wildly over one another. But the timer indicated a break of 5/100ths of a second between Thompson taking off from his block and Davis touching the pool's end.

So when the p.a. announcement was made that Canada's record-breakers were dead in the water, Victor charged across the pool's tile apron, heading for the locker room. And when the white plastic chair loomed in his path he booted about a 20-foot field goal. He steamed past us waiting scribes, shoving one guy roughly aside and refusing to be interviewed. And the rest of the team stomped off even before the official results were announced.

Next morning, the Games over, it occurred to me that the press officers would be arranging a meeting with Victor. I saw that the Aussie morning papers were having a picnic with his outburst. I got a cab to the Games village and on arrival spotted some of the swim guys waiting at the village bus stop.

Victor was there, in shorts and a T-shirt and wearing dark glasses, and the team manager, Trevor Tiffany, was there, too.

"Where's everybody off to?" I asked Trevor.

"Surfers Paradise," Trevor said. "We figured a day of surfing ought to cool everybody out."

Surfers Paradise is a broad beach on the so-called Gold Coast south of Brisbane. On the one hand it resembles the beaches of south Florida with tall condominiums and amusement parks; on the other hand, it doesn't resemble south Florida in that the women often neglect to wear their swimsuit tops.

Victor was seated on a low concrete wall, arms resting on his outstretched thighs. He seemed somber, eyes only dimly visible behind the dark shades.

"Things a little brighter this morning?" I said.

Victor replied readily enough.

"It was an impulsive reaction to an enormous disappointment," he blurted. "Then when I saw all those vultures waiting to pounce I couldn't believe it. I'm sorry I pushed that guy. If I offended anybody I apologize. It all built up."

Victor said the team had gone to the home of a Brisbane couple after the fiasco for a long, late party. "I still feel kind of wrangy," he said. "I'm gonna have to learn to watch myself when things don't go right, especially in these international meets where everybody's watching."

We spoke a while longer and I took notes and then a minibus arrived to take the swimmers to Surfers Paradise and I went back to town.

It was my notion that if the swimmers didn't get back to the village by five o'clock I was in the clear with my Victor interview. That would make it three o'clock in the morning in eastern Canada, safely past the deadlines for the rival morning papers. I'd worked out the time difference soon after arriving in Australia when Alex Baumann set a world record in a 100-metre medley heat. He did this a couple of minutes before 1 p.m. and I was watching from the pool's press box. The *Sun*'s deadline was 11 p.m., and being unsure of the time difference I picked up the phone and dialed the *Sun*'s sports department, an immediate connection via satellite.

John Iaboni, our hockey writer, was on the other end. "John," I said, "what's the time?"

"A couple minutes to 11. You forget your watch?"

"Ha," I said. "Alex Baumann just set a world's record. Can you take it?"

"Sure," Johnny said. "Shoot."

So the way I stored the time difference into my massive brain was to recognize that when the sky was daylight bright in Australia it was inky dark in Toronto – minus two hours. Thus, one o'clock in the afternoon in Brisbane was 11 o'clock at night in Toronto.

So to keep my Victor Davis interview safe from the wolfpack, all that was needed was Victor's absence until five o'clock in the afternoon, 3 a.m. back home.

And that's what happened. I said nothing until dinner that night when around seven o'clock I told Matthew Fisher how I'd stumbled into my Davis interview.

"Hey, nice going," enthused Matthew, who was doing some freelance stuff for the *Globe*. "What'd Victor have to say?"

I told him briefly.

The next morning, preparing to leave for home, I ran into Matthew in the hotel lobby. He said he was taking a train trip across Australia to Perth. Then the chubby fellow broke a wide smile.

"Thanks, pal," Matthew said.

"For what?"

"Oh, I've been doing a daily piece for CFRB in Toronto. After I talked to you last night I phoned them the stuff you told me about Victor. It was on my 6 a.m. newscast about the time your stuff was on the street corners, maybe a little sooner."

I thought back. Matthew and I had eaten around 7 p.m. That would be 5 a.m. in Toronto. Which meant he still had an hour to spare in phoning his 6 a.m. broadcast, which was probably taped and repeated at 7.

"Son of a bitch," I grumbled. "Did you give me credit?"

"Credit? After what you did? No way. I just said Victor told this stuff to a Canadian journalist." Matthew chuckled again. "Have a nice da-ay," Matthew said, walking out the door.

The 1984 Olympics in Los Angeles were Hollywood's idea of what the United States looks like, a combination of schmaltz and chauvinism to glaze the eyeballs. When Pierre de Coubertin revived the ancient pastime of fun and games in 1896, he had a couple of thoughts about them. "The important thing is not to win but to take part," was one. Another was, "The essential thing is not to have conquered but to have fought well."

Pierre was just a little bit ahead of the time of Vince Lombardi, the football coach, who dreamed up the current American doctrine. "Winning isn't everything," Vince said. "It's the only thing."

Even so, for three hours at every Olympic opening everybody pretends that de Coubertin knew what he was talking about, and the thing that makes this hilarious hypocrisy work is the matchless cast – thousands of young, shining, and unlined faces to remind people that there is still innocence.

For the opening ceremonies at the L.A. Olympics there were 7,500 of these young, shining, and unlined faces from countries around the world parading into the Coliseum, a horseshoe bowl seating 92,655 in brilliant sunshine. But missing were scores of world-class athletes from Communist countries of the peaceful pre-1989 revolutions – the Soviet Union and East Germany in particular, two nations that for 20 years had dominated Olympic scoreboards. Nonetheless, through the two weeks of the Games the American bullshit was everywhere – in the stands, on the airwaves, in the newspapers.

Typical was a 2,500-word piece on the sprinter and long-jumper Carl Lewis in *Time* magazine the week of the opening. "What he does is so simple, and how he does it so complicated, that Carl Lewis is a basic mystery. How fast he runs, how far he jumps, may serve to establish the precise lengths to which men can go. Gentler than a superman, more delicate than the common perception of a strong man, Lewis is physically the most advanced human being in the world."

To produce the opening ceremonies the organizing committee hired, what else? a film producer, a mortal named David Wolper, who had produced the boffo hit television smasheroo (not to put too fine a point on it) *Roots*. David said what he wanted was "a show that is majestic, inspirational, emotional – a 20 goose-bump experience."

For one goose-bump experience there were these 84 guys in powder-blue dress suits sitting halfway up a wall banging out George Gershwin's "Rhapsody in Blue" on 84 grand pianos. Another goose-bump experience was an instant Old West town, bang, right there on the stadium's freshly painted grass, from zero to the O.K. Corral in nothing flat.

The tableaux were designed to invoke the American spirit, the official program said, a spirit which in a *Globe* piece I suggested might also have been demonstrated a couple of days earlier in a nearby hamlet called San Ysidro. There, a guy left home with a pistol, a rifle, and a semi-automatic weapon, walked into a McDonald's, and killed 21 people, including kids arriving on bikes to buy a Big Mac.

It was a mean-spirited parallel to draw, I suppose, and I got my share of mail denouncing my "personal harangue," as one reader termed it. I guess it was the blatancy of the ceaseless chauvinism that got to me.

Speaking of chauvinism, the *Globe* made a front-page fuss over Linda Thom, a 40-year-old sharpshooter from Ottawa who on the first day of competition won a gold medal in sport-pistol shooting. It was Canada's first Olympic gold since the Canadian equestrian team managed not to fall off the horses at Mexico City in 1968.

In mid-afternoon that day I came out of press headquarters and saw one of the Canadian press officers, Pam McFarlane, standing with a half-dozen Canadian news guys. I knew something was up but didn't know what so I joined the group.

We stood talking about the absence of smog and other terrific topics and then Pam said to me, "Are you coming with us, Trent?" And I said, "You bet, you can count me in."

Soon a Canadian Olympic minibus arrived and we headed off into the wilds of inland California, finally pulling up at a place called Chino where a big crowd was assembled in an open field.

"What's going on?" I asked a spectator.

"A shoot-off for the gold," this woman said.

"Who's in it?"

"Four of them, women from the States, Australia, Canada, and China."

"Canada?" I said, the light going on. "Which one is Canada?"

"I think the tall blonde woman. That's her husband over there."

I walked over and introduced myself and he said, "Hi, I'm Don Thom." He said that Linda, the sharpshooter, was a great cook. "I worked in Paris for the Canadian government in 1972 and Linda got interested in food over there. She does a real mean truffle soup."

"Truffle soup?"

"Yep. Costs 15 bucks a bowl when you make it at home."

While we waited for the minibus back to Los Angeles I

started writing my *Globe* piece in a notebook: "A gourmet cook and mother of two, Linda Thom of Ottawa won a gold medal for Canada yesterday on the opening day of the Olympic Games." And so forth, using the stuff Don Thom had told me. The *Globe* ran it under this head:

> Canada's first Olympic gold
> Captured by mother of two

Sure enough, the roof caved in. Feminists across the land fired letters to the paper denouncing the male chauvinist pig (a big phrase in 1984). "What's this mother of two stuff?" one wondered. "Would you call a male medalist *father* of two?"

As it happened, yes. On November 19 that year a Winnipeg-born head coach led the Blue Bombers to the Grey Cup on an ice floe in Edmonton, and on purpose I described him as "Cal Murphy, father of seven," and not a voice was raised in the land.

In Los Angeles in 1984, who had heard of Ben Johnson? Only the closest followers of track were paying attention and there weren't many of those. It wasn't that Ben didn't make an impression; indeed, he came home with two bronze medals. He was third behind Carl Lewis and another American, Sam Graddy, in the 100 metres and he ran a leg of the 4-by-100 relay with Desai Williams, Tony Sharpe, and Sterling Hinds for the other bronze. By Canadian track standards until then, this was a very good showing. But, still, third was third.

Ben began breaking the sound barrier in 1985. He won the 100-metre sprint in the World Cup in Canberra and a year later left the coiffed Carl Lewis behind for the first time. The Dubin Inquiry in the summer of 1989 established that Ben, like scores of other athletes of many countries, had been using anabolic steroids, in his case since 1981, but, really, the idea that they alone turned him from a 98-pound weakling into Samson is ridiculous.

Ben trained zealously for 10 years before becoming the world's fastest human, day after grinding day of lifting weights and performing an eyeball-popping exercise routine. One afternoon I watched him work at the Metro Toronto track centre on the York University campus when from a deep squat position he hoisted a steel bar with large, round discs of iron at each end.

"How much was that?" I asked when he dropped the bar with a thud.

"A little over 500," Ben said.

"*Pounds?*"

"That's right." He was obviously proud.

His coach, Charlie Francis, stood nearby. I said I could appreciate that Ben needed powerful legs but why those terrifying muscles on the chest and shoulders?

Charlie was never a guy to mince words.

"For Crissakes, you run with your arms, too, you know," he barked. "You don't think your body just moves along like some damn giraffe's neck, do you? You got to *pull* it. You got to make it work as hard as your legs."

Accordingly, with Ben lifting a ton of iron over the years it didn't dawn on me that the muscles on his muscles were being fuelled by drugs banned by the IOC. And, after Seoul and his disqualification, the thing that bugged me was how the Canadian government's sports minister, Jean Charest, instantly declared Ben banned for life from competing for Canada, and how for months and months so many scribes and broadcasters preceded his name with such adjectives as disgraced and dishonoured, as in "The disgraced Ben Johnson is still working out . . . " "Dishonoured Ben Johnson said today . . . " And so forth.

I didn't read those words in front of the name of Harold Ballard or the name of George Steinbrenner, both of whom were convicted of breaking federal laws. I didn't read them in front of tough guy Bob Probert's name. Nobody took away Ballard's hockey club after his jail term or Steinbrenner's baseball club after his conviction. Yet Ben Johnson was stripped of his gold medal and of recognition of his world-record time of 9.79 seconds at the Seoul Olympics and the mark of 9.83 at the world championships in Rome in 1987.

The Detroit hockey player Probert served a three-month jail term for transporting cocaine across the border from Windsor. The night he returned to the Red Wing lineup the 19,875 loonies in the Joe Louis Arena stood and brayed their affection and the intensity climbed to the rafters when he knocked a rival player into the boards. By contrast, what Ben Johnson received for breaking *an IOC house rule* that scores of athletes were breaking all around him was scorn and abuse in his homeland.

The only sensible official voice belonged to Juan Antonio Samaranch, the IOC president, who said Ben would be welcome to compete in the 1992 Olympics following his two-year post-Seoul suspension. "Johnson was treated like any other athlete in Seoul when we suspended him," Samaranch said with a reasonableness uncharacteristic of any of his predecessors in the IOC waxworks. "Now we have to do the same. He must not get more sanctions because he is Johnson. This is not fair."

Before Seoul, Ben received little of the attention squandered on the American dandy, Carl Lewis, partly because Ben was a tough interview, partly because track was not a big sport with the public, and partly because a lot of us were too lazy or too impatient to sit down with him. To me and a lot of other scribes Ben always seemed a shy person with a stammer in a Jamaican accent that confused the impatient ones among us. A lot of guys stayed away because of it.

But on the track, Ben's speed was the only language he needed. If you blinked you were apt to miss him. Running the 100, sprinters vaulted out of the starting blocks like hungry bulldogs, legs and arms pumping and thumping, and they thundered across the red rubberized tracks in short, straining, staccato bounds. In the stands it seemed that in the time it took to stand up and start shouting, it was over, the runners had pulled up in long jarring strides and were walking in small gingerly steps back toward the finish line, heads down, chests heaving. For anybody on Earth but Ben the whole business took slightly more than 9.9 seconds. For Ben, slightly less.

Chapter 16

The fourth estate

In my early days in the CP's Winnipeg bureau I'd sit at a typewriter with a copy of the day's *Winnipeg Tribune* folded open at the sports page. I was so dazzled by the prose in Ralph Allen's daily column, One Man's Opinion, that I'd type out a couple of paragraphs. I really wasn't sure what I was up to – hoping somehow that the style would rub off, I suppose.

And then one day years later I read a book called *No Cheering in the Press Box*, a collection of taped interviews with 18 veteran American sportswriters on their work habits. The book was put together by an earnest, painstaking, cigar-chomping acquaintance of mine, Jerome Holtzman, a baseball writer then and now for the *Chicago Tribune*, and in it was this paragraph from Red Smith:

"When I was very young as a sportswriter I knowingly and unashamedly imitated others. I had a series of heroes who would delight me for awhile and I'd imitate them – Damon Runyon, Westbrook Pegler, Joe Williams. I'd read one daily, faithfully, and be delighted by him. Then someone else would catch my fancy and slowly, by what process I have no idea, your own writing tends to crystallize, to take shape. Yet you have learned some moves from all these guys and they are somehow incorporated into your own style. Pretty soon you're not imitating any longer."

So when I was starting out I was trying to learn from Allen. I think what I liked most about him were the attributes that I still admire most about sportswriters: his sense of humour, the rhythm of his sentences, a certain self-deprecation, and a wariness of anybody above the rank of general manager, especially owners. Owners are the newspaper publishers of sports. Look out for them.

Ralph, who died of cancer at age 53 early in December, 1966, was a complex guy. He was a beautiful writer and if there are any editors anywhere who are better than he was they must have dropped down from heaven (or by now have gone back there). The people Allen assembled and dealt with at *Maclean's* during the decade of the 1950s are still prominent and some still influential today – Pierre Berton, Peter Gzowski, June Callwood, Peter Newman, Harry Bruce, Christina McCall, W.O. Mitchell, Janice Tyrwhitt, David MacDonald, Barbara Moon, to recall a few.

In his personal life Allen wasn't so accomplished. One of his sons, a friend of mine whom I greatly respect, says he was a terrible father and not a very good husband. He was shy and he was awkward socially, and yet he was a very funny guy, too. Chris McCall wrote of him, "He was a humanist who loved to go to war." As a war correspondent for the *Globe and Mail* he went places he didn't have to go, which happened to put him in a perfect position to survive and write about what it was like to be bombed by the RAF.

On this frightening day he had nosed so far toward the battlefront that when a wall-to-wall cloud of 700 RAF bombers mistook advanced Canadian troops for German infantry he and the Canadian soldiers were continuously bombed for an hour and five minutes. People who wondered about the chilling experience found this in the *Globe*:

"Beyond recording that everybody else in the dugout behaved magnificently, the only further light I can throw on the question, 'How does it feel to be bombed by the RAF?' is to say I think my head was clear, but when I left the dugout I was wringing wet from head to toe; that I did not pray but would have prayed had I not felt it would be presumptuous; that I never ceased to hope I would get out alive and never ceased to suspect that I would not."

In peacetime and back in the sports department, he wrote light-hearted stuff. This was just before he became the boss at *Maclean's* in 1950 after a year at the *Toronto Telegram*. I remember once between periods in the Maple Leaf Gardens press room he nudged my arm and drew me aside.

"What kind of a game is this?" he asked.

"What kind of a game?" I said. "Whattayuh mean, what kind of a game?"

"I mean, is it any good, is it bad, is it typical? I haven't been coming much, you know."

"Oh, yeah. Well, typical, I guess. About as usual."

"That's what I was afraid of," he muttered. "I don't mind writing the bloody column; it's the goddam *games* I can't stand."

For a time at the *Tely* the sports department and the business department shared a large room on the third floor of the old red brick pile at the corner of Melinda and Bay streets whose architecture and plumbing were from roughly the 14th century. Though the room was reasonably large, it was not large enough for the proper accommodation of two departments.

One day Allen wrote this paragraph at the top of his column:

"Wanted: Six to 12 go-getting, clean-living midgets to work in sports department of established metropolitan newspaper. Maximum height 3 feet 6 inches, maximum weight 35 pounds. Knowledge of English grammar, hockey, baseball and football an asset but not essential. Here is a real opportunity for the midget of vision and ambition to enter a career with a genuine future. Interested midgets should apply, giving waist, chest and calf measurements, to Personnel Dept., *The Evening Telegram*, Bay Street, Toronto."

Another time when George McCullagh, the dashing publisher of both the *Tely* and the *Globe*, swept into our crowded cell, his eyes caught me at my desk in a corner beyond three desks.

"By God, what a disreputable looking bunch," he grunted. "Don't *you* own a tie?" staring straight at me.

This was back in an era when I didn't know much about newspaper publishers, and I was speechless until Allen ended my embarrassment.

"Hell, if he'd worn a tie in here," Ralphie said, "he couldn't have reached his desk."

Also at the *Tely* was the singular Ted Reeve, for 50 years revered by thousands of sports fans in Toronto, almost a cult figure with a giant hooked nose and a twinkle in his good eye and the creator of inspired doggerel. He had been a truly accomplished lacrosse and football player and once when he was growing a trifle long in the tooth he was slouched, wracked and bent by injuries, on the bench of his Balmy Beach team in the Grey Cup final.

Time was running out with the Beaches narrowly ahead but the rival team was closing in for a winning field goal. On third down Ted hobbled from the sidelines into the Balmy Beach defensive line and he got through to block the kick that would have sunk his team. On Monday he wrote:

> When I was young and in my prime,
> I used to block kicks all the time.
> But now that I am old and grey
> I only block them once a day.

One spring Reeve, who called himself the Moaner, and Jim Coleman went to New York with the Maple Leafs for a playoff series against the Rangers. Coleman had succeeded Ralph Allen at the *Globe* when the latter went into Conn Smythe's so-called Sportsman's Battery in 1941. There was a lot of heavy drinking in those days in the newspaper business, something that is less general nowadays. As the inevitable party grew in intensity in the hotel suite in New York, it dawned on the Moaner that he'd better get his column off to the *Telegram*. He went to an adjoining room to work, placing the pages of copy on the bed as he completed them.

In tottered Coleman, nose red, eyes bleary. He picked up a sheet of Reeve's prose and was reading it when suddenly he tossed his cookies.

The Moaner glanced over his shoulder but continued his work. "If that's intended as criticism, old chap," he said amiably, "you're not being very subtle."

Some of these tales have been told and retold. It was never a secret that Reeve drank rum and Coke from dawn to dusk (and then some). He'd occasionally hop gingerly into the office in the morning to write his column (the *Tely* was an afternoon paper with a 9 a.m. deadline) and five minutes later hop gingerly out to visit his friend Del Worsnop, who ran the King Edward Hotel parking garage a couple of blocks away and was personally responsible for the Moaner's morning fix when the need arose. In that five minutes in the office Ted would have clipped a column from, say, the *New York Herald-Tribune*, pasted it to a sheet of copy paper, written in a stubby little pencil at the top of the paper, "What does Red Smith mean by this?" and sent the works to the composing room. Or he might paste up one of his own old columns and write at the top, "Reprinted by Request." Then he'd speed to the King Edward garage as fast as his varicose veins would permit.

In this era of my youth, drinking was part of being a newspaperman. In Winnipeg after a game Herb Manning and I often went to the comfortable bootlegging apartment of a woman named Fanny Mogul. Manning was the *Trib*'s columnist who succeeded Ralph Allen. After a couple of hours we'd take a cab to the *Tribune* and ask Jack Gordon, the night editor, to wake us at 5 a.m. We'd turn off the lights in the sports department, climb onto a couple of desks, and go to sleep with our round little heads on piles of old newspapers. By then, a third man on our staff, the widely known Vince Leah, who worked for some 60 years at the *Tribune* and later the *Free Press*, would have sent the wire copy plus his own column to the composing room. When Jack Gordon woke us at five we'd do our work until the seven o'clock deadline for the provincial edition. At seven the sports editor, Johnny Buss, came in.

Buss was a jovial, round-faced, large-bellied fellow in his late 40s who could (and often would) drink a quart of beer from a pitcher in a prolonged series of non-stop gulps. Manning and I would sit in the office with him, doing the odd bit of work for the afternoon city edition, until the pub opened at noon in the St. Regis Hotel half a block down Smith Street. There we'd sit for an hour or two, drinking beer and telling lies with an assortment of football referees, hockey scouts, and other suspects. Then we'd either go home and sleep the afternoon away or occasionally play golf at one of the friendly clubs where we could play free and they had a bar. Sometimes we didn't bother with the play free part of it.

In those days, sanity usually returned to young sportswriters around the age of 22 or 23. These days, not many drink so foolishly, although there are still a few eldering juveniles around who impart thrilling tales when they return from road trips of how drunk they got in Seattle or Baltimore or wherever.

The current sportswriters are superior to those of my youth. It used to be that there'd be a handful of outstanding ones such as Allen and Coleman and Reeve and Scott Young in Toronto and Dink Carroll and Elmer Ferguson in Monreal, and the rest were scarcely more than hometown fans forced by avaricious publishers to live on the handouts of promoters.

Most of the modern publishers I've encountered are as penurious as they ever were but the newspaper guild has compelled them to pay sportswriters a sufficient amount that they no longer need to pander to club owners. That fact alone has raised the quality of modern writing. And there are a lot of really good ones – Cam Cole in Edmonton, Mike Farber in Montreal, Jim Taylor in Vancouver, Steve Brunt, Dave Perkins, and Jim O'Leary on Toronto's three papers, Eric Duhatschek in Calgary, Jane O'Hara and Earl McRae in Ottawa, to name half a dozen or so, a couple of whom go over $100,000 a year. And it's my notion that the *Globe*'s Al Strachan writes the best hockey stuff I've ever read.

And then, of course, there's the indefatigable Milt Dunnell, heading into his 85th year in 1990 and still writing three pieces a week for the *Toronto Star*. Not just three pieces, which a lot of us old dudes can handle, but three *topical* pieces that haven't come off the top of his head but which he has gone out and extracted from somebody involved in a current event or controversy. Milt began writing his sports column in the *Star* 40-odd years ago when he was tranferred from the news side at age 43 to succeed Andy Lytle as sports editor.

What a lulu Lytle was, a robust, ruddy-faced, sarcastic hulk from Vancouver who managed to keep his staff constantly agitated by inserting his own little witticisms into the copy that appeared in the paper under their names. Then the beat men, Annis Stukus, Joe Perlove, Ed Fitkin, Red Burnett, Gord Walker, and others, would have to try to placate the people gouged by Lytle under their names.

One day three years after I'd gone to the news side of the *Globe* from Winnipeg and was writing occasional bits for the Maple Leaf Gardens hockey program, I got a telephone call from Lytle asking me if I'd like to write a column for $100 a week. That was mighty heady stuff for a guy making $45 as a news reporter, and I leaped at it. Lytle cautioned me that I wasn't to use his offer as a lever to get a raise at the *Globe*, that either I accepted or rejected it right then. I assured him I was accepting. He said there was a formality of clearing his proposal with the gruff and feared *Star* managing editor, H.C. Hindmarsh, who, Lytle assured me, did not make a practice of rejecting proposals from him.

A couple of days later, seated at my desk on the *Globe* editorial floor, I was beckoned by the publisher, McCullagh, who was strolling through the newsroom. I followed him to the sixth-floor cafeteria where he provided two cups of coffee and advised me that the city editor, Tommy Munns, was about to become the new sports editor and had recommended that I be transferred to sports.

Aghast, I had to interrupt the publisher to tell him of the Lytle proposal.

"How much did he offer?" McCullagh asked.

"A hundred dollars a week."

He got to his feet. "You're not worth that here," he said. "Good luck to you."

After a week, not having heard from Lytle, I called him at the *Star* and asked when I should report for work.

"For what?" he said.

"For work, for the column," I said.

Can you believe this? His next question was, "What column?"

I said, "The one we talked about on the phone. The one you called me about."

And he said, "I don't know where you got such a notion. We have no need for additional people here. Good day."

What happened at the *Star*, I suspect, was that Hindmarsh told Lytle he had no interest in putting another hundred dollars a week into the sports budget. Lytle, in turn, was too vain to let me know he had no real authority upstairs.

This was the man Milt Dunnell replaced and Milt turned the department around. He gave the men full responsibility for their beats, didn't inject insults or anything else into their prose, gave them full backing when necessary, and left them alone. Peace broke out.

Nobody worked like Dunnell. After he settled into Lytle's chair he wrote six columns a week and another one for the old *Star Weekly*. He did two sportscasts a day five days a week on radio and each week on television he did a sports editorial on one channel and a barbed interview program called *Sports Hot Seat* on another. Among Milt's admirers was John Bassett, the publisher of the *Star*'s afternoon rival, the *Telegram*, and at various times a principal owner of the Argonauts and of the Maple Leafs. It wasn't the least unusual for Bassett to phone Dunnell with news that scooped his own *Tely* sports department. Not long ago I asked Bassett why.

"Well, why wouldn't I?" snorted Big John. "He had great integrity and he was a great pal of mine. If I had a story today, I'd call Milt."

On the opposite end of the age scale was Allen Abel, a shining light. After six years of sports at the *Globe* and a two-year stint as the paper's Far East correspondent in Beijing, Abel decided in 1987 to turn to television. He joined the CBC's high-budget *Journal*, where these days you can see him doing documentaries from around the world.

Abel and I travelled together frequently when he was in sports and I was at the *Sun*, and I often wished, sometimes fervently, that the geniuses at the *New York Times* or some other enlightened enclave would come to their senses and hire him. He was in his early 30s, inquisitive, perceptive, tireless, had a brain like a steel trap, and owned a wonderful ear for the flow of a sentence. As I often used to tell myself, though, apart from that what did the son of a bitch have to offer? Just curly hair and youth and a terrific wife named Linda.

The American sportswriter I grew up in awe of was John Lardner. He lived in the shadow of his father, the humorist and novelist Ring Lardner, whose work became an American classic (he once wrote a baseball novel called *Shut Up, He Explained*), but I always liked John's stuff better. Years ago he wrote a magazine piece whose lead itself is a classic, a piece on the fighter, Stanley Ketchell, that has been quoted many times, by me and others:

> Stanley Ketchell was 24 years old when he was fatally shot in the back by the common-law husband of the lady who was cooking his breakfast.

When John Lardner died of heart disease at 47 in 1960 *The New Yorker* said of him: "He was one of a kind. As a humorist, reporter, sportswriter and critic, he found his style – a mixture, unlike any other, of dignity and gaiety, precision and surprise. He was a funny writer, and, though he would never have admitted it, an artist."

He was one of four sons of Ring, and three died long before they should have. The youngest, James, was killed at 24 as a volunteer in the International Brigade in 1938 in the Spanish

Civil War, the war Hemingway wrote about in *For Whom the Bell Tolls*. Six years later David, a war correspondent for *The New Yorker*, was killed by a land mine outside Aachen, Germany. He was 31. The fourth brother was Ring, Jr., who didn't die young and, as far as I know, hasn't died yet. It was Ring who adapted a book called *MASH* into a hit movie called *M*A*S*H* on which the vastly successful television series of the same name was based.

John, the sportswriter, did a weekly column for *Newsweek* and reviewed television and the Broadway theatre for *The New Yorker*. He had a gentle humour. When a woman friend of his had her gall bladder out, he sent a telegram to her in the hospital, "You look better without it."

I first came upon his work around 1940 when he and Grantland Rice each wrote three columns a week for the North American Newspaper Alliance. They arrived by mail each week in the *Trib* sports department. I threw away Rice's stuff, which was full of purple passages, and doted on Lardner's, which soothed the ear. As I mentioned earlier, I talked to Lardner before going to Boston to interview Sam Langford. This came about as a result of reading a collection of his fight pieces called *White Hopes and Other Tigers*. I wrote to him, care of *Newsweek*, and in due course he wrote back that he'd be home on a certain July afternoon and I could see him there.

A gentle all-day rain brought a shine to the streets as I rode a cab to his apartment building in Greenwich Village. There was no reply when I pushed the lobby button so I stood outside in the shelter of an awning running from the entrance to the curb until a yellow cab drew up and this angular bespectacled figure emerged. I was nervous in the elevator standing with a man whose work I'd been reading for 20 years. He made small talk about the rain, staring at the elevator floor. He seemed shy and reserved.

The apartment was unoccupied except for us. He said his wife and two daughters and one son were at a summer place of theirs on Fire Island. It is a measure of how naive, or stupid, I was that I said I'd written him because I'd admired the boxing pieces in his book and wanted to know whom I should see to get the same sort of information about Sam Langford.

He looked at me strangely but he didn't laugh aloud, which he well might have. Seated opposite me, long-legged, slim, pushing his black hornrims higher on his nose, he advised me patiently that you don't *see* anybody; you go to the New York Public Library, as he had done, and patiently leaf through back copies of newspapers to ferret out information on old fights, fighters, managers, and promoters.

"It isn't written out for you anywhere," he said quietly. "It's there to be panned and you're the prospector."

Or, he said, I could go uptown to the office of *Ring* magazine where one of the fight game's oldest historians, Nat Fleischer, was the editor and might have something on Sam. He said he had once talked to the fight manager Joe Jacobs there "and got some usable stuff." I don't know if it was on that occasion but one time he encountered Jacobs and wrote about an incident in Hamburg, Germany, in 1935 when Adolf Hitler was reaching his apex of power.

It was a source of distress to Hitler that a favourite of his, Max Schmeling, needed an American manager to get rewarding fights in the U.S. and even more distressing that Schmeling's manager was this Jew, Joe Jacobs, widely known as Yussel the Muscle. On the night in Hamburg, Schmeling beat a guy named Steve Hamas, and the next day Jacobs was in the German headlines:

FUEHRER INSULTED BY NOTED NON-ARYAN

"It was a tough position," Jacobs said when Lardner encountered him a few weeks later. "Hitler came in and the whole crowd raised their right arms and yelled 'Heil!' Even the people in the ring did it, and I was right up there in plain sight. I was smoking a heater and I have my hat on.

"If I held my hat in my left hand and took my cigar out of my mouth, I saluted with the cigar in my right hand. If I held the cigar in my left, I saluted with my hat. If I saluted with nothing in my right hand, I had my hat on. So I saluted with the hat in my left hand, and my right hand empty, and the cigar in the middle of my kisser. They didn't like it."

In 1947 John Lardner brought out a collection of his sports pieces in a book whose title, as far as I'm concerned, can serve as a legacy for the whole business of writing sports for a living – *It Beats Working*.

Epilogue

It is an axiom of sports that the legs go first. For sportswriters, it's the enthusiasm.

When I was a young sportswriter in Winnipeg all the athletes were nine feet tall. When I became a very old one in Toronto, they had shrunk considerably.

I remember an autumn afternoon in 1940 bouncing into the *Winnipeg Tribune* office from the Marlborough Hotel where I'd interviewed three players from the previous spring's Stanley Cup champions, the New York Rangers, whose fall training camp was in Winnipeg's ancient Amphitheatre rink. Let's see, there was Dave Kerr, the all-star goaltender, Babe Pratt, the local-boy defenceman, and Neil Colville, the star centre.

Mine eyes had seen the glory. When my boss, Johnny Buss, looked up from the Underwood he was pummelling he paused and regarded me in a long, reflective glance. My flushed and downy kisser had tweaked a long-buried chord.

"Ah, Billy boy," he said softly. "You're a hero-worshipper, aren't you?"

I retained that, oh, *reverence* for famous athletes as long as they were remote and my imagination could play with their deeds. Foster Hewitt's radio broadcasts kept the illusion alive and even after television brought the games into living rooms the players were still unreal figures, distant as movie stars.

But, little by little, the tingle dwindles and, one day, standing at a batting cage watching a home-run hitter or sitting in a dressing room hearing a goal-scorer, the scene somehow has grown too familiar, has become too repetitious. It's not the hitter's fault, or the goal-scorer's. It's time that's to blame. Time has chipped away the enthusiasm.

What is left are the memories of high moments such as the ones resurrected here. What is left, too, are the remarkable characters and the things they said and did. Such as the grizzled old manager Casey Stengel, who once barked at a straggly herd of rookies when he took over the newly franchised New York Mets in 1962, "Line up alphabetically by height."

Earlier, the Yankees had won 10 pennants in Stengel's 12 years as the skipper. Praised on all sides, the old man modestly allowed, "I couldn't have done it without the players."

And Yogi Berra, the catcher, who may or may not have said half the things attributed to him, one of which related to a favourite restaurant, "Nobody goes there any more," Yog may have said. "It's too crowded."

I'll remember and be grateful to Tony Kubek forever. He was Yogi's teammate in nine years of playing shortstop and the outfield for the Yankees during which he appeared in six World Series. Then he came to Toronto, to the Blue Jays, as a broadcaster until 1990 and he taught all of us more about baseball than we knew existed. He never stopped being patient with us print guys bugging him for anecdotes and education about the game. He even gave us his home phone number in Appleton, Wisconsin, the ultimate courtesy.

Looking back, it occurs to me again that no game has the lore of baseball, and I don't really know why. Maybe it's the rhythm of the game. For one thing, it's timeless; it can go on all day or be over in two hours. Except for the pitcher and the catcher, nobody does much of anything for long periods except stand around and wait. This creates a kind of leisureliness. Scribes can mingle with the millionaires in the hours before games, asking what they think of this or of that and how are their bunions. Hockey, our national pastime, is a wonderful game but it's a bang, bang business in a cold, cold climate, conditions not conducive to standing around for a chat.

Some people with nine-to-five jobs may regard the sportswriter's life as a ride on the gravy train taking her or him free and on an expense account to events of wide interest where fans' seats are expensive and hard to come by. The reality is that working sportswriters actually *work* in a competitive, repetitive field. Most times, meeting tight deadlines, they see about half the events they're attending, often stuffing conditional leads into their computers – if this team wins use this one and if that team wins use that one, occasionally glancing up from the machine to see how the game's progressing.

Most sportswriters are partial to the teams they cover because of their constant exposure to them, and the familiarity often produces an unintentional emotional involvement. Even so, a certain detachment is essential because readers often don't own the same sentiments and also because half the writers are from out of town and have a different favourite. Accordingly, there's no cheering in press boxes. Sportswriters grow accustomed to keeping quiet even when they're not working.

I can recall hearing myself cheer only twice and both times I was surprised to recognize my own voice. Until then, it had not occurred to me that I was a fervent nationalist.

The first occasion was in 1964 when Northern Dancer won the Kentucky Derby. I got to Louisville a couple of days before the race and heard the endless speculation on the abilities of the two favourites, the Dancer and the California champion, Hill Rise, which always ended in favour of Hill Rise. The bluegrass bluebloods couldn't countenance the notion of a *Canadian*-bred colt winning their cherished Run for the Roses. He might as well have been a yak from darkest Tibet.

So when this full-chested little middleweight was fighting off the heavyweight champ from Lotusland in the duel down the long stretch at Churchill Downs I became aware that someone was screaming over and over in my ear, "He's going to make it! He's going to make it! He's going to make it!"

And when he did, when he charged under the wire a neck in front, I sat back down and finally shut up.

The only other time I can recall yelling at a sports event was eight years later in Moscow when Paul Henderson put the puck behind the accomplished Soviet goaltender, Vladislav Tretiak.

Remember? The series was knotted at three wins apiece and one tie when in the decisive eighth game the Russians vaulted ahead by 5–3 with two goals late in the second period. I sat watching in dismay beside Jim Coleman on one of the long polished benches that served as seating in the big arena in the Luzhnicki sports complex.

When the period ended we climbed down to the crowded smoky lobby under the seats and joined a few other newspaper guys, Red Fisher and Ted Blackman from Montreal, Jim Taylor from Vancouver, Fran Rosa from Boston, maybe a couple of others. After nearly eight games, we were finally prepared to accept the evidence that the Soviet speed and conditioning were obstacles too large for the Canadians to handle.

"I just hope it isn't a blowout," I said to Taylor. He nodded grimly. We were a gloomy bunch.

And then there was the astonishing comeback. Phil Esposito scored. Yvan Cournoyer scored. And finally, with 34 seconds left, there was Paul Henderson and his stunning goal.

Four thousand Canadians in one end and corner of the arena went berserk. "*Take that, you sons of bitches!*" a guy was screaming in my ear. Yep, me, filled with enthusiasm.

That was a long time ago.